Meeting Difficulties in Literacy Development

This timely and thought-provoking book addresses the sensitive issue of difficulties in literacy development. The authors begin by exploring different conceptualisations of literacy and their implications in terms of addressing the barriers to literacy acquisition. They then go on to discuss practical strategies and programmes to help reduce these barriers at school, family and community level. Throughout, the authors relate cognitive, psychological and socio-cultural perspectives to current curriculum policies, controversies and ethical considerations.

This book enables practitioners to reflect critically upon the choices available to them in assessing and supporting students who experience difficulties in literacy development. It will be essential reading for students on initial teacher training courses, and teachers on CPD courses in the area of special needs, literacy and dyslexia.

Janice Wearmouth is a Lecturer in the Faculty of Education and Language Studies at The Open University.

Janet Soler is a Lecturer in the Faculty of Education and Language Studies at The Open University.

Gavin Reid is a Senior Lecturer in the Department of Educational Studies at The University of Edinburgh.

Meeting Difficulties in Literacy Development

Research, policy and practice

Janice Wearmouth,
Janet Soler and Gavin Reid

RoutledgeFalmer
Taylor & Francis Group

LONDON AND NEW YORK

The Open
University

KH

First published 2003
by RoutledgeFalmer
11 New Fetter Lane, London EC4P 4EE

Simultaneously published in the USA and Canada
by RoutledgeFalmer
29 West 35th Street, New York, NY 10001

RoutledgeFalmer is an imprint of the Taylor & Francis Group

© 2003 Janice Wearmouth, Janet Soler and Gavin Reid

Typeset in Goudy by Taylor & Francis Books Ltd
Printed and bound in Great Britain by TJ International Ltd,
Padstow, Cornwall

British Library Cataloguing in Publication Data
A catalogue record for this book is available from the British
Library

Library of Congress Cataloging in Publication Data
A catalog record for this book has been applied for

ISBN 0–415–30470–9 (hbk)
     0–415–30471–7 (pbk)

10/25/04

Contents

Preface

In recent years there has been an awareness of the importance of competence in literacy to individuals' life chances and the socio-economic well-being of the nation. This has resulted in a growing focus on national standards in literacy internationally. As a consequence, the issue of difficulties in literacy has assumed increasing importance. Debates over how to address difficulties in literacy have increasingly become the focus of policy-makers and central government agencies as well as practitioners in many countries, and have provided an impetus for particular initiatives and interventions in the literacy curriculum. The perceived need to draw up coherent policy frameworks for raising standards of literacy has led to approaches to national curricula which are very different in their level of control and prescription in different countries. These curricula also reflect differing emphases on, and recognition of, cognitive and socio-cultural views of literacy.

This book breaks new ground by drawing upon a wide range of perspectives related to cognitive, psychological as well as socio-cultural viewpoints and critical literacy to help inform practice, policy and research into difficulties in literacy development. It relates cross-disciplinary research in the area of difficulties in literacy to current curriculum policies, controversies and ethical considerations. The book explores different conceptualisations of literacy and their implications for what might constitute barriers to literacy acquisition from both individual and social-cultural perspectives. It highlights the important issues for practitioners that stem from these different views of literacy. From the perspective of the practitioner who is dealing with literacy in complex, real-life learning situations, these issues encompass both psychological and social factors. For this reason the book explores different psychological models that underpin the process of literacy acquisition, particularly reading, and outlines a cognitive viewpoint on difficulties in literacy which underpins the concept of dyslexia. It also sets out to present socio-cultural approaches and approaches drawn from critical literacy to address power, equity, inclusion and legal issues alongside these psychological models.

This interdisciplinary conceptual framework is drawn on to theorise the practical interventions and programmes that are described in the second half of the book. The intention is to enable practitioners to reflect critically upon the choices available to them in assessing learning needs and supporting students who experience difficulties in literacy development at school, and in family and community contexts.

Chapter 1

Models of, and debates over, the reading process

Introduction: models of reading

Learning to read is the initial stage of becoming literate. The skills involved in reading can be quite complex, and different views exist on how children read and the relative importance of each of these skills and processes in reading. An understanding of different models of reading is essential in order for the teacher to make decisions about appropriate strategies for facilitating success in learning to read. Reading programmes and interventions are underpinned by different models of reading, and it is crucial to know what these are before deciding which programme or intervention to implement to address difficulties students may have with literacy.

Bottom-up (phonics) and top-down (whole-book/whole-language) approaches

As Reid (1998) notes, there are two principal models of the reading process:

1 The 'bottom-up', data-driven model, which suggests fluent readers look first at the stimulus – that is, the component features of the letters in the words – before they move on to consider the meaning of the print.
2 The 'top-down', concept-driven model, which assumes that fluent readers first anticipate the meaning of text before checking the available syntactic and graphic cues.

These contrasting theoretical perspectives on the act of reading each lead to a different approach to the teaching of reading to students who experience difficulty. From the bottom-up perspective, the reconstruction of the author's meaning is achieved through the process of decoding the abstract and complicated alphabetic code. Reading is a series of small steps to be learned one by one. In order to learn how to do this, children must first learn the letters of the alphabet and establish the principle of sound-symbol identification and then apply this in order to decode words. The teaching of bottom-up skills emphasises the mastery of phonics and word recognition. M.J. Adams notes that the bottom-up approach was the earliest method of teaching reading (1994, p. 21). There was little need to be concerned about reading comprehension since the Bible constituted most reading matter for children and the text was predetermined.

In a major US report commissioned by the Center for the Study of Reading in Champaign, Illinois, to review all aspects of phonics and early reading instruction, Adams argues that research indicates that readers of English thoroughly process the individual letters of words easily and quickly because they are well acquainted with the sequences of letters they are likely to see (*ibid.*, p. 108). What separates good from poor readers is their ability visually to recognise frequent spelling patterns and to make visual–sound correspondences automatically.

Adams concludes that phonics has a crucial place in competent reading. Beginning readers should first learn to recognise individual letters quickly in order to optimise their ability to recognise whole words. They also need to pay attention to the sequence of letters in a word, not simply the whole word. The implication of this view is to highlight the significance of 'synthetic' phonics, writing and spelling of whole words, 'exercise with frequent blends and digraphs, practice with word families' and attention to every letter of the word, in left-to-right order. Adams also advocates exercises on frequent digraphs, letter blends and word families.

In contrast, Goodman (1976) advocated a top-down approach to reading and his approach became known as the 'psycholinguistic guessing game'. The implication of this, according to Goodman, is that good readers will have less need to rely on graphic cues and therefore do not have to process every characteristic of the word and letter. The top-down, whole-book/whole-language approach implies that children learn to read through reading, being read to and being immersed in a literacy-rich environment.

The second perspective views reading as the active *construction* of meaning. This perspective is influenced by psycholinguistics, with its emphasis on how we make sense of our world through the use of language. Goodman likens the way in which the human mind makes sense of print to the way in which it makes sense of any other aspect of the world (1996, pp. 110–11). The strategies that the mind uses for making sense of print are called psycholinguistic because thought and language continuously interact in this process. Beginning with written text, the mind constructs meaning drawing on cues 'from the various language levels' (*ibid.*). He calls the process a 'psycholinguistic guessing game' (Goodman 1967) because the reader has a hypothesis of what a text might be about, and then tests this hypothesis and confirms or rejects it as s/he reads through the text.

Goodman describes four cycles between the visual input supplied by the eyes to the brain and the meaning constructed by the brain: visual, perceptual, syntactic and semantic. Those learners in the early stages of literacy development should be encouraged to decide for themselves whether they have read text correctly by continually monitoring for meaning in order to develop useful strategies for self-correction. Only miscues that cause a loss of meaning need correction.

A number of other researchers, for example Adams's colleagues Strickland and Cullinan (1994), follow a similar top-down model of reading and criticise the use of terms such as 'pre-readers', 'reading readiness' and 'prerequisite skills' as implying that children acquire literacy skills suddenly and as a result of formal instruction in phonics. They prefer the term 'emergent literacy' because they feel that children's literacy emerges out of their interaction with language and their experience of the world of print around them. Studies showing a strong relationship between linguistic awareness and literacy development do not provide conclusive proof that competence in phonics should be acquired before children are taught to read, because competence in phonics develops as a result of access to stories and print rather than the other way round. Strickland and Cullinan feel that the emphasis should be on literacy-rich environments for early literacy acquisition rather than direct instruction in phonics. Instruction in reading should include phonics but should begin from an emphasis on meaning.

According to Harrison (1994), current views of the reading process turn Goodman's model on its head. They stress that, when it comes to word recognition, it is the good reader who has less need to rely on context as s/he can recognise the word because s/he has mastered the elements of reading. The poor reader cannot recognise the word and therefore needs context to aid recognition. Harrison suggests this takes up valuable processing capacity, which reduces the potential for comprehension. Fluent readers are therefore more efficient than poor readers, but they do not use less visual information.

The interactive approach

Despite her advocacy of the importance of phonics in initial reading instruction, it should be noted that Adams also acknowledges the importance of semantic cues in reading and other 'critical sources of information':

> In the reading situation, as in any effective communication situation, the message or text provides but one of the critical sources of information. The rest must come from the readers' own prior knowledge. Further, in the reading situation as in any other learning situation, the learnability of a pattern depends critically on the prior knowledge and higher-order relationships that it evokes. In both fluent reading and its acquisition, the reader's knowledge must be aroused interactively and in parallel. Neither understanding nor learning can proceed hierarchically from the bottom up. Phonological awareness, letter recognition facility, familiarity with spelling patterns, spelling–sound relations, and individual words must be developed in concert with real reading and real writing and with deliberate reflection on the forms, functions and meanings of texts.
>
> (M.J. Adams 1994, p. 422)

Stanovich (1988) also suggests that both top-down and bottom-up methods have limitations because readers draw on both processes when reading. He suggests that readers use information simultaneously from different levels and do not necessarily begin at the graphic (bottom up) or the context (top down) level. During the development of reading skills some readers may rely more heavily on some levels than others. Additionally, Stanovich argues that the readers' weaknesses are compensated for by her/his strengths. He called this process the 'interactive compensatory model' because the various processes interact and also because the reader can compensate for weaknesses in one area by relying on strengths in the other aspects. Therefore the argument is that poor readers rely on context to compensate for their difficulties in processing the individual sounds of words. Stanovich (1986) argues that those children who are not proficient in the subskills of reading will not have the opportunity to acquire these skills because they do not have easy access to reading, the so-called 'Matthew effect'.

Basically there are three processes interacting when children read. These are:

1 Sound – the sound pattern of the letters or word. This is called the phonic aspect of the reading process.
2 Sight – the visual characteristics of the word are focused on or a word is read as an entity. The 'whole-word' method of teaching reading was designed to reinforce this process.
3 Meaning – context, both semantic (meaning) and syntactic (grammar) aspects of text.

The interaction between the three of them constitutes 'reading'. This model of the reading system highlights the reciprocal relationship between content, meaning, orthography (print) and phonology (speech). Processing at the level of orthography includes sequencing the letters in a word, whilst at the phonological level it encompasses matching those letters to the letter sound. Processing of meaning relates to the reader's knowledge of meaning at word level, and processing of context provides a framework for understanding the text.

A number of factors are involved in the process of reading: linguistic, auditory and visual. It is important to have some idea of how these factors contribute to the difficulties some children have with reading.

Linguistic factors

Reading is expressed in language form and this can present a difficulty for some children because:

- the flow of oral language does not always make the break between words clear;
- they may have difficulty breaking the words into constituent sounds and sequencing these sounds;
- they may have problems retaining the sounds in memory;
- they may have difficulty in articulating sounds;
- they may have difficulty in recognising the sounds in written form.

Visual factors

Children when reading must:

- recognise the visual cues of letters and words;
- be familiar with left–right orientation;
- recognise word patterns;
- recognise letter and word shapes.

Difficulty in any of these areas may inhibit reading acquisition.

Auditory factors

These include:

- recognition of letter sounds;
- recognition of sounds and letter groups or patterns;
- sequencing of sounds;
- corresponding sounds to visual stimuli;
- discriminating sounds from other sounds;
- discriminating sounds within words.

(Adapted from Reid 1998)

Once again, difficulty in any of these areas may inhibit reading acquisition.

Connectionist models of reading

The dual-route model

Coltheart (1978) developed a somewhat different model of the reading process, the so-called 'dual-route model'. Basically he suggests that children have at their disposal two routes to the written word (lexicon). These are:

- a direct route in which they use a visual strategy to read whole words which are already familiar to them; and
- a phonological route which is used to break words down into their component sounds and is used with unfamiliar words.

Reappraisal of the dual-route model

There has, however, been a reappraisal of the dual-route model which suggests that children read through the use of 'parallel distributed processing' (PDP). This is sometimes referred to as the connectionist model of reading and offers a different framework for understanding the reading process. This model suggests that, rather than through different routes, children learn to read through the interaction of each of the processing elements in reading.

According to Snowling, a critical feature of the connectionist model is that it is possible to associate the input patterns (written words) with the output patterns (spoken words), and children can eventually generalise from this association to read words they have not been explicitly taught to read (2000, p. 61). However, Snowling argues that training in phonology is important and that children who come to the reading task with 'well specified phonological representations are well placed to establish links between the letters of printed words and the sounds of spoken words'. One of the difficulties with models such as the connectionist model is that they may explain the processes involved in reading but they do not inform about the conscious reading strategies readers may adopt. This is particularly important in English because there are a great number of irregular words which may not conform to logical processes, and these words are those which are most challenging for dyslexic children. Additionally, the connectionist model implies that the connections which are regularly used will be stronger, so reading practice will help to develop the connections. The phonological representations hypothesis suggests that children with dyslexia approach the task of learning to read with poorly specified phonological representations. As a result they have difficulty in establishing the connections between the letter strings of printed words and the phonemic sequences of spoken words, and difficulty in generalising this knowledge when they meet new words. This would imply that dyslexic children would need to gain practice at using connections, particularly with irregular words. This, however, can be particularly challenging for dyslexic children and underlines the need for an early systematic structured programme to develop phonological representations.

Developmental model of reading

Another approach to understanding the process of acquiring literacy is through the developmental model of learning to read. From a developmental perspective, learning to read consists of the acquisition of different kinds of skills at different points in the learner's development. In order to chart a child's development in reading acquisition it is important to be able to identify the sub-skills involved in the reading process itself.

Ehri (1999) suggests that there are three essential interrelated ingredients in the knowledge base for teachers in order to inform them in making decisions on reading instruction. These are: knowledge about the reading process; knowledge about teaching methods and how these facilitate the reading process; and knowledge about observational procedures to identify the processes readers are facilitating and the processes they have difficulty with. As Snowling suggests, children read in different ways so it is important to gather data on the reading skills and the reading processes of individual children and to map these onto their reading development. Although Ehri stresses the importance of the word-learning process, she also suggests that this knowledge can be used by teachers to create relevant instructional activities to help children store sight words in memory. Ehri therefore hypothesises that explanations about beginning reading processes can help teachers gain insights that can prove useful in their classrooms.

There is a very strong similarity between Ehri's and Stanovich's description of the reading process and the 'top-down' and 'bottom-up' models. Ehri refers to four developmental phases which occur in the development of sight-word reading. Each phase reflects the type of connection that links the written forms of words to pronunciation and meaning that is stored in memory.

Ehri stresses the fundamental importance of children gaining mastery over phonics. However, despite her discussion of the interactive model of reading she does not highlight the place of learning to read through reading – that is, the top-down approach. This leads us to reflect on the applicability of the interactive model, as Ehri discusses it, to the practice of teaching reading when her discussion of implications for reading instruction omits key aspects of the interactive reading process and emphasises phonics alone.

The 'Great Debate' over reading

Differing models for conceptualising literacy have resulted in conflicting views and diverse positions over how to teach reading which have often been energetically attacked and rigorously defended. Many adults involved in the field of education will have encountered such 'great debates' and 'literacy wars' over the teaching of reading during their lifetime. These educators would be able to give a personal account of their professional encounters with the issues thrown up by such conflicts and the way in which they resolved these in their practice.

The debates over the best way to teach a young child to read and how to overcome barriers to developing reading skills have stretched over the entire period during which we have had compulsory schooling. Carson's personal account of her grandmother's and her own experiences of teaching reading from the 1880s to the present (Carson 2002, pp. 117–32) highlights the impact of these debates and the tensions they create for individual teachers in classroom settings. Carson argues that her experiences as a teacher and a university teacher responsible for educating future teachers from the 1950s to the present have led her to believe that the 'Reading Wars' over phonics and whole language are essentially the same issues debated again and again, as they resurface in new forms and are rephrased as new ideas.

In her account of these personal experiences of teaching reading Carson notes the lack of an integrated approach between the 'sight-word' method and writing which existed in the 1950s during her own teacher training. She also writes about the lack of connection between how to conduct reading instruction in reading-methods classes and approaches to literacy experienced in language arts in her pre-service training. In her initial years of teaching in the 1950s and 1960s she was aware of the dominance of 'whole-group instruction' and 'round-robin reading'. She was also aware of the resulting difficulties in assessing each child's individual knowledge and use of individual instruction. Her training contrasted with her own experiences of learning literacy through an exploration of the potential of printed text for literate traditions. Carson also experienced this tension in her initial years of teaching as she sought to combine the teaching of skills and grammar with an interest in the meanings, narratives and purposes embodied in literacy.

During the 1960s and 1970s Carson explored phonics-based methods of teaching and increasingly sought to integrate these into developing a literature-rich creative exploration of literature and stories. By the 1980s she had further developed her integrated approach and explored the use of whole-language, oral-language approaches whilst maintaining an interest in phonics and word-identification strategies. In reviewing her experiences, Carson feels that the concerns expressed over reading tend to push educators to the extremes of each position.

Her own experiences of balancing and resolving the tensions implicit between whole-language and phonics approaches and 'top-down' and 'bottom-up' models of reading has led her to believe that there is a need for an intermediate position between these two theoretical stances, one more in line with the 'interactive' view which has been developed in New Zealand's 'Balanced Reading Programmes'. Moreover, she argues that such a balanced programme needs to be implemented 'fully in a comprehensive, seamless blend of factors related to reading success, rather than to swing with the pendulum, defining anew what balanced literacy means' (Carson 2002, p. 130). During her career she has arrived at the conclusion that there is a need to 'merge constructivist and behaviourist methods of teaching children to read'. She also advocates the recognition of teachers' experience of teaching reading as well as a knowledge of the research literature in order to develop a balanced approach to teaching literacy. Her own teaching experiences have led her to believe that different children learn through different approaches and by one or the other model of reading acquisition. Since there is no one right method and one model cannot necessarily be more effective than the other in conceptualising the process of learning to read, Carson believes that she needs to give the children she teaches and the university students she trains 'the opportunity to reflect upon and construct and validate their learning, just as I did', so that the students can respond to children's literacy development needs.

At the beginning of Carson's career the focus of attention was on the 'Great Debate over Reading'. From the 1950s to the 1970s experimental behavioural psychology, with its claims to be a 'scientific' approach, and an associated view of literacy as a neutral technology precipitated and shaped views of how to teach reading and prevent difficulties with reading (see Rassool 2002, p. 19).

Writing at the end of the 1960s in the United States and looking back on the previous two decades, Chall begins her influential book *Learning to Read: The Great Debate* (1967) with a chapter on 'The Crisis in Beginning Reading'. 'The Great Debate' over reading set the contexts for the 'Reading Wars' in the 1970s and more recent debates over reading models and methods in the 1980s and 1990s. The 'Great Debate' emerged at a time when psychometrics and experimental behavioural psychology were developing into major influences in literacy education through their claims to scientific validity. It rested upon claims of scientific validity for particular methods over others in order to establish the most efficient and effective way to teach reading. The extract below from *Learning to Read: The Great Debate* describes the situation in the US and England, which impacted upon Carson's early years as a teacher and any students who were in the English education system and/or teaching in primary schools in the 1950s and 1960s.

Despite thousands of research studies and scholarly discussions on reading since the turn of the century, it has been difficult for researchers to state with any degree of confidence that one particular method or approach to beginning reading is really better than another. From time to time there has appeared to be a consensus on how and when to begin and what to emphasize at the beginning stages of reading instruction. Then a period of disagreement and confusion sets in.

Such a period began in 1955 in the United States with the publication of Rudolf Flesche's *Why Johnny Can't Read*. This book took the nation by storm. It stayed on the best-seller lists for over thirty weeks and was serialized in countless newspapers. Although the general press reacted favorably to it, reviewers in educational periodicals almost unanimously rejected it (Riedler, 1962).

Flesch challenged – strongly, clearly, and polemically – the prevailing views on beginning reading instruction, which emphasized teaching children by a sight method. He advocated a return to a phonic approach (early teaching of correspondences between letters and sounds) as the best – no, the *only*-method to use in beginning instruction. He found support for this view in his interpretation of the existing reading research, particularly the research comparing sight and phonic methods. (Oddly enough, this same body of research formed the basis for the prevailing methods, and proponents of those methods used it to defend themselves.)

Several years later the conclusion reached in other popularly written books – Sybil Terman and Charles C. Walcutt's *Reading: Chaos and Cure* (1958) and Walcutt's *Tomorrow's Illiterates* (1961) – perhaps with less anger but with equal force and certainty, was essentially the same: that the prevailing approach to beginning reading, with its stress on sight reading was incorrect.

England saw the beginnings of a similar controversy in 1956 with the publication of the first experimental report of J.C. Daniels and Hunter Diack. These authors concluded that their newly devised approach, which they called the 'phonic-word method,' produced better results than the prevailing mixed methods (sight, then phonics) then in use in England.

(Chall 1967, pp. 3–4)

Chall notes that, in her view, in the US dissatisfaction continued to spread. The general public was becoming increasingly concerned about the methods by which children were being taught to read. Various 'experts' were proposing a wide range of solutions:

> In the fall of 1959, when the debate was at its most bitter point, the National Conference on Research in English called together a special committee on research in reading for a three-day conference at Syracuse University. The purpose of the meeting was to map out programs of needed research. Participants generally agreed that the problem of beginning reading, although acknowledged to be a difficult one, desperately needed more attention from researchers. They felt that the research then available provided evidence so vague, contradictory, and incomplete as to encourage conflicting interpretations. No serious researcher could state with any degree of certainty, on the basis of such evidence, that either one or another approach to beginning reading was indeed the best or the worst.
>
> (Chall 1967, p. 4)

The conceptualisation of literacy as neutral and scientific helped foster a view in the media and political debates of an interpretation of literacy as 'the learning of "basic" literacy skills of the "Three Rs"' through 'direct instruction and rote learning' (Rassool 1999, p. 27). The promotion of this view of literacy and the resulting emphasis on the correct method to teach reading in the 1950s and 1960s inevitably gave rise to a cycle of public debates and political concerns over literacy 'standards' in the following decades.

In the 1950s there began a series of claims backed up by 'objective data' and 'scientific findings' that standards of reading are declining and that the main cause of this decline in reading could be attributed to the methods of teaching reading. If practices to promote literacy development are seen primarily to be a matter of finding the one best scientifically proven method to teach reading, it follows that literacy educators who do not utilise the 'best method' run the risk of lowering literacy standards. This was at the heart of the arguments that there was a decline put forward by Flesch in the US and Daniels and Diack in England in the 1950s and 1960s.

The literacy wars

As Rassool notes, the 'literacy wars' developed in the 1970s as an 'attack by experimental psychologists on the orthodoxy that evolved during the 1970s around the emphasis placed by psycholinguists on the reading process and the production of meaning through the use of contextual cues' (Rassool 1999, p. 27). He argues that in the 1970s psycholinguistic influences upon the conceptualisation of literacy resulted in a move from viewing literacy as the neutral decoding of print. Psycholinguists critiqued this behaviouristic, experimentally inspired view of literacy. They argued that it should be replaced with a view of literacy as a 'range of meanings produced at the interface of person and text, and the linguistic strategies and cultural knowledges used to 'cue' into meanings embedded in the text' (*ibid.*, p. 28). This view formed the foundation for the 'whole-language' and 'real-book' approaches that were advocated by literacy educators such as Goodman and Smith in the 1970s and 1980s (see, for example, Goodman 1986 and F. Smith 1971).

The 'whole-language' or 'real-book' approach draws upon psycholinguistics and represented a 'top-down' approach to teaching literacy. In this approach meaning was seen to develop from 'whole to part' {meaningful units of language}, from vague to precise, from gross to fine, from highly concrete and contextualised to more abstract (Goodman 1986, p. 39).

The 'literacy wars' of the 1970s and 1980s resulted from behavioural, experimental psychologists such as Stanovich (see, for example, Stanovich 2000) attacking this top-down, whole-language, real-book approach. They argued that it lacked scientific validity because it was seen to be 'operating on broad assumptions and not having sufficient empirical data' (Stanovich and Stanovich 1995, quoted in Rassool 1999, p. 27). They have argued for a 'bottom-up' model of reading, where children are seen to build their knowledge of words from part to whole. This approach, as noted above, leads to an emphasis on phonics and phonological awareness, common letter-strings and initial sound blendings in order to decode and write text.

Concerns over the dominance of phonics

The conflict between 'bottom-up' and 'top-down' approaches lies at the heart of the 'Great Debate, the 'reading wars' and subsequent political storms over reading instruction. It is often referred to as the phonics versus whole-language debate, particularly in the United States and Australasia, and the phonics versus real books in the United Kingdom. As we have seen, during this debate the emphasis has swung from one approach to the other, but by the late 1990s – particularly in America –

phonics had become dominant so that there was a strong advocation of phonics as the 'one best system in American education for the initial teaching of reading' (Davis 2002, p. 3).

In his article, which addresses the implications of this for teachers and administrators, O.L. Davis Jnr argues that in previous debates between whole language and phonics the teaching profession in the United States has managed to adopt a middle ground. Teachers have attempted to integrate the two approaches depending on the method they felt was most appropriate and what made sense for the individual children they taught, while also endeavouring to adopt 'as their own some elements of the "new" procedures which made sense to them' to further develop the 'very best ways they knew' to teach reading (*ibid.*, p. 83). As discussed earlier, this is the approach Shirley Carson describes adopting during her fifty-year career as a teacher and teacher educator. Davis notes that administrators in the United States have tended to support teachers 'intense and balanced' efforts to address the failure of some students, despite 'mindful diagnosis, and the use of carefully crafted, individually designed programmes' (*ibid.*).

Davis is concerned, however, that the more recent public debates over phonics versus whole language in the United States have been more intense, with more ideological zealots than in previous periods of the 'reading wars'. In the current battle those who promote phonics-only instruction can be seen to have captured the high ground and have the potential to produce a 'nightmarish vision of government intrusion into higher education' where all teacher educator programmes will have to have 'common syllabi that feature phonics only reading instruction', so that 'in the current situation phonics proponents appear to be following a "take no prisoners" position'. He argues that already in the United States they dominate 'several key state governors and state boards of education' so that phonics-only could become mandatory for these particular states. Davis is concerned that this will lead to a situation where teachers will be legally forced to teach phonics so that they would lose their ability to make decisions and to integrate the two approaches:

> This dismal vision of the near future appears at once to be outrageous and monumentally bizarre. On the other hand, it could happen and it could occur soon. Legislated phonics instruction must define legal and illegal instructional practice and establish punishments for violations of the law. Some agency (and it could be a new 'Corps of Phonics Police') must be the enforcer of the law.

Violators – in this case, teachers and college professors, perhaps administrators, school systems and universities – must be prosecuted.

(Davis 2002, p. 84)

Davis warns teachers that if the proponents of phonics-only become successful in implementing a 'one size fits all' strategy in approaches to reading, then their success in this area could lead to the undermining of balanced approaches to other areas of the curriculum. He argues that teachers must ignore and refuse to participate in the current round of the reading war. They need to become politicised and enter the debates to ensure that the politicians, policy-makers and legislators are aware of the need to utilise a number of research-based approaches to teaching reading, and the need for individualised programmes, literature-based programmes, whole-word approaches and a combination of these approaches, as well as phonics-based approaches.

The literacy standards debate: clarifying the issues

In the 1990s the public debate over declining standards surfaced again in England when the *Times Educational Supplement* carried a front-page story reporting that educational psychologists had found that reading standards among 7-year-olds were falling rapidly in London local education authorities (LEAs). This story was subsequently reported in all the national English newspapers. Stierer describes the impassioned coverage of this claim as follows:

> On 29 June 1990, *The Times Educational Supplement* carried a front-page story reporting a claim made by nine unnamed educational psychologists that reading standards among seven-year-olds had declined dramatically in their LEAs. The story was picked up by all the national newspapers and by many television and radio news programmes, leading to emotive accusations of unstructured and uninformed teaching in schools, inflexible 'bandwagoning' amongst teacher-trainers and LEA inspectors and advisors, and lax control by politicians and policy-makers.

(Stierer 2002, p. 75)

One of these press reports is reproduced below to give an indication of the style of the initial press coverage of this particular crisis over falling standards. The press-report rhetoric which surrounded this crisis carried the implicit assumption that 'falling reading standards' were due to the inappropriateness of 'modern reading methods', particularly the whole-language/real-book approach.

> Tests on 350,000 seven-year-olds in England and Wales have revealed the biggest drop in reading standards for more than 40 years. Secret data collected by a cross-section of nine local education authorities shows that average reading scores fell from 100 in 1985 to 96.8 last year. The fall – said to be the biggest since a sharp decline in reading standards between 1937 and 1945 – is bound to fuel parents' growing concern about modern methods of teaching children to read. Such is the secrecy surrounding pupils' reading scores that the findings, which are the most detailed to have been published since the early 1970s, emerged only by accident from an informal meeting of the senior educational psychologists who administer the tests. Brought together by shared worries about their own results, they discovered, in the words of one, 'that we were all staring at the same problem'.
>
> (*Daily Telegraph*, 29 June 1990)

In this press report, representatives of the nine authorities were said to have agreed to summarise their data and publish their results without the permission of their employees:

> The nine areas have not been named but are understood to include Surrey, Suffolk, Norfolk, Croydon, Derbyshire and South Glamorgan. They are among the shrinking number of education authorities that still measure the reading ability of seven-year-olds annually. Most others, including such Conservative-controlled counties as Hampshire and Kent, have abandoned the practice in the belief that the information collected is 'unhelpful'. Mrs Mona McNee, an acknowledged expert, said a seven-year-old should be able to read nursery rhymes and books like Noddy, Little Red Engine and Billy Goat Gruff with ease, having to ask for help with only the occasional word. An example of a sentence a seven-year-old ought to be able to read was: 'The string had eight knots in it which I had to untie.' An eight-year-old should be able to read: 'The people could scarcely obtain enough food to remain healthy.' ... Mr Martin Turner, the educational psychologist who convened the meeting of the nine, said

their figures showed that the proportion of seven-year-olds with a below-average reading score of less than 85 had doubled in some areas and risen by at least half in the rest. The proportion scoring more than an above-average 115 had fallen overall. A score of 100 means a seven-year-old has a reading age of seven; approximately two-thirds of the age group would then score between 85 and 115. 'By the time they are seven, children should have made a good start with their reading,' Mr Turner said.

... Those areas that have statistics going back many years can show that the rot set in during the early 1980s. But we are all agreed that the fall since 1985 has been pronounced. ...

'You have to ask why education authorities won't release the information. What are they hiding? Parents can see that their children aren't making progress with their reading and it worries them. Schools should be accountable for what they're doing.' Some experts attribute the decline in standards to an approach to teaching reading known as the 'look-say' method, which has been widely used since the 1960s.

The method requires children to memorise words by their shape, as if they were learning Chinese characters, instead of learning to sound them out, as in c-a-t. Others put more of the blame on the time children spend watching television.

(Clare 1990, p. 1)

The great debate over literacy standards is inextricably linked to a particular view of literacy and reading which continued into the 1990s and underpins current concerns over literacy standards. Turner's (1990) arguments that there was a decline in reading standards and that this could be attributed to the widespread take-up of what he considered the ill-conceived method of teaching with 'real books' can be viewed as a continuation of the earlier debate and its associated conceptualisation of literacy, as the newspaper report indicates.

This media attention was followed by Turner's publication of *Sponsored Reading Failure: An Object Lesson* (1990). Turner was Senior Educational Psychologist in the London Borough of Croydon and one of the nine who made the initial claims outlined above. The pamphlet was intended to provide evidence to substantiate the original claims that reading standards had suffered a serious decline by the early 1990s.

Stierer looks at this particular episode in depth and argues that an analysis of the evidence in this pamphlet shows that these claims were based upon 'a fairly small number of children chosen only from those authorities which showed a decline', yet the media reports and statements made by Turner and the other LEA representatives misleadingly implied that the claim was 'based upon a large and representative sample' (Stierer 2002, p. 75). Stierer also argues that the claims were based on false assumptions related to the way the reading tests were interpreted, the standardisation of differing scores, and the underpinning assumption that the data and the psychologists' agenda was politically neutral and scientifically objective and rigorous, when their analysis was 'bound to be guided by their assumptions and preconceptions' related to particular views about how children should be taught to read (*ibid.*, p. 76).

Having shown how tenuous the evidence was for declining reading standards, Stierer goes on to explore the way in which Turner forged a link between this evidence and the claim that reading standards were declining because of the introduction of whole-language/real-book-based approaches to teaching reading, so that to Turner, the real-books or whole-language approach 'is synonymous with "no teaching"'. Stierer argues that there could be alternative explanations for Turner's data. He notes that the standardised tests used to gather this evidence 'no longer reflect the psychometric conceptions of reading built into the tests', so that children who have been taught by the real-book/whole-language method may not do as well as children who have been taught in traditional ways which the traditional tests are designed to measure.

At the conclusion of his article Stierer notes that in the aftermath of the controversy the teaching profession has tended to ignore the ideological political motives that underpin Turner's position in the phonics versus real-books/whole-language debate. This stance, he argues, needs to be challenged if we are to advance our understanding of literacy and related teaching practices:

> The mainstream professional response to Turner's position has been to ignore its wider professional and ideological underpinnings, and to treat the debate as an unnecessarily polarised comparison of the two techniques for teaching reading. 'Moderates' quoted in the press refuted Turner by reporting that most teachers use a combination of methods, and that the world of reading is not as fraught a battleground as Turner would have us believe. ... [I]n its claim to impartiality, this response falls into the same trap that Martin Turner does: it is blind to its own ideological underpinnings ... so this response seems to me to be a spurious

attempt to reconcile fundamentally irreconcilable philosophical positions, under the guise of impartiality, by reducing the debate to one of techniques and by accepting implicitly all of the assumptions about teaching, learning and schooling underpinning Turner's stance. It leaves unanswered the really crucial questions about literacy, which stand at the frontiers of practice, crying out to be investigated.

(Stierer 2002, p. 80)

Stierer's examination of this specific example of the 1990s literacy-standards crisis in England shows that the 'Great Debate' and the subsequent 'literacy wars' are inextricably part of the wider debates about schooling, education and its role in society. Debates over appropriate methods of literacy often turn into debates over falling literacy standards. Claims about 'falling literacy standards' tend to lie at the centre of this confrontation between competing disciplinary, professional and sectional interest over what will be defined as acceptable levels and forms of competence in decoding and writing text. Such 'literacy crises' highlight the contesting interests at the heart of the politics which surround literacy education.

The discussion above included one recent English example of a 'literacy crisis' with which many English educators will be familiar. It is also possible to examine 'literacy crises' from an international viewpoint in order to generate some explanations for the regular occurrence of assertions that literacy standards are falling. Welch and Freebody, in their chapter 'Explanations of the Current International "Literacy Crisis"', like Stierer in the article discussed above, point out that psychology, human development and educational measurement have been the disciplines which have traditionally informed our understandings of how to teach reading and have upheld an implicit assumption that the teaching of reading and writing is politically neutral, objectively quantifiable and technicist (Welch and Freebody 2002). However, more recent cross-disciplinary accounts, which draw upon history, politics, linguistics and economics, counter this traditional view of the teaching and evaluation of literacy and link them to differing dominant visions of what literacy is for and how we must teach it:

The perspectives on literacy arising from this comparatively new cross-disciplinary attention in turn provide the grounds for critiques of both technicist and progressive accounts of literacy education. The 'great debate' between so-called skills and meaning approaches to literacy teaching (presented by Chall, 1967) has been put into its historical and ideological context (Christie, 1990), and the ways in which it has blinkered the exploration of literacy practices are beginning to be documented (Gee, 1990). ... It is fast becoming commonplace, therefore, to assert that literacy practices are not ideologically innocent. They do not merely meet cultural and individual needs: rather they shape both the ways in which cultures develop socio-economic arrangements and the ways in which literate individuals develop 'adaptive psychological dispositions and cognitive strategies'. ... In a literate culture, neither inter- nor intra-personal conditions are unaffected by the technologies of literacy. This idea – which may be expressed by the slogan that literacy practices are culturally and psychologically emergent – is a central scaffold that is taken for granted by a growing number of scholars, educators and policy makers.

(Welch and Freebody 2002, p. 61)

Welch and Freebody argue that there are four possible hypothesis that may help us understand what underpins the recurring phenomena of the debates and literacy crises across national and international contexts:

1 *The Slide Hypothesis*: That the rhetoric of concern about literacy standards is indeed a result of genuinely declining standards in the recent past in the literacy competence of school students or perhaps of nations or sub-national groups;

2 *The Demands Hypothesis*: That, while competences have not declined, the requisite literacy competencies for effective civil, social, and cultural functioning have increased and diversified in our society;

3 *The Credentials Hypothesis*: That, while neither competences nor cultural demands have changed significantly, the increased competitiveness of the labour market, and/or the decline in work-force numbers of low-literacy occupations in a society have led to an increase in the necessary formal credentials for any given job;

4 *The Invention Hypothesis*: That the rhetoric of concern about literacy standards is, like the concept of 'standards' itself, a confection, designed or at least functioning to undermine certain progressive or socially powerful educational trends that have developed in the recent past.

(Welch and Freebody 2002, pp. 62–3)

All of these hypotheses, apart from the first one – concerns over standards, which is the hypothesis Turner promoted during the 1990s – suggest that Stierer is correct to caution us to take a critical look at the way in which crises over reading standards and subsequent debates over reading standards are motivated by wider social, cultural and national agendas. Welch and Freebody note that research into literacy crises over falling standards in Canada and the United States matches the arguments put forward by Stierer, that literacy crises and claims of falling literacy standards can be linked to wider social and economic changes – for example the emergence of periodic demands for a more skilled workforce and greater economic progress when there are concerns over the schooling system producing workers to participate in a competitive economy. Studies of other international examples of literacy crises and debates over falling literacy standards also show, as Stierer notes, the differing political agendas of various groups as they seek to pursue their own particular interests. Welch and Freebody's chapter reiterates Stierer's assertion that the teaching profession needs to take a critical perspective when considering the debates surrounding literacy standards. We need to be aware that such debates are usually related to contemporary social and economic changes, and develop a 'critical understanding of literacy practices through an analysis of their material and visible relations to knowledge, culture, and power' (Welch and Freebody 2002, p. 71).

Conclusion

This chapter has investigated theoretical and political conflicts and tensions that have arisen over views of a fundamental aspect of literacy development – that is, how children learn to read. It has explored the conflicts and tensions that arise over how to teach reading by researchers and practitioners who are drawing upon psychological-based models of reading, as well as exploring the political agendas that have shaped the debates over reading and the teaching of reading. Although the models of reading examined in this chapter are derived from a common disciplinary focus on the individual, they offer differing understandings of how to facilitate the process of learning to decode text. This in turn has given rise to differing and often conflicting notions of what might cause difficulties with literacy and how we should address this in our literacy programmes.

Chapters 2 and 3 will continue to explore the tensions and issues associated with psychological models and their views of what might cause students to experience individual difficulties in literacy development. These chapters critically examine the notion of dyslexia. This much-debated and frequently used concept focuses on the cognitive ways in which individuals process text-based information. The term 'dyslexia' and the research associated with it are often drawn upon by educational psychologists and practitioners to devise programmes and techniques designed to overcome barriers experienced by individuals in their endeavours to decode and produce text.

Chapters 4 and 5 will move beyond cognitive psychology to explore wider disciplinary and interdisciplinary views of reading. In these chapters we will draw upon understandings of literacy derived from social psychology, social linguistics and sociological perspectives to further explore the differing and conflicting notions of social and cultural factors that might contribute to particular groups of students experiencing difficulties in literacy.

Chapter 2

Concepts of dyslexia

Introduction

Dyslexia is a psychological conceptualisation of difficulties that, most commonly, refers to the way in which individuals process cognitive information. In this conceptualisation the information-processing system of 'dyslexic' individuals is conceived of as different from that of non-dyslexics in ways which have an impact on a number of areas of performance, and in particular on reading and writing.

'Dyslexia' is also a concept about which there is much debate, characterised by controversy with regard to both scientific research and educational policy. Some of the current controversies related to dyslexia and dyslexia research are associated with whether or not there is an identifiable entity that we might term 'dyslexia' and, if so, what its precise nature, causes and explanations might be (Stanovich 1996). Pumfrey (1996), for example, describes dyslexia as a 'variable syndrome'. This implies that definitions of dyslexia may vary and be interpreted in different ways. Much of the controversy in policy-making relates to issues of equity in resourcing individual learning needs by privileging certain groups of students.

The controversies associated with dyslexia may at times present a picture of confusion and uncertainties regarding best practice in assessment and teaching. It is therefore important that the conceptual and practical considerations relating to dyslexia are considered within a framework of critical appraisal. Assessment of the barriers to literacy learning experienced by individuals needs to be comprehensive, and forms of educational support need to be justified against particular perceptions of need. For example, one might ask whether a particular explanation has arisen because of the responses from research, or because it has been developed to fit into existing practice. One might also question whether a particular explanation of dyslexia views dyslexia mainly as a reading difficulty or as a more wide-ranging concept incorporating a range of other factors.

Research into dyslexia

Fawcett (2002) traces the history of research into dyslexia and relates this to current and emerging practice. She notes how in the 1980s researchers in the US changed the focus to 'reading disability' rather than 'learning disability'. As a result resources were devoted to analysing the reading process rather than the learning processes which underlie reading methodology and practice. Inevitably, this resulted in divisions between those researchers who were investigating the causes of 'dyslexia' and those investigating the roots of reading problems. For a mature theory of difficulties in literacy development it is clear that both approaches are needed.

Fawcett (op. cit.) has expressed views on what, in her opinion, constitute the current key issues for research in the area of dyslexia. She notes that one of the 'major' tensions in dyslexia research is the potential conflict between the viewpoints of individuals and interest groups, all of whom have different agendas: researchers and practitioners, parents and teachers, teachers and educational psychologists, schools and local education authorities (LEAs), and LEAs and governments. She notes the significance of the issue of funding in forcing academic researchers into opposition. One might also add that this issue often forces parents and LEAs into opposition. This issue of resources as a major source of debate in relation to notions of equity for all students is discussed below.

Fawcett highlights these issues by referring to a series of round-table discussions held at the international conference of the British Dyslexia Association (BDA) in 2001. These involved professionals from different countries, with different agendas and varying perspectives. The purpose of the round-table discussions was to identify a set of proposals which might be put forward as a plan of action for both the BDA and others in the field. While the consensus reached after the discussions was that considerable progress had been made, there were also concerns, principally the need to transform the scientific developments and the 'spirit of co-operation into a reality'. The gulf between intention and practice may still be wide in some areas. Policies, whether at national government or local level, may deliver the appropriate rhetoric, but they also need to be translated into reality in daily classroom practices, as well as at a systemic level, in all schools. In one of the other round-table discussions at the same conference (Reid 2001) the different needs and different practices in all sectors of the UK education system was apparent. The discussions centred on issues such as inappropriate curriculum and assessments for young people with dyslexia, the need for teacher training and a heightened aware- ness of dyslexia at the classroom level, and equity in terms of formulating policy and provision at local level. These issues engen- dered considerable debate, which highlighted Fawcett's concern that different agendas drive different interest groups into opposition. The challenge, then, is to develop uniform, equitable and constructive multidisciplinary practices involving professionals and parents in order to, as Fawcett suggests, 'work towards a common understanding'.

Nicolson (2001), commenting on his own experience as a researcher in the area of dyslexia, refers not only to the disagreements between scientists working in the field of dyslexia research but also to the increasing range of alternative and vigorously marketed 'treat- ments' for dyslexia. Sometimes claims for the success of a particular treatment are based on 'research' which may in fact confuse and mislead practitioners and parents:

> When I first entered dyslexia research I naively assumed that dyslexia research was science, science was the search for truth and that nothing else really mattered. This is not so. Even in academia, scientific research is at least as much about academic politics as about science – as Medawar put it science is the art of the soluble. If no one will fund the research, the scientific progress will not be made. Consequently astute academics spend much time cultivating influential acquaintances and building their power base. Dyslexia research spans a particularly broad spectrum, including a range of 'pure science' theories to a range of treat- ments and support that if successfully marketed might make their inventors millionaires, to overt lobbying of governments. ... It is all too easy to apply the logic of politics (or worse, marketing) to matters of science. Perhaps the best way forward to maintain the credibility of the field is to introduce some system of 'kite marking' or declaration of interests, allied to clear disassociations of func- tion, so that lobbying, marketing and science are kept well apart.
> (Nicolson 2001, p. 6)

In relation to adults, Reid and Kirk (2000) convened a series of task-group discussions of over 200 professionals and occupational psychologists throughout the UK in order to identify 'best practice' in assessment and support in relation to dyslexia and employment. The research mainly focused on the work of the Employment Service, and it was noted that much of this type of assessment in the employment service is carried out by disability employment advisers and occupational psychologists. The research was conducted through questionnaires and through task-group discussions, which were held in around twenty locations throughout the UK. Participants at these discussions were invited to provide views on current working practices in relation to dyslexia and suggest possible improvements to the process and the provision. Reid and Kirk reported that:

> A range of professional perspectives on dyslexia existed among participants. These ranged from on the one hand a broad conceptual view of dyslexia to a narrow, sceptical view of dyslexia.
> (Reid and Kirk 2000, pp. 78–9)

It was also noted that many occupational psychologists were very familiar with the literature on dyslexia but chose to highlight ambiguities and controversies in the literature as evidence of a weak theoretical foundation for the concept of dyslexia and believed this justified their scepticism. Some justified dyslexia from a neurological standpoint, were familiar with neurologically based tests and so found the educational model 'unhelpful' (Reid and Kirk 2000, p. 79). This research also noted that many of the sample in the discussion groups viewed dyslexia as a redundant concept for those dealing with work factors, because their primary concern was to match the individual with the workplace and therefore an assessment of workplace needs was the priority, not a diagnosis of dyslexia. Clearly this can be a controversial perspective, as in many cases, both in tertiary education and in the workplace, the individual requires the label 'dyslexia' before adequate supports can be generated.

Silver, reviewing controversial therapies for the International Dyslexia Association's *Perspectives* periodical, suggests:

> The process from initial concept to acceptance of a particular treatment approach is slow and can take years. Research must support a particular approach and the results should be published in a peer-reviewed journal. Often replication studies are undertaken. Then there is the process of publicising best practices and incorporating these approaches into standards of care. When

research data are not available and the approach is based on an individual's beliefs and writings, information on such treatment approaches is usually found in a popular book, the newspapers, lay magazines, or in discussions on television shows. Often parents hear of such approaches before professionals.

(Silver 2001, p. 1)

Nicolson (2001) also teases out the significance of distinguishing between description and cause in the area of research into dyslexia. He suggests, like Fawcett, that the medical model differentiates between cause, symptom and treatment and can provide a reasonable starting point for an investigation of 'abnormal states', but a full investigation requires the integration of all three aspects – the cause, the symptom and the treatment. This is similar to the cognitive neuroscience model developed by Frith (1997), which focuses on the biological, cognitive and behavioural levels of explanations of dyslexia. The biological focuses on causes, the cognitive on symptoms and the behavioural on observed difficulties and possible 'treatments'. Nicolson emphasises that no one element is more important than the other – all three are important and a complete explanation would involve all three. This emphasises the key role of multidisciplinary research involving professionals from different fields and with varying specialisms. It also emphasises the need to integrate different theoretical perspectives to provide a fuller picture. In the case of dyslexia, a scan of the literature reveals that the following groups of professionals and 'specialisms' have been involved in some way in helping to provide a 'fuller picture': speech and language therapists, medical researchers, optometrists, neuroscientists, teachers, educational psychologists, cognitive psychologists, occupational psychologists, occupational therapists, psychiatrists, researchers in literacy, parents, dieticians, physiotherapists.

This list is not exhaustive but it serves to underline the potential for disparate views and potential confusion in relation to the cause and description, the possible hypotheses and the interventions which can be associated with dyslexia. The British Psychological Society (BPS; 1999) described ten different hypotheses which have been associated with dyslexia from the literature. This serves to emphasise the importance of integrating the different perspectives into an operational definition which can promote a working and fuller understanding of dyslexia and other similar conditions.

Fawcett, like Nicolson, suggests that the detailed description of phenomena enables researchers to derive hypotheses which can account for these phenomena. The hypothesised cause is then evaluated against the description of new data, and scientific progress can be made towards a more accurate explanation. Fawcett uses the term 'medical model' of abnormal development to distinguish between cause, symptom and treatment, and makes an analogy with allergies, where different symptoms in different people can result from the same allergy and where the link between them is unclear. Appropriately trained, qualified specialists need to administer more sensitive tests to uncover the real cause and, consequently, an appropriate 'treatment'. Practitioners are concerned with 'treatment', educational psychologists with 'symptoms', and academic researchers with uncovering cause(s). The integration of all three aspects is essential to supporting improved pupil learning. For example, in the area of early identification of dyslexia it might be appropriate to rely on theoretical research into the predictors of dyslexia outside the domain of reading in order to develop a screening test. The alternative is to wait until children fail to acquire literacy despite access to regular teaching, and to risk a negative impact on future life chances.

Discrepancy definitions of dyslexia

As was noted earlier, dyslexia as a syndrome is not without controversy. One of the major debates in relation to education policy and provision concerns the following:

- the difference between the cut-off and regression methods of identifying individuals as 'dyslexic';
- the significance of these two definitions for making appropriate provision to meet pupils' difficulties in literacy development.

This controversy relates to discrepancy definitions and is encapsulated in the statement made by Nicolson and Siegel for contributors to consider in preparation for a special edition of *Dyslexia*, an international journal of research and practice on dyslexia and intelligence:

> Most of those involved in dyslexia research and practice believe that, although the precise symptoms of dyslexia vary from individual to individual and there may indeed be different subtypes of dyslexia, it is nonetheless a 'syndrome', different in kind from reading problems attributable to generally low intelligence. Recently, however, this view has been challenged strongly by

research which has failed to find qualitative performance differences between dyslexia and the 'garden variety' poor readers.

(Nicolson and Siegel 1996, p. 153)

This has implications for how education authorities define dyslexia, and
particularly for how this definition is used to allocate resources. For
example, two methods used to define dyslexia, both of which utilise IQ,
can be compared to highlight the implications for practice. These are
the 'cut-off' method and the 'regression' method. Both have resource
implications, particularly for the type of teaching programmes and
provision allocated. The regression method essentially looks at the
discrepancy between IQ and the reading level which would be *predicted*
based on a child's IQ score. This means that a child with a high IQ
score who may be around or only slightly below his age level in reading
can still be identified as dyslexic because the reading level may still be
below that expected for the IQ level. On the other hand, the cut-off
method means that any child with an average or above IQ who is
lagging in their reading level by at least eighteen months can be
described as dyslexic. Both these methods can be problematic, for two
reasons: they rely on the validity of the IQ measure as a robust indicator
of a child's abilities; and both cut-off and regression methods can
change over time, and a child who qualifies for additional help on
account of any of these measures may make an improvement in reading
which would exclude them, using the discrepancy criteria, from continuing to use the label dyslexia or to qualify for extra help. In practice,
therefore, a child receiving additional help may lose this support if s/he
makes a gain which narrows the discrepancy gap between reading and
IQ. Some researchers, such as Fawcett and Nicolson, take the view that
dyslexia is not only a reading difficulty but also affects other aspects of
learning and should be seen as more than reading. This also has implications for resources, as has the view from researchers such as Stanovich
(which is discussed later in this chapter, p. 30) that there is no qualitative difference between the phonological pattern of errors between
dyslexia readers and readers with low IQs.

Differences in definitions given by researchers in the field

Below are seven views from researchers working in this field, relating to
the notion of dyslexia as a syndrome and how the syndrome can be
precisely defined. These views differ in relation to the role of intelligence

in identifying dyslexia and the nature of dyslexia in relation to the reading processes between poor readers with low and high IQ scores. On the one hand, researchers such as Stanovich focus almost exclusively on reading, while Nicolson and Fawcett link dyslexia with other cognitive processes. This highlights the fact that some explanations of dyslexia may explain reading difficulties but not spelling and writing. They have therefore included the role of the cerebellum and the cognitive processes influencing automaticity in their theoretical understanding of dyslexia. This results in a broader definition of dyslexia.

View 1: Stanovich

In response to this question presented by Nicolson, Stanovich (1996) questions the assumption that poor readers of high and low intelligence need different explanations for their reading difficulties. He suggests that the primary sub-component of reading that presents difficulty for children with severe reading problems is word recognition, and that the main psychological process underlying such word-recognition difficulties is a problem in phonological coding due to weak segmental language skills. He suggests that these factors are independent of intelligence: 'We are now in a position to ask where intelligence comes in as an explanation of reading difficulty. The answer is: nowhere' (*ibid.*, p. 161). In defence of his argument Stanovich cites a number of empirical studies which indicate that the nature of the processing within the 'word-recognition module', including the reading of pseudowords, phonological segmentation skills, orthographic processing and the spelling–sound regularity, is quite similar for poor readers of high and low IQ. Stanovich therefore poses two crucial questions relating to the identification of dyslexic children. He asks:

i) why is a low I.Q. child, with demonstrated speech segmentation problems, with poor phonological coding skills, with poor word recognition skills and hence reading comprehension below their listening comprehension not dyslexic? ii) what is the specific information processing model that bars this child from the label and what are the specific processing mechanisms that differentiate this child's poor word recognition from that of a high I.Q. poor reader?

(Stanovich 1996, p. 161)

In view of the questions he poses above, Stanovich therefore concludes that 'if we have decided to keep the term dyslexia in our conceptual lexicon, then all children with problems in phonological coding resulting from segmental language problems are dyslexic' (ibid.).

In this argument Stanovich is not actually disputing the presence of dyslexia as a syndrome, but rather which population of children we regard as dyslexic and how these children are identified.

View 2: Miles

Miles, however, argues that the notion of a global IQ figure is misleading, and that this is certainly the case for children with dyslexia. He suggests that:

> [C]entral to a diagnosis of dyslexia ... is the fact that dyslexics are strong at some tasks and relatively weak at others; and the purpose of giving them suitably selected items from traditional intelligence tests is to obtain evidence about their strengths, evidence which of course often transforms their lives.
>
> (Miles 1996, p. 177)

View 3: Tunmer and Chapman

Tunmer and Chapman argue that:

> [I]t may be possible to define dyslexia as the condition that arises from being unable to respond appropriately to formal reading instruction despite access to linguistic and environmental opportunities, because of an initial weakness in phonological processing that is due to an executive dysfunction (ie a deficit or delay in metacognitive functioning) and/or a deficiency in the phonological processing module.
>
> (Tunmer and Chapman 1996, pp. 185–6)

This statement implies that dyslexic children may be prone to acquiring and utilising inefficient cognitive strategies. They suggest that:

[F]or a considerable period of time disabled readers have been using ineffective learning strategies that may be difficult to 'unlearn'. Moreover as a consequence of repeated learning failures, many disabled readers develop negative reading-related self-perceptions and therefore do not exert as much effort as other children because of their low expectations of success. Emphasis must therefore be placed on making these children aware that they can achieve success by using more effective word identification strategies.

(Tunmer and Chapman 1996, p. 187)

View 4: Nicolson

Nicolson's view is that:

[B]y the late 1980's the phonological deficit account was the consensus view of most dyslexia researchers. On the other hand it is clear that the PDH [Phonological Deficit Hypothesis] could never be a complete account of all three critical difficulties of dyslexic children, namely reading, writing and spelling. Reading is well handled (at least in the early stages where phonological onset/rime problems dominate). Spelling is poorly handled, in that PHD predicts problems only with phonological aspects of spellings, whereas it appears that all aspects of spelling are impaired. Handwriting problems are not predicted at all, in that they reflect motor skill problems.

(Nicolson 1996, p. 193)

I consider that serious damage is done to the concept of dyslexia if dyslexia is viewed merely as one end of the poor reading continuum, or if all children who read poorly are considered dyslexic. ... I.Q. is crucially relevant to dyslexia theory. If (as Stanovich suggests) we were no longer to distinguish between poor readers with low I.Q. and dyslexic children we would no longer be able to investigate the issue of whether dyslexic and PR/MLD [Poor Readers/Mild Learning Difficulty] children differ in terms of the cause of their phonologically-related domains other than reading ... My belief is that the overall goal for a ... research programme (in dyslexia) is to develop a clear framework of cause, diag-

nosis and treatment, in which the elucidation of the underlying cause(s), which almost certainly eventually [are] at the
neurological level[,] will lead to the development of positive
indicators for dyslexia that can be administered before a child
starts to learn to read. Early identification should lead in turn
to structured support that should avoid, or at worst mitigate,
subsequent reading problems. Once this is achieved, but not
before, neither I.Q. nor poor reading need to be central to the
diagnosis of dyslexia!

(Nicolson 1996, pp. 199, 203–4)

View 5: Working Party of the Division of Educational and Child
Psychology (DECP), British Psychological Society
The working party of the British Psychological Society which
investigated evidence relating to discrepancy definitions
concluded that:

[T]he validity of identifying dyslexia in terms of statistically
unexpected contrasts between actual literacy attainments and
those predicted on the grounds of I.Q. scores, is not supported
by the body of evidence showing that children of different
I.Q. scores perform similarly on a variety of measures of
reading and spelling ... profiles of test scores obtained from
batteries of tests of designed to assess cognitive performance
(eg the BAS [British Ability Scales] and the WISC [Wechsler
Intelligence Scale]) can aid understanding of the learner's
particular strengths and weaknesses. No cognitive profile
however can adequately discriminate between children with
or without literacy difficulties of a dyslexic nature.
Furthermore, it is important to consider the validity and reliability of test results in relation to children's cultural
experiences and life events.

(British Psychological Society 1999, p. 67)

View 6: Snowling
Snowling feels that characteristic features of dyslexia relate to
phonological processing and are independent of notions of intelligence:

[I]t is rare to find a dyslexic child who does not have some kind of phonological problem if they are tested using sensitive measures. A unitary definition of dyslexia with phonological impairments at its core therefore still seems tenable.

(Snowling 2000, p. 137)

[D]yslexia need not be a definition by exclusion. There are positive signs of dyslexia that persist throughout the life span. Dyslexia is a specific form of language impairment that affects the way in which the brain encodes the phonological features of spoken words. The core deficit is in phonological processing and stems from poorly specified phonological representations. Dyslexia specifically affects the development of reading and spelling skills but its effects can be modified through development leading to a variety of behavioural manifestations.

(Snowling 2000, pp. 213–14)

View 7: Cline

Cline looks at this issue in relation to children for whom English is an additional language (EAL). He suggests that:

[S]ome early definitions [of dyslexia] relied on exclusionary criteria, e.g. including a requirement that a child has 'adequate intelligence' and excluding those whose intelligence fell below an apparently arbitrary point on the normal curve. On this basis it became common to restrict the term 'dyslexia' to situations where a discrepancy was found between measured I.Q. and reading achievement. There are strong reasons for doubting the validity of diagnosing dyslexia in this way. In addition there are specific problems in employing this approach for children who are learning English as an additional language. I.Q. tests administered in English tend to under-estimate the potential of children for whom English is an additional language (Cummins 1984). As a result these children may fail to meet criteria for access to additional resources where these are based on I.Q.-achievement criteria (Cline and Frederickson 1999). Definitions that make no reference to I.Q., such as that proposed in the British Psychological Society (report 1999), avoid this problem.

(Cline 2002, p. 205)

It is clear, therefore, that dyslexia as a syndrome attracts controversies and disagreements in relation to an understanding of the research and research priorities in causes and explanations, as well as in assessment, teaching approaches and policy. It is important to consider how the views of the researchers mentioned above actually differ and what the implications of these differences are for policy and practice.

Stanovich suggests that dyslexia is related to reading, and particularly phonological awareness, and that this is independent of IQ. One implication for policy, according to this view, is that the notion of IQ should not be used to determine provision. Second, Stanovich takes the view that dyslexia is only related to the phonological skills associated with reading. Third, and very important for Stanovich's argument, is his view that the nature of the phonological errors displayed by children with general learning difficulties (garden variety readers) is qualitatively no different from that shown by dyslexic readers. Miles, however, feels that although the notion of global IQ may be misleading the cognitive profile revealed by the IQ test can highlight a pattern of strengths and weaknesses, which can both identify a typically dyslexic profile and help to inform teaching. Tunmer and Chapman, like Snowling, however, suggest that phonological awareness is the primary characteristic in dyslexia, but Tunmer and Chapman also suggest that difficulties with phonological awareness can be partly due to a delay in metacognitive functioning. This means that the child, because of his/her phonological difficulties, selects inappropriate strategies and learning habits which stay with them over time, and, once learned, these become difficult to unlearn. This has implications for learning skills as well as programmes on phonological awareness. Nicolson's view differs still further, as he argues that dyslexia involves more than literacy. He suggests that the phonological explanation ignores the importance of visual errors in spelling and motor factors associated with handwriting skills. The implications of Nicolson's views for practice are that neurological factors need to be taken into account in order for the underlying causes of dyslexia to be understood, and that a policy of early intervention with widespread screening could minimise the disruption to reading development experienced by dyslexic children. This means that positive indicators of dyslexia, particularly at an early stage, would be more useful to determine policy and practice than IQ scores, although Nicolson (unlike Stanovich) suggested that in the present situation there is a role for IQ scores – principally to distinguish between poor readers with low IQs and dyslexic readers. The report of the working party of the British Psychological Society rejects both of the discrepancy definitions described by Fawcett. They prefer to focus on cognitive profiles, as well as classroom-based curriculum factors, including learning opportunities and environmental aspects. This view, if transformed into policy and practice, would have considerable implications for classroom teachers, and indeed staff development for teachers, as it implies that the classroom should be the focus of both the identification of and the intervention in the presenting literacy difficulties experienced by the dyslexic child. Similarly, Cline suggests that IQ/discrepancy definitions can be misleading, particularly when dealing with children whose first language is one other than English, and as a result this group of children may be deprived of additional resources because they may not meet the discrepancy criteria using an IQ measure, which may in fact underestimate the potential of this group of children.

Clearly the explanations provided above, although they share some similarities, also have considerable differences, which consequently have implications for identification and for policy and practice. The BPS viewpoint supported by Cline will have considerable implications for the use of the curriculum as a vehicle for both identification and intervention – this is not too far removed from Nicolson's view of using early intervention in order to minimise the underlying neurological factors associated with dyslexia and preventing them from disrupting the child's literacy development. Yet in reality much of the current practice in dyslexia is reactive – dealing with literacy failure – although there are some positive signs that widespread early-intervention strategies may eventually prove effective in both identification of and intervention in potential and early literacy, and therefore become cost effective.

A theoretical framework for understanding dyslexia

As we can see, there are many perspectives on dyslexia. For example, the scientific researcher may have a different view from the policy-maker or the teacher, or indeed the parent. Each has a legitimate claim to ways of understanding the term. However, unless these views are organised into a systematic framework which can be understood by all, we are left with contradictory and disparate opinions, which can be unhelpful and confusing for those involved in the dyslexia field. One very useful framework for understanding these different perspectives and the significance of their diversity is described in the BPS's (1999) investigation of the concept of dyslexia, models of assessment and the practical implications of these for educational psychologists. The working party report which resulted from the enquiry utilised the 'causal modelling framework' (Morton and Frith 1995) and its three levels of theory as a means of understanding, explaining and organising the potentially disparate views and elements which contribute to dyslexia.

Three levels of theory

The 'causal modelling framework' developed by Frith and Morton forms a particularly useful model for understanding the different domains within which causal factors and the different perspectives in dyslexia research and practice might be categorised. Three 'levels' of theory stemming from the Morton and Frith framework on which research into dyslexia must focus include: the biological level, the cognitive (processing of information) level and the behavioural level (Frith 1997). What is meant by the 'biological level' is the physical brain mechanism, with abnormalities in the language areas of the cortex (outer layers of grey matter), magnocellular pathways and the cerebellum (the part of the brain below the cerebrum). The behavioural level relates to what students identified as 'dyslexic' commonly do, or cannot do – for example, their reading, rhyming and spelling may be poor. Explanations at the cognitive level are associated with information processing and might include deficits in short-term or working memory, phonological awareness, automatisation and slow speed of processing. Hypotheses about the way the brain processes the information it receives from sensory receptors are the essential link between brain and behaviour. Specialists working at all three levels need to collaborate towards a common understanding of dyslexia (Fawcett 2002). In this framework, the environment plays an overarching role, mediating as it does all three aspects.

Frith (2002b) suggests that the causal modelling framework 'can solve some seemingly intractable problems and confusions'. When all three factors are considered together, paradoxes disappear and a satisfactory definition of dyslexia can be achieved. The framework acknowledges that a large number of conditions can cause poor reading performance. Frith justifies the framework as a means of understanding not just dyslexia but also other conditions, because the same three factors – biological, cognitive and behavioural – together with overarching environmental influences, can affect most other conditions in varying degrees. For example, Frith suggests that 'biological causes may include genetic contributions and neuro-anatomical factors' (2002b, p. 46). The sorts of causes that qualify for the label 'cognitive' have to do with information-processing mechanisms. Although the way in which such mental mechanisms work can, in principle, be specified in computational language, in fact these mechanisms and their faults are still extremely sketchy. Nevertheless, there is sufficient understanding of them to make testable predictions. 'Theoretical propositions include difficulties in speech processing, in visual or auditory perceptual processing, and in motor or temporal processing' (*ibid.*, p. 47).

In relation to dyslexia, Frith acknowledges the existence of often apparently competing explanatory models of dyslexia, such as, for example, the hypotheses relating to phonological and magnocellular deficits. However, Frith suggests that these hypotheses need not be in conflict with each other; nor need they be mutually exclusive. The causal modelling framework can be used as a means to explain the linking levels. The phonological deficit theory focuses on the cognitive level of explanation, while the magnocellular deficit theory stakes a claim at the brain level. Frith therefore suggests that 'the two theories are compatible with each other' (*ibid.*).

Frith suggests that the framework can be applied readily to the idea of dyslexia as a syndrome. The evidence at the biological level, which assumes that dyslexia is a condition with a genetic origin and a basis in the brain, can link with the cognitive level and be used as a bridge to explain behavioural factors. These need to be seen as the outcome of the interaction of a great many factors. According to Frith, if dyslexia is to be represented as a neuro-developmental disorder, explanations should not be confined to one particular level. Cognitive theories therefore need to take into account biological and environmental risk factors as well. Frith suggests that:

> [C]ognitive theories need to make novel predictions in all direc-
> tions which means they have to be anchored within current
> knowledge of brain function. At the same time they have to
> systematically take account of environmental factors that influ-
> ence behaviour. In this context ideas about cognitive causes
> should act as a vital bridge in causal models and should lead to
> ideas for remediation.
>
> (Frith 2002b, p. 48)

These levels therefore are not discrete. At times it is difficult to separate out one level from another.

Biological level

New techniques in neuroscience, brain imaging and genetics have led to outstanding progress in theoretical dyslexia research at the biological level. The work of Galaburda (1989) has had a significant impact on both the conceptualisation of dyslexia and the implications for practice. Essentially Galaburda suggests that the processing patterns of dyslexic people in the hemispheres of the brain show differences in relation to non-dyslexics. Right-hemisphere processing relates to tasks that require a 'global' holistic approach, while left-hemisphere processing involves analyses of detail and small chunks of information. Those individuals who are right-hemisphere processors will therefore be stronger in performing tasks that need a holistic approach. The implication of this is that dyslexic children and adults can have right-hemisphere skills that can place them at a disadvantage in left-hemisphere tasks such as reading accuracy. There may be advantages in greater reliance on right-hemisphere processing, however. For example, West (1997) has utilised Galaburda's research to show that dyslexic people who are right-hemisphere processors can actually be at an advantage in some situations.

In addition to hemispheric processing, there has been some recent interest in the role of the visual systems in reading and in dyslexia (Stein 2002). Eden et al. (1996b) has also shown how dyslexics can have abnormalities associated with the magnocellular subsystem of the visual cortex. This has been followed by further work which relates the auditory and the visual magnocellular systems to the cerebellum, phonological processing systems and the role of nutritional factors, particularly the essential fatty acids (Stein 2002; Richardson 2002). Stein (1995) has also shown how convergence difficulties can affect reading for the dyslexic individual. Wilkins et al. (1994) have shown how some dyslexics may benefit from, for example, coloured overlays due to difficulties in some visual processes, and Jordan (2002) has highlighted the beneficial uses of a visual magnifier in reading.

Everatt (2002) notes the apparently logical rationale underlying theories of perceptual dysfunctions, for example Pringle-Morgan's (1896) term 'word-blindness', as being a major cause of reading difficulty: if a child cannot correctly see the text, s/he will not be able to read it. Errors commonly made by dyslexics such as mirror-image or reversal errors – 'b' for 'd', 'p' or 'q'; 's' for 'z'; 'was' for 'saw' – led to Orton's (1937) argument that the two hemispheres formed mirror-image representations of visual stimuli. Usually the left hemisphere is dominant, and the letter/word is read correctly. However, dominance of the right hemisphere in the dyslexic brain leads to the processing of an image-reversal. Later research led to increased understanding of the functions of the hemispheres that challenged Orton's theory, although aspects of Orton's ideas remain in the causal explanations of some recent theories.

Everatt notes that evidence from research studies in the 1970s and early 1980s challenged visual discrimination theories because it showed that students identified as 'dyslexic' can search, locate, recognise and compare visual stimuli as competently as non-dyslexic students, and therefore cannot have a visual impairment of the sort outlined in theories such as Orton's. It was only when verbal correspondence was necessary that dyslexic individuals achieved less well than non-dyslexic peers. In addition, non-dyslexics, in particular beginning readers, also often made reversal errors.

As the focus of research shifted away from recognition processes, research evidence indicating that individuals identified as 'dyslexic' often have greater difficulty than non-dyslexics in naming pictorial representations of familiar objects led to a sense that these naming deficits may be due to phonological rather than visual representations in memory. Non-dyslexic individuals outperformed dyslexics when individuals were required to use linguistic labels for memory tasks, but not for memory tasks involving sequences of non-linguistic, spatial locations. Generally, dyslexic individuals remember visual-based information as well as non-dyslexic, although there are exceptions to this rule.

Everatt comments on the fact that the two subtypes of dyslexia (phonological versus surface) are based on the framework of the dual-route model of reading (Castles and Coltheart 1993). Individuals identified as 'surface' dyslexics are over-reliant on the relationships between letters and sounds, and will assume pronunciation regularity to the point of error. Everatt offers the example of reading 'pint' as though it rhymes with 'mint'. This research finding supports the argument that direct access to a word via its visual form is one route to reading. 'Phonological' dyslexics, on the other hand, have difficulty in recoding letters into sounds.

Everatt highlights the changing views of dyslexia based on developing research, but also indicates a level of conflict among researchers and differences in outcomes. As indicated earlier, the area of visual dyslexia has gained some momentum from the magnocellular deficit hypothesis. This is described as being very influential both in the research into causes and explanations and as a link to practice. Everatt describes this as 'an alternative visual-based theory' which proposes that dyslexia may be the consequence of an abnormality in the neural pathways of the visual system. He notes how one of these pathways, the magnocellular (M) system is sensitive to gross (lower spatial frequency), rapidly changing (high temporal frequency) or moving information. He quotes the research of Chase (1996), Hogben, (1997) and Lovegrove (1996), who conclude that individuals identified as 'dyslexic' tend to be relatively poorer than non-dyslexics at performing tasks designed to assess the functioning of the magnocellular pathway. In addition, post-mortem investigations of the magnocellular layers of the visual system of individuals who had had difficulties in reading (Livingstone *et al.* 1991) found abnormal organisation and size of cells. When visual stimuli are presented quickly, dyslexic individuals require longer gaps between two stimuli and longer presentations of each stimulus to identify items. Both of these findings appear to indicate poorer processing by the magnocellular pathway of 'dyslexic' people.

Individuals identified as 'dyslexic' are also less reliable in their ability to detect the coherence of movement among moving dots. When they carry out such tasks there is a lower level of activity in the areas of the cortex thought to be responsible for identifying the direction of movement, as assessed by functional magnetic resonance imaging, according to Eden *et al.* (1996a).

However, the magnocellular pathway deficit hypothesis is challenged by the fact that some good readers perform relatively poorly in tasks related to the functioning of the magnocellular pathway and not all dyslexic individuals perform badly. In addition, there is input to processes performed by the visual cortex from the parvocellular pathway as well as the magnocellular. Lower levels of activation in the visual cortex cannot be assumed to arise from differences in the magnocellular pathway alone. Everatt quotes findings from his own, and other, research to conclude that dyslexic individuals perform worse than non-dyslexics only in tasks involving interaction between magnocellular and parvocellular pathways.

There is also a view that visual difficulties may be caused by oversensitivity to light. Such an oversensitivity is usually confined to certain wavelengths (or colours) of light and is sometimes referred to as scotopic sensitivity syndrome (Irlen 1991). The importance of this is that accessible tools for practitioners, such as coloured filters, overlays or lenses which are said to alleviate reading problems (see Wilkins *et al.* 1994), have increasingly been incorporated into practitioners' remediation programmes and this is said to alleviate reading problems.

According to Everatt, although theories in this area are not well specified they do incorporate ideas associated with the magnocellular
pathway deficit hypothesis and may need to be viewed against the
background of this research.

Nicolson and Fawcett (1994) developed the cerebellar deficit
hypothesis in order to account for common patterns of difficulties
among individuals identified as dyslexic: problems in balance, speed and
phonological skill. Fawcett and Nicolson (2001) note that the cerebellum is a densely packed and deeply folded subcortical brain structure,
also known as the 'hind brain'. In humans it accounts for 10–15 per
cent of brain weight, 40 per cent of brain surface area and 50 per cent of
the brain's neurones. The cerebellum is made up of two cerebellar hemispheres, and the lateral zone, known as the neocerebellum, has evolved
more recently and is much larger in humans than in other primates in
relation to overall brain size. It is involved in the control of independent limb movements, and especially in rapid, skilled movements.
Damage to different parts of the cerebellum can lead to different symptoms in humans, ranging from disturbances in posture and balance to
limb rigidity, loss of muscle tone, lack of co-ordination and impaired
timing of rapid pre-planned automatic movements.

However, one of the key features of cerebellar damage is the plasticity of the system, which means that near-normal performance can be
regained within a few months of damage. This concept that the cerebellum is involved in cognitive skills has led to considerable
controversy, because the cerebellum has traditionally been seen as a
motor area involved in learning and the automatisation of motor skill.
However, the human cerebellum has evolved enormously, being linked
with areas in the frontal cortex, including Broca's language area. There
are claims that the cerebellum is central to the acquisition of language
dexterity, and there is now evidence of specific cerebellar involvement
in reading. Fawcett and Nicolson therefore believe that:

• their behavioural studies show a common symptom of performance
  in dyslexic children regarding automaticity in a variety of tasks,
  including literacy tasks;
• the cerebellum has a key role in skill learning and automatisation,
  and the evidence also suggests that the cerebellum plays a central
  role in language-related tasks.

Research studies over a long period concluded that the cerebellum was
involved in speed, in learning and in becoming automatic in motor

skill. As Fawcett (2002) notes, evidence from the US also suggested the possibility of cerebellar involvement in language dexterity through interconnections with the language areas of the brain, in particular Broca's area. Fawcett and Nicolson (2001) therefore tested the hypothesis that cerebellum functioning might be implicated in dyslexia.

Fawcett and Nicolson sought to investigate the role of the cerebellum and its implications for dyslexia. In a study reported in the literature (Fawcett *et al.* 1996) the researchers replicated an earlier study on cerebellar impairment (Dow and Moruzzi 1958), but unlike this earlier study Fawcett *et al.* used a dyslexic sample. The tasks in the study included posture and muscle tone, hypotonia of the upper limbs and complex voluntary movement, fourteen tasks in all. The results indicated that the performance of children with dyslexia was significantly worse than that of chronological-age controls on all fourteen tasks, and significantly worse than reading-age controls in eleven out of the fourteen tasks. Nicolson and Fawcett (2000) carried out further tests with other groups, and these studies supported the earlier conclusions. The most noticeable results of this study – which was conducted on a sample of 126 dyslexic children and controls from age 8 to 16 divided into four age bands – were the exceptionally poor performance of all four groups with dyslexia on postural stability and limb shake. These findings were used as behavioural evidence that dyslexic children do indeed show cerebellar abnormalities. Further studies by Nicolson and Fawcett on neuro-anatomical studies of dyslexic brains (Finch *et al.* 2002) revealed a different pattern of the neurons in the cerebella of the dyslexic brains. Brain-imaging studies (Nicolson and Fawcett 2000) found that the dyslexic group activated their cerebellum less both in pre-learned and novel sequences.

To summarise, the studies conducted by Fawcett and Nicolson indicate that dyslexic children showed:

- clinical symptoms of cerebellar abnormality;
- abnormalities in cerebellar activation in automatic processing and in new learning;
- greater frontal-lobe activation, suggesting they were bypassing the cerebellum to some extent.

This suggests that dyslexic children use different methods in sequential learning and automatic performance.

Fawcett and Nicolson hypothesise that the causal chain between cerebellar problems, phonological difficulties and eventual reading problems accounts for three criterial difficulties of dyslexia: writing, reading and spelling. Lack of automaticity is only a real problem if rapid processing – fluency – or multi-tasking is required. Fluency is the ability to repeat previous actions or thoughts more and more quickly without conscious thought. Reasoning ability is not dependent on fluency. Fawcett concludes that there is sufficient evidence to provide strong support for the cerebellar deficit hypothesis. One implication is that dyslexic individuals are likely to face broader barriers to their literacy learning than simply phonological difficulties.

THE 'BALANCE MODEL' OF READING AND DYSLEXIA

The 'balance model' of reading used in dyslexia research and practice is an example of a biological model based on research which can be translated into practice. The balance model of reading was first introduced at a time when neuropsychological research into the lateral representation of brain function was prevalent. The authors (Robertson and Bakker 2002) discuss research evidence that challenges the hypothesis that the division of language and visual–spatial perception functions runs completely parallel with the left–right division in the brain, as was first thought. The balance model hypothesises that early and advanced reading will be mediated by the right and left hemisphere, respectively. This model predicts that some children, P (perceptual)-type dyslexics, rely too much on the perceptual features of text because they may not be able to shift from right to left in the hemispheric mediation of reading. Some other children, L (linguistic)-type dyslexics, rely on linguistic features of text to read fast, but pay too little attention to perceptual features of text.

The research focusing on the question whether P- versus L-dyslexia does exist in reality have provided positive and useful data which supports this notion and also provides pointers for practice. The results of these investigations do indicate that P- and L-dyslexics differ with regard to the lateral distribution of hemispheric activity elicited by words flashed in the central visual field – that is, in the field normally used to read a text. The groups also differ with regard to the speed of processing of reading-related information. P-types, for instance, are faster than L-types in deciding whether all letters in an array are the same or different, but P-types are slower than L-types when it comes to the question of whether a word is real or not (Licht 1994; Bakker 1986; Fabbro et al. 2001).

These studies have been used to support neuropsychological treat-ment, as there is overwhelming evidence now that the brain is able to change capacities according to stimulation from the learning environ-ment (see Robertson and Bakker 2002). The balance model hypothesises that while learning to read P-dyslexics took the role of the left hemisphere somewhat for granted and that L-dyslexics did so with regard to the right hemisphere; thus, stimulating one or the other hemisphere seems appropriate. Hemisphere stimulation as a treatment for P- and L-dyslexia started more than twenty years ago (Bakker *et al.* 1981; Bakker and Vinke 1985). The techniques, applied ever since, are hemisphere-specific stimulation (HSS), through the visual channel (HSS-vis), the tactile channel (HSS-tac) or, occasionally, the auditory channel (HSS-aud), as well as hemisphere-alluding stimulation (HAS) for P- or L-types.

According to Bakker and Robertson, one of the strengths of the neuropsychological approach is that the allocation to subtypes is based largely on observation of pupil performance in the particular aspects of the reading process which are causing concern. Intervention can there-fore aim directly to adapt learning behaviour in line with the identified weaknesses in reading behaviour. An intervention programme for the L-type learner will therefore focus on the perceptual aspects of letters and symbols, whereas the P-type learner will focus on the acquisition on fluency for speedy access to print. In reality skilled reading requires competence in both accuracy and speed.

The studies reported by Robertson and Bakker indicate that it is possible for neuropsychological intervention to be seen as a useful addition to the repertoire of specialist teaching approaches available for dyslexic pupils. Essentially, this involved identifying the P-type and L-type readers and providing them with text and tasks to stimulate the weaker hemisphere. In their studies both pupils and teachers were posi-tive about the method and several pupils voluntarily commented on the impact derived from the method on their reading generally.

Knight and Hynd (2002) suggest that investigation of anatomical and genetic differences can provide insights into our theoretical under-standing of dyslexia. They consider reading to be a complex activity, as a number of brain subsystems are involved in reading words. Different types of studies have attempted to show the neuro-anatomical charac-teristics of dyslexia. These studies include post-mortem studies and imaging techniques such as magnetic resonance imaging (MRI) and positron emission tomography (PET). The findings from these studies provide some evidence for abnormalities such as misplaced cells, particularly in the left hemisphere, smaller neurons in the thalamus and differences in patterns of cellular symmetry. These factors, as Knight and Hynd suggest, could explain some of the visual, auditory, sensory and perceptual differences which can be associated with dyslexia.

One of the uncertainties and controversies relating to neurological research in dyslexia concerns the aspect of cause and effect. This is particularly important as different parts of the brain interact and affect the function of others. It is therefore difficult to determine the exact effect or activation directly related to the experimental task. Knight and Hynd pinpoint some of the controversies in neurological studies such as that above: the difficulty of isolating a task, and also the differences in the apparatus used in different experiments, which can make interpretation across studies difficult. In addition, they note that some neuro-imaging techniques have good spatial resolution but not temporal resolution, and this can affect the sequence of a process or activity such as reading. This may, in fact, provide a distorted interpretation of the activation patterns observed in the experiment. Nevertheless, they firmly hold that these should not detract from the view that there is a significant biological basis in reading disabilities.

Knight and Hynd show how studying neurological process can inform and confirm knowledge about the reading process. They propose that three major circuits are involved in reading words: a ventral circuit, which is word specific; a posterior dorsal circuit, which integrates visual and phonological information; and an anterior circuit, which has been associated with recoding the phonological aspects of visually presented information. The authors conclude that these findings agree with Ehri's (2002) view that the phonological and orthographic processes are bonded to one another. Significantly, however, they describe studies which imply that the connections between the circuits bonding visual and phonological information may be under-active in dyslexic people. In addition, they refer to Eden's studies (Eden et al. 1996a and 1996b) that indicate that dyslexic readers have reduced activation in the magnocellular pathways, and point out that this could affect reading speed. Knight and Hynd also refer to genetic studies that consistently appear to indicate that dyslexia is hereditary, or at least that factors placing an individual at risk of dyslexia are hereditary.

The authors conclude by suggesting that, although genetic, morphological and functional studies have offered evidence of significant differences in the brains of individuals identified as dyslexic, there are still many unanswered questions about dyslexia. Nevertheless, they claim that with increased understanding of the brain of such individuals there is greater promise of effective identification, diagnosis and teaching.

Cognitive level

Since the 1980s the dominant theoretical framework to explain dyslexia has been the phonological deficit hypothesis, derived from seminal research in the UK by Bradley and Bryant (1983) and Snowling *et al.* (1986), and by Stanovich (1988) in the US. As Fawcett (2002) notes, from a phonological deficit explanation the solution lies in intensive training in phonological awareness.

Hatcher and Snowling (2002) consider the phonological representation hypothesis as an explanation of dyslexia and discuss the implications of this for assessment and teaching of dyslexic children. Phonological representations are the attributes or the knowledge about sounds which the child brings to the task. Learning to read is an interactive process in which the child uses all her/his language skills. Phonological processing seems, according to Hatcher and Snowling, to be strongly related to the development of reading. Deficits at the level of phonological representation constrain children's reading development. According to Hatcher and Snowling, one of the effects of this is the inability to generalise knowledge about the phonological properties of sounds and words they are taught. This means that activities such as non-word reading are problematic because of the difficulties associated with sound–symbol relationships. The authors support the notion that this can be viewed as one of the most robust signs of dyslexia. They suggest that the persistent difficulties dyslexic children have with phonological awareness appear to be more obvious when children are learning to read in irregular orthographies such as English. The fact that dyslexia can exist in virtually all countries would perhaps indicate, however, that phonological awareness is only part of the range of difficulties associated with reading which can be experienced by dyslexic children.

The evidence for Hatcher and Snowling's view of the importance of the phonological representation hypothesis comes from studies some of which investigate the development of dyslexic children before they fail to read. This can be achieved by following the progress of children with a higher risk of dyslexia, by virtue of having a dyslexic parent, and doing retrospective analysis of the children's early language skills. The studies found differences between children with and without reading difficulty at the age of 7. For example, the children with reading difficulties made more speech errors and had limited use of syntax at the age of 2½. The authors also refer to a study by Gallagher, Frith and Snowling (2000) which demonstrates that children with significant reading impairments at 8 years of age showed slow speech and language development in the pre-school years.

Hatcher and Snowling suggest that the phonological representation hypothesis is also compatible with differences between the profiles of individual children which are characteristic of dyslexia. They suggest that the crucial factor in the individual profile of dyslexic children is not criteria relating to subtypes of dyslexia but the actual severity of the lack of development in phonological representations. This can account for the differences and the different presenting characteristics of the dyslexic group. In addition, dyslexic children with poorer phonological representations will have less compensatory word-attack strategies to draw on, which will further undermine their reading performance.

Hatcher and Snowling conclude that assessment of phonological skills is therefore necessary, and they provide examples of tasks: rhyme recognition, rhyme production, phonological manipulation such as phoneme deletion and letter knowledge, which can be found in some of the established tests available for this purpose. This view has considerable implications for practice, and particularly for intervention programmes in the early years. They outline examples of phonological awareness training such as rhyme activities, identifying words as units within sentences, syllable awareness and blending tasks, but also indicate that it is insufficient to train phonological awareness in isolation as it is important to establish the relationship between sounds and written forms of words.

TASKS TO ASSESS PHONOLOGICAL AWARENESS

Some of the tasks suggested by Hatcher and Snowling that will provide an indication of a child's underlying phonological representations include phonological awareness tasks such as:

- rhyme recognition and detection tests that can assess the ability of a child to identify rhyme in words;
- rhyme-oddity tasks, which present the child with a set of three or four spoken words and require the child to identify which is the one that 'does not belong' – for example 'sun', 'rub', 'fun', 'bun';
- alliteration tests that assess the ability to isolate initial sounds in words – for example 'sun', 'sock', 'cow', 'chip'.

In addition, Hatcher and Snowling also suggest phonological production tasks such as:

- rhyme production, which requires that the child understands the nature of rhyming words and is able to produce a rhyming word – for example, which words rhyme with play?
- syllable blending, which requires the child to be able to assemble segments of words that have been presented to them – for example, which picture goes with [snow]–[man]; [win]–[dow]?
- phoneme blending, which measures the child's ability to blend a sequence of sounds into words – for example /d/ /o/ /g/; dog;
- phoneme segmentation tasks to assess a child's ability to segment words into separate sounds – for example sand; /s/ /a/ /n/ /d/.

Hatcher and Snowling also provide some examples of packaged programmes for this purpose and some evaluative data on their effectiveness. They suggest that, despite the importance of phonological awareness in the early development of reading, interventions that rely exclusively on training in phonological awareness are less effective than those that combine phonological training with print and meaning in the context of sentences in text.

Wolf and Bowers (1999) suggest that, in addition to their phonological difficulties, dyslexic children process information more slowly. This is the so-called 'double deficit' hypothesis. Fawcett supports the view that dyslexic children take longer to learn a skill than non-dyslexic children:

> Our analysis of how dyslexic children learn (Fawcett and Nicolson 2001) suggests performance can become automatic, but strikingly, our 'square root rule', suggests that this takes longer in proportion to the square root of the time normally taken to acquire a skill. So, a skill that normally takes 4 sessions to master, would take a dyslexic child 8 sessions, whereas if it normally took 400 sessions, it would take the dyslexic child 8000 sessions!
>
> (Fawcett 2002, p. 18)

She suggests that it is important to differentiate instruction for dyslexics in 'small, easily assimilated steps', and to assess existing practice for its suitability in this regard.

PREDICTING READING DIFFICULTIES FROM COGNITIVE MEASURES

Singleton (2002) examines the cognitive factors associated with literacy and draws a close parallel between cognitive skills and literacy performances. According to Singleton this means that competence in cognitive skills can be used as an indicator and predictor of literacy difficulties.

Singleton suggests that dyslexia may be regarded as a form of learning difficulty arising out of specific combinations of cognitive limitations. This, however, can raise some questions regarding the use of the label 'dyslexia', as using this criterion as the basis for determining dyslexia rests on quantitative rather than qualitative differences. This can present challenges to educational psychologists and others involved in diagnosis. Singleton, however, argues that the advantage of viewing dyslexia from an information-processing perspective is that it shifts the focus away from a label to a description of the cognitive profile.

There is a close, and well-researched, relationship between cognitive skills and reading, particularly focusing on phonological skills and working memory. These two factors in particular have potential as indicators of difficulties in literacy acquisition. One of the notable factors of approaching dyslexia from an information-processing perspective is, according to Singleton, that the abilities as well as the difficulties are highlighted. For example, research evidence suggests that visual memory has an important function in reading, and studies have shown that many dyslexic readers have skills in visual processing.

Behavioural level

Fawcett (2002) comments that, from her experience as the parent of a child identified as 'dyslexic', she had noticed that dyslexic pupils seemed to face barriers to their learning beyond a difficulty with phonological awareness. Dyslexic children experience difficulty in acquiring a wide range of skills, including sensitivity to rapid movement, rapid auditory discrimination, fine and gross motor co-ordination such as threading beads and balancing, and phonological awareness and skills associated with working memory. In particular, there seemed to be a difference in the 'fluency' with which such pupils carried out all tasks. With Nicolson, she tested the hypothesis that dyslexic children seem to find it difficult to acquire any skill to a level of competency at which it becomes automatic, whether related to reading or not (Fawcett and Nicolson 2001). This hypothesis is called the dyslexia automatisation deficit hypothesis (DAD), which was referred to above (pp. 42–4) in the discussion of the role of the cerebellum. Evidence from a series of tasks involving balance, chosen because it had no obvious relation to reading, supported this hypothesis. Especially when they had to perform another task simultaneously, dyslexic children experienced particular problems in balancing.

Future trends in dyslexia research – consensus or conflict?

Fawcett (2002) and Nicolson (2002) both express views about what they feel will or should be the direction of research in the area of dyslexia in the future. Further investigation is needed for all major hypotheses, from underlying cerebellar deficits and/or magnocellular deficits to the overarching symptoms of phonological deficit, and to the double deficit hypothesis. Systematic rigorous research is needed, based on analyses of the incidence of these deficits across different populations. All aspects of language should be addressed in addition to phonology. Additionally, there needs to be a focus on the impact of the linguistic environment on the manifestation of dyslexia. Further research is needed on the interaction between genetic inheritance and the environment, with particular reference to deprivation. In order to assist the early identification of dyslexia that is needed to prevent ongoing difficulties, with the likelihood of both emotional and academic consequences, specific tasks for particular theories of dyslexia should be produced. Fawcett, in particular, advocates a non-adversarial approach, based on careful evaluation of other theoretical viewpoints, while maintaining healthy critical discussion. Both Fawcett and Nicolson suggest that multidisciplinary co-operation is essential to reflect the diversity of the underlying factors associated with dyslexia and the implications of these for early identification and intervention. The distinction they make between cause and description is a useful one – teachers focus on descriptions, which assist them in identifying dyslexia, while researchers are interested in 'cause' as a means of explaining the characteristics and the 'descriptions' of dyslexia. At the same time, both Fawcett and Nicolson take a long-term proactive perspective. They argue for a system-controlled approach which sees the proactive benefits of comprehensive screening, enlightened policy and collaboration between government and all groups, ensuring a 'win–win' situation (rather than 'zero sum') – which would pave the way for innovative practices and cost-effective interventions. Although there has been progress and scientific advances have provided additional theoretical elements in relation to dyslexia, some of these are still developing in terms of widespread replication and how they fit into the existing body of knowledge and understanding. For example, there is some evidence that the magnocellular deficit may be implicated in much more than visual processes, but also with auditory stimuli (Stein 2002).

Similarly with the role of essential fatty acids and the cerebellum, both of which may have a more influential role in the neurological functioning of other processes which contribute towards learning and literacy (Richardson 2002). This underlines the view of both Fawcett and Nicolson that some form of synthesis needs to be embedded into the dyslexia 'ecosystem'.

This clearly has implications for practice, and one important distinction in relation to practice can be drawn between literacy and life support. While dyslexic children and young people require intervention strategies directed at enhancing their literacy levels, they also need support throughout life – particularly as the society we live in places a high value on literacy, and employers are still not fully aware of the nature of the strengths and difficulties which may be experienced by a dyslexic person (Reid and Kirk 2001). An understanding of dyslexia is therefore not only a concept for scientists to understand, but one which penetrates classrooms, workplaces and the community at large. The social and economic effects can be considerable. Nicolson alludes to this by referring to an attitude of partnership to enable real inclusion and the development of multidisciplinary, multi-perspective projects to ensure collaboration and cost-effective research and practice among those involved in the field at all levels.

Policy development

Policy in relation to the educational provision for dyslexic students in schools and colleges is the area in which the most consistent progress has been made. In the UK, for example, some years ago there was no recognition of 'dyslexia', but in recent years an increasingly widespread acceptance of the term has been evident. The Warnock Report in 1978 highlighted the issue of dyslexia:

> Although there are no agreed criteria for distinguishing those children with severe and long-term difficulties in reading, writing and spelling from others who may require remedial teaching in these areas, there are nevertheless children whose disabilities are marked but whose general abilities are at least average and for whom distinctive arrangements are necessary.
>
> (Warnock Report; quoted in Young and Tyre 1983, pp. 5–6)

The Warnock Report in 1978 highlighted the issue of dyslexia by suggesting that, although there were no commonly agreed criteria for distinguishing between individuals who experience severe and long-term difficulties in literacy acquisition and others who may require additional teaching in literacy, nevertheless there were those who experience marked difficulties despite the fact that their ability overall was at least average. For those, special arrangements were deemed necessary.

Although these reports are now dated and have been overtaken by more recent legislation, it is important to consider the objections to attempting to define and promote the widespread use of the term dyslexia and the points which were made at the time to describe children with dyslexic difficulties. Before we do that let us also consider the following quote, from a debate on the proposals for the 1981 Education Act, which utilised much of the Warnock Report: 'Whatever the cause or nature of the condition commonly called 'dyslexia' the local authority will have to make appropriate arrangements for meeting the individual educational needs of these children, whatever the cause' (House of Lords debate, 5 March 1980).

From the short quotations above and the comment made in the House of Lords the key points which governed policy at that time seem to be as follows:

- There are no agreed criteria for distinguishing dyslexic children from other children.
- There are children whose difficulties are marked but whose general ability is at least average.
- Distinctive arrangements are necessary (for those children).
- The term 'dyslexia' is used too loosely.
- The term is not descriptive enough to be helpful to the teacher.
- 'Specific reading difficulties' is a more appropriate term.
- Reading abilities in this population of children are discrepant with other abilities.
- The cause is not as important as meeting the needs.
- It is the responsibility of the education authority to meet the individual needs of these children.

These views seem to have characterised the debate, the perception of dyslexia and the provision which was suggested for dyslexic children. Essentially, because the research in dyslexia at that time was sparse and much of it had a medical slant it was difficult to formulate a precisely

...ed policy for a group which at that time could not be readily defined, although it was commonly acknowledged that it did exist. Interestingly, in a survey of education authorities in England and Wales in 1984 organised by the Division of Child Psychology of the British Psychological Society it was revealed that 32 authorities (58 per cent) had a formulated policy for dealing with children with specific learning difficulties and 15 (27 per cent) had produced documents specifying this policy (British Psychological Society 1983). The report in fact recommended that all education authorities should formulate a policy for specific learning difficulties, as they would with other special educational needs. The perceptions of specific learning difficulties/dyslexia at the time were further fuelled by the results of the Rutter studies in the Isle of Wight in the 1970s. In one of those studies (Rutter and Madge 1976) it was suggested that socio-economic class was a factor which related to reading failure. This, however, ran counter to some views at the time. For example, a 1986 study by Grampian Region reported that '[t]here is little reason for doubting that specific learning difficulty is evenly spread in frequency of occurrence throughout the population as a whole' (Grampian Region Psychological Service 1988, p. 34). Similarly conflicting views can be noted at the time in relation to those involved in researching reading; for example:

> Children who experience difficulty in learning to read are frequently called dyslexic, but their difficulty does not arise because they are dyslexic, they are dyslexic because they cannot read and therefore the cure for dyslexia is to learn to read.
>
> (F. Smith, quoted in Young and Tyre 1983, p. 18)

Miles (1983) suggests, however, that dyslexia should be seen as a discrete condition, and not as a normal variation of reading performance.

The debate has moved on since the 1970s and 1980s. The dyslexia debate gained momentum in the late 1980s and 1990s. Whatever the controversy regarding labels and terminology, there does appear to be a conviction by the various governments in the UK that they should accommodate the needs of dyslexic children in some way. For example, in 1987 the BDA was asked to submit a memorandum to the House of Commons Select Committee on Education concerning the implementation of the 1981 Education Act. The government minister Robert Dunn said in the House of

Commons on 13 July that the 'government recognises dyslexia ... the important thing is to be sure that something is being done about the problem' (quoted in Ott 1997, p. 11). Further, the Education Act 1993 and the subsequent Code of Practice (1994) focused on provision to meet the needs and the importance of early identification. Much of this seems to have been well received by various groups around the country, including the BDA. When the BDA reported to the House of Commons Select Committee on Education in 1996, its spokesperson indicated that:

> In a nutshell, we said that several issues need to be addressed if the commendable Code is to become a reality: issues such as the prompt identification of dyslexia by properly trained teachers, investment in Individual Education Plans and consistent and fair treatment at Tribunal Hearings.
>
> (Cann 1996, p. 2)

This indicates an approval of the 1994 Code of Practice and optimism that it will go some of the way to satisfying the needs of children and parents in relation to educational provision for dyslexia.

In Scotland the debate swept along similar lines, but again there was a quest to find out the views of those holding important posts in education. Some of this debate was encapsulated in a study conducted by Stirling University on *Policy, Practice and Provision for Children with Specific Learning Difficulties* (Duffield *et al.* 1995). The research questions addressed three main aspects:

1   To what extent are pupils with specific learning difficulties recognised as a group with distinctive needs and how is the nature of their difficulties perceived?
2   Where specific learning difficulties are recognised, how are they identified?
3   How are the needs of these pupils met and their identified difficulties remedied?

In attempting to answer these questions, the research drew on perspectives from local policy-makers, who included principal educational psychologists, education officers and special educational needs advisers; parents and voluntary associations; learning support teachers; teacher educators and pre-service teachers; and Scottish Examination Board officers and medical personnel.

A measure of the controversy and disagreement which existed at the time can be seen in Table 2.1, which shows the differences in the conceptual understanding of specific learning difficulties between those occupying key policy-making positions in education authorities.

It is interesting to note the views of learning support teachers, who occupied a key teaching role in relation to children with specific learning difficulties. There was clear disagreement within this group regarding the use of labels in particular, and also in other issues such as assessment and in teaching strategies. These differences are perhaps encapsulated in the following statement from one learning support teacher:

> I dislike the term specific learning difficulties: it is unwieldy, vague and nobody understands what it means. Having used it, you have to launch into further explanations. I actually prefer 'dyslexia' but only use it with qualification because of people's varying reactions. Learning support colleagues are aware of the ambiguities and controversy surrounding the word.
>
> With regard to identification, the responses indicated that the majority of learning support teachers were apprehensive about their abilities to identify specific learning difficulties (dyslexia). From a sample of 206 learning support teachers, around 75% were able to make at least one means of diagnosis of specific learning difficulties in their school, but a total of 50 different tests were named! In the B.P.S. report ([British Psychological Society] 1999) twelve tests were described which draw on theoretical rationales of dyslexia.
>
> (Reid 2001, pp. 257–8)

Table 2.1   Definition of specific learning difficulties: local authority views

	Discrete	Continuum	Anti-categorisation	Total
Psychologists	3	12	2	17
Education officers	4	5	2	11
Advisers	6	4	6	16
Total	13	21	10	44

Source: Duffield et al. 1995; reproduced with permission

One can note, then, that the differences regarding professionals' understanding of dyslexia, the use of the term, and the identification criteria have been evident for many decades.

Since the publication of *The Code of Practice for the Identification and Assessment of Special Educational Needs* (Department for Education 1994; Department for Education Northern Ireland 1998) it has been clear to everyone that it is the responsibility of schools to identify and support children with dyslexia and other difficulties in learning. Pupils now have a legal entitlement to have their special educational needs identified, assessed and met. The Code categorised dyslexia as a 'specific learning difficulty (for example, dyslexia)' when considering criteria for making a statutory assessment (*ibid.*). A key requirement is that 'there is clear, recorded evidence of clumsiness, significant difficulties of sequencing or visual perception; deficiencies in working memory; or significant delays in language functioning' (Department for Education 1994, para. 3:61, iii). Similarly, in Scotland and the Republic of Ireland, although they do not have a code of practice, a commitment to recognise the needs of children with dyslexia is implicit in the recent legislation and consultative documents.

Local authority level

In the area of policy development, some LEAs have addressed the issue of dyslexia specifically. Many throughout the UK have well-documented policies on dyslexia. One such policy is that of East Renfrewshire LEA, whose policy document on specific learning difficulties reads as follows:

> Definitions vary greatly but there is agreement that dyslexia is a subset of specific learning difficulties, is a difficulty with aspects of reading and spelling and that attainment in these areas is discrepant with the child's level of performance in other areas. Writing and number work may also be affected. It must however be emphasised that dyslexia exists on a continuum, and while there are distinctive patterns of difficulties, individual dyslexic children's strengths and weaknesses may vary considerably. The authority has in place a stepped process for the identification of children who may have difficulties in learning. Class teachers should recognise when a child is showing difficulties with learning, and it is the responsibility of the teacher to investigate further, and arrange for an appropriate assessment. This should be performed in

co-operation with the school's learning support co-ordinator and the head teacher, and may involve the bi-lingual support service where appropriate. Parents also need to be made aware of the problems the child is encountering at school and their views should be sought.

(East Renfrewshire Council 2000, p. 2)

Some of the implications of this policy at LEA level are:

- the availability of key staff with knowledge and expertise in dyslexia who, preferably, are familiar with current research, to inform school practice through ongoing consultation and staff development;
- clear procedures for the formal assessment of students;
- flexible arrangements for communication with parents;
- liaison between support services.

Policy for provision for dyslexic adults

There is now little doubt that provision for dyslexic adults is 'improving'. The 1998 Disability Act has now taken effect in education as well as employment. The Moser Report (Moser 2000) on adult literacy has initiated a funded programme of government support. Recently the Employment Service also funded a programme of research and training in dyslexia for occupational psychologists and other key staff in the employment service (Reid and Kirk 2000). This research suggested that 'many of the commercially produced language programmes for dyslexic people are inappropriate for adults' and the report recommended that 'a structured language programme should be made relevant to the person with dyslexia, promote top-down approaches based on development of language experience and exposure to relevant print material' (Reid and Kirk 2000, p. 122).

The research highlighted the actual and potential confusion between provision in basic skills and provision for those adults with dyslexia. It was hypothesised that the priorities and methods of dealing with these groups differed. Interestingly, in a survey of over a hundred chartered psychologists who deal with adults the researchers (Reid and Kirk 2000) found that two-thirds of the sample rated their knowledge of dyslexia as average/low. Over 90 per cent of the same sample rated employers' knowledge of dyslexia as low. In addition to the Disability Discrimination Act, this low awareness may be reversed in time through the work of a number of advisory groups. Two councils have been set up to advise the government on discrimination against disabled people: the National Disability Council and the Northern Ireland Disability Council. In addition, a separate group, the National Advisory Council on Employment of People with Disabilities (NACEPD) targets the provision of advice to the government on the Disability Discrimination Act. In December 1997 the Disability Rights Taskforce (DRT) was set up with the aim of reporting to the government on how best to secure the civil rights of disabled people, including those with dyslexia. A Disability Rights Commission has also been set up with a number of aims, including the promotion of good practice among employers and service providers. Clearly, therefore, although hitherto a fairly neglected area, some recent emphasis has been placed on adults with dyslexia in relation to assessment, training of professionals, employers' awareness and equity issues affecting the training and employment opportunities of adults with dyslexia.

Reid and Kirk (2001) report on the heightened awareness in further and higher education regarding the need to provide for students with dyslexia. In addition, it appears that it is not unusual for young dyslexic adults to obtain a dyslexia diagnosis after leaving school. Singleton (1999) reported on a survey of over a hundred institutions which revealed that a significant number of dyslexic students were diagnosed after admission to university. Institutions of further and higher education now have a legal obligation to provide for students with disabilities, including dyslexia. Some of this support can be in the form of extra time for examinations, but other supports can be provided, such as study skills help, counselling, printed notes, taped lectures and detailed feedback on assignments. Reid and Kirk highlight two models of support – the individual model and the social model. The first portrays the individual as the person who has to deal with difficulties, and this is essentially a deficit model which implies that the individual has to somehow make up these deficits to cope and compete with others. The social model provides the necessary supports and adaptations to integrate the dyslexic person fully into the learning or work environment. There is a difference here on the issue of 'whose responsibility?' The question is whether the responsibility lies with the individual or the institution. Take some time to consider this issue and consider the ways in which society can help to accommodate and integrate adults with dyslexia into education and employment.

Issues of equity and resources

The issue of resource allocation in relation to dyslexia is one that has generated much heated debate. Pumfrey acknowledges that 'establishing a resource allocation decision making model that is explicit, open, fair and theoretically defensible, requires considerable professional knowledge' (Pumfrey 1996, p. 20), but Reid qualifies this:

> In practice however criteria used to allocate resources for dyslexia often have a reactive as well as a proactive element. The reactive element usually emerges from parental pressure (Heaton 1996) and the proactive attempt from an objective attempt from education authorities to establish some form of working criteria for identifying and dealing with dyslexia within their budgetary considerations. This however usually results in discrepancy criteria being employed – for example, reading scores two standard deviations below prediction from I.Q., or perhaps reading accuracy at or below second percentile for age.
>
> (Reid 1998, pp. 5–6)

The extent of the differences between those lobbying for recognition of dyslexia as a causal factor in contributing to difficulties in literacy development that require the allocation of additional or alternative resources, and those who feel that dyslexia is used as an excuse to attract unwarranted additional resources for some students can be judged by reference to the following newspaper article:

> Last Christmas the British Dyslexia Association (BDA) held a fundraising event, a concert by the choir of King's College Cambridge that filled the Royal Albert Hall. Such an event would be beyond the reach of most education charities, and is a mark of the BDA's success.
>
> In the 1970s the debate about dyslexia hinged on whether it really existed or was just a polite term applied to middle-class children who could not read ...
>
> Success has made dyslexia the cuckoo in the nest of special educational needs. It accounts for over 40 per cent of cases coming before the SEN [special educational needs] Appeals Tribunal. ... It is determining case law in special education as a whole. The question of whether a local authority could be sued for negligence was decided last year in the Lords over a dyslexia

issue. Huge injections of funds have enabled the lobby to buy up teacher training courses en bloc. Advertising columns in specialist journals are now overwhelmed by posts for 'specific learning difficulties' ...

At the same time, there is a permanent field day for paid advice and consultancy. Parents may be charged several hundred pounds for 'independent' professional advice by a psychologist who will diagnose dyslexia, even if that was not the parents' original concern, and who will then obtain an LEA-funded place in a private residential school for dyslexics where he or she sits on the board of trustees.

The lobby's new-found vigour diverts funds and attention from children who have genuine disabilities or difficulties worthy of being covered by a statement. In local authorities which have taken inclusion seriously, pupils who simply have a problem learning to read may be competing directly for mainstream support with those who have, say, autism or profound hearing loss. In any LEA area, they have a distorting effect on the special needs' budget.

In our view, the BDA's success is a cultural and political phenomenon, rather than proof of any clinical facts about reading abilities ... the recent head of steam coincides with the encouragement of 'market forces' in the education system.
(Tony Booth and Chris Goodey, 'Dyslexia: Playing for the Sympathy Vote', *Guardian*, 21 May 1996, p. 5)

The authors of the newspaper article go on to add:

The power of the dyslexia lobby reflects the hierarchy of social esteem in which various disabilities are held, with severe learning difficulties at the bottom. The Down's Syndrome Association and the Autistic Society are grassroots organisations with a few administrators. The lesser stigma of physical disability and sensory impairment creates lobbies with more professional structures and greater fundraising powers. But these cannot match the BDA. Sir Nicholas Monck and Paul Cann, its president and director, were both educated at that Cambridge college which entertained at the Albert Hall Christmas concert; its roots and funding sources lie deep in the British establishment, with its distrust of state education.

(*Ibid.*)

This article provoked a number of replies. Typical of a number of them was the following:

> Tony Booth and Chris Goodey note that the 1970s debate about dyslexia hinged on whether it really existed. It is obvious they have read little of the scientific literature since then. There is now irrefutable evidence that dyslexia is a disorder which has a biological basis and affects around 3 per cent of the population. It has been known for years that dyslexia runs in families – not just middle-class ones – and there is good evidence that it is a heritable disorder. Indeed, gene markers have been located on chromosomes 6 and 15, and there are also brain differences, both in structure and function between dyslexic and normal readers. A vast amount of literature shows that, at the cognitive level, dyslexic children have difficulties with specific aspects of language processing, namely difficulties with the processing of speech sounds. These difficulties show up in family studies of children at risk of dyslexia well before they go to school, and they also account for these children's failure to learn to read. None of this evidence should be taken to indicate that dyslexia cannot be remedied or that its negative effects cannot be prevented. The 'nettle' that LEAs have to grasp (and indeed have done so) is that early intervention can avoid the negative spiral of poor reading, poor writing, poor self-esteem, disaffection and probable unemployment. The costs both in social and financial terms of not intervening are enormous. It is indeed regrettable that the more articulate parents are the only ones able to shout loud enough to assert the rights of their children. To set the record straight, we were educated neither in the private sector nor at Oxbridge. As scientists we need no convincing that dyslexia can be accurately diagnosed, and moreover, that its effects can be alleviated. We are actively involved with local schools and LEAs in the early identification of children who are at risk of dyslexia, and in advising on methods to promote their early development of literacy.
>
> Professor Margaret Snowling (Chairman of the International Conference Committee of the British Dyslexia Association) and Dr Kate Nation (Centre for Reading and Language, University of York).

(Professor Margaret Snowling, 'Not a Middle-class Myth; Dyslexia: A Powerful Response from Readers to Last Week's Discussion', *Guardian*, 28 May 1996, p. 7)

Conclusion

This article and the response to it highlight some of the aspects concerning the nature of the controversies and conflicts surrounding dyslexia research and practice. This chapter has encapsulated many of these controversies and highlighted the positive directions in dyslexia research, and the implications for practice which have emerged from the debate and the research. There is no doubt that now there is a much clearer notion of dyslexia – one which is shared by both practitioners and researchers – and it is also becoming clear that the responses to these controversies, which are discussed in Chapter 3, indicate that the developments of the last few decades, such as assessment procedures, intervention programmes and strategies and policy frameworks, are all having an effect in classrooms throughout the UK.

Chapter 3

Responses to dyslexia

Introduction

Different perspectives held by researchers and practitioners need to be reconciled and converted into practice to satisfy the demands of legislation, policy-makers, school management, teachers, psychologists, parents and, above all, to support all pupils to engage in learning within educational settings and outside. Pupils, however, must first be assessed in ways that determine the nature of the difficulties they face in literacy development. Then there must be an equitable use of resources and consideration of what might constitute appropriate responses to meet the needs of dyslexic children at the level of the school and the classroom. Above all, it is extremely important to consider the social and emotional development of the child, and particularly the emotional consequences of being diagnosed as dyslexic.

Assessment

Tests of dyslexia

It is important to note how research initiatives in the area of dyslexia have influenced practice both in terms of screening tests and also in practical responses to meeting individual students' learning needs.

Phonological awareness

From the research already discussed in the previous chapter, one can note that, for example in the cognitive and classroom areas, there has been considerable activity in the study of phonological awareness in relation to dyslexia. This is reflected in the development of assessment and teaching materials such as the phonological abilities test (Muter *et al.* 1997), the phonological assessment battery (Fredrickson *et al.* 1997) and many phonological teaching approaches such as sound linkage (Hatcher 1994), the Phonological Awareness Training Programme (Wilson 1993) and the multisensory teaching system for reading (Johnson *et al.* 1999). Some of the studies which highlight these factors include Hagtvet's (1997) Norwegian study, which showed that a phonological deficit at age 6 was the strongest predictor of reading difficulties. Other studies, such as Hulme's (Snowling and Nation 1997), have shown speech rate to be a strong predictor of dyslexic difficulties and this is reflected in the development of the phonological abilities test (Muter *et al.* 1997).

Wolf and Bowers (1999) highlight the 'double deficit' hypothesis, indicating that dyslexic children can have difficulties with both phonological processing and naming speed. It is interesting that speed of processing and semantic fluency are included in some of the recently produced tests for dyslexic children. Badian (1997), in a further study, provides evidence for a triple deficit hypotheses, implying that orthographic factors involving visual skills should also be considered.

Early intervention measures

Fawcett, Nicolson and Dean (1996) have shown how cerebellar impairment may be implicated in dyslexia, and may be linked to difficulties in phonological processing as well as automaticity. These factors are represented in the battery of dyslexia screening tests (Fawcett and Nicolson 1996). Fawcett comments that each of the screening tests, the dyslexia early screening (4.5–6.5 years), the dyslexia screening test (6.5–16.5), the dyslexia adult screening test (16.5–65) and the pre-school screening test (3.5–4.5), was designed as the first of a series of stages in a structured screening–assessment–support procedure. These tests were intended to be used by teachers in schools and, as such, were deliberately designed to be quick, cheap and effective in providing all the 'positive indicators' for dyslexia, and attractive to pupils as they were 'fun, varied, and non-threatening'.

One of the strengths of the screening tests developed by Fawcett and Nicolson is that they can be readily used and understood by the teacher. One of Fawcett's aims was therefore to empower teachers to take responsibility for this particular element in the diagnostic procedure. Fawcett acknowledges that their aim was to produce tests that were not only cheap and effective and fitted into the code of practice, but also provided 'positive indicators' for dyslexia. Nicolson suggests that it can be almost an 'impossible juggling act' (2001, p. 13) to obtain a balance. This balancing act involves tests that:

- appealed to educational psychologists in that they were normed, reliable and provided important and objective information,
- appealed to school teachers in that they empowered them to undertake the tests themselves ...,
- appealed to schools in that they were cheap, quick and effective, and fitted into the code of practice,
- appealed to the dyslexia community in that they represented all the positive indicators of dyslexia, ...
- appealed to the children in that they were fun, varied and non-threatening and [ones] that could be administered in the child's first year at school ... before dyslexia can formally be diagnosed.

(adapted from Nicolson 2001, p. 13)

Clearly there is considerable benefit in using such pre-literacy screening tests as they can, through early recognition, either prevent failure from becoming deep rooted or at least identify early signs of literacy difficulties and provide recommendations for appropriate intervention.

Another of the strengths of the dyslexia screening tests is that the specific subtests are all rooted in current and established research findings and are sufficiently comprehensive to incorporate a wide variety of elements from the research. For example, the naming speed subtest relates to an element of the double deficit hypothesis discussed earlier. The scoring system has been developed in a manner which can provide an 'at-risk quotient' and the profile can be clearly indicated so that the strengths and weaknesses can be clearly identified. In addition, because the subtests also include phonological tests one can note the extent to which the phonological area is presenting the most difficulty, or whether the scores indicate a typical dyslexic profile of problems in phonology, speed and motor skills. These factors can provide pointers for intervention. Fawcett suggests that an at-risk quotient of 0.9 or more can indicate that the child is 'at risk of dyslexia' and most certainly would be regarded as a candidate for extra and appropriate support in relation to the code of practice.

Singleton appears to have attempted something equally ambitious in relation to early screening by producing a computer-based cognitive profiling system which attempts to identify children at high risk of literacy failure and dyslexia at 4 years of age. The theoretical basis of the cognitive profiling system (CoPS; Singleton *et al.* 1996) is that some cognitive factors such as visual/verbal memory, auditory/verbal memory associations, phonological awareness and colour discrimination are key determinants of early literacy. This would mean that children who have difficulty in these cognitive tasks will very likely have difficulty acquiring literacy. The CoPS therefore, according to Singleton, should have a predictive value for the teacher.

To highlight the potential of predictive and early identification using cognitive measures, Singleton describes the development and use of early-identification measures such as the computer-based test – 'CoPS' – which he suggests, from research studies, outperforms conventional tests in prediction of poor readers at various ages. One of the key points made by Singleton is that individual differences in cognitive ability can be assessed before children learn to read, and this can highlight children who may be at risk of literacy failure at an early age. This can also pinpoint potential areas of early intervention, which in many cases is the key to a successful outcome in literacy and learning.

The Listening and Literacy Index (Weedon and Reid 2001) is a group screening test for specific learning difficulties which can be administered by the class teacher in a classroom setting to the whole class at the same time. It contains four subtests: listening, regular spelling, sight spelling and reading comprehension. A screening procedure of this nature can clearly be advantageous in assisting the class teacher gather the type of data which can help to inform teaching and make diagnostic conclusions about a child's literacy development.

A holistic perspective

Burden (2002) suggests that the dyslexia perspective should be broadened, and makes a strong case for the application of Feuerstein's deficient cognitive functions (DCF) model as an alternative cognitive assessment and intervention approach (Feuerstein *et al.* 1980).

He feels that the term 'dyslexia' is at best a shorthand form of convenience that can provide a vehicle for discussion and promote positive intervention, and that it may be a barrier to helpful communication and appropriate action. Therefore, according to Burden, the way in which concepts are defined and used in everyday speech will inevitably shape our thoughts and action: 'Thus, the difference between describing someone as "having dyslexia", "being dyslexic" or "displaying learning difficulties of a dyslexic nature" becomes highly significant' (Burden 2002, p. 271).

Burden comments that dyslexia should be seen as a comparative term, not an all-or-nothing phenomenon:

> Rather than stating that a person 'has dyslexia' or even 'is dyslexic', it is considered more helpful to indicate that that person displays specific learning difficulties of a dyslexic nature, and then to identify exactly how and in what specific areas those difficulties are occurring.
>
> (Burden 2002, p. 272)

This approach emphasises intervention rather than causation, action rather than labelling, and this can help to minimise the harmful effects of the controversies which can accompany a diagnosis and a label. According to Burden this kind of approach can be described as 'holistic and humanistic rather than fragmented and mechanistic' (*ibid.*). This view lends itself to utilising Vygotskian models of intervention within a socio-cultural framework. Within that framework Burden argues for the use of information-processing models to understand dyslexia and avenues of intervention.

He feels, for example, that learning difficulties may arise at the *input* phase of information processing. He suggests this could occur because the learner has an impulsive learning style or may have only a general perception of the material to be learned. At the *elaboration* phase in the information-processing cycle Burden notes that difficulties may arise because the learner cannot identify the salient points. Similarly, at the *output* stage there could be some difficulty with identifying the needs of the task and the actual outcomes expected.

The key point being made by Burden is that these information-processing factors are not permanent, but can be modified through teaching and learning experiences. Hence Burden's view that programmes such as Feuerstein's DCF, which aims to modify the learning experience for the individual, can be effective in terms of information processing, and can provide both an enhanced learning experience and diagnostic information which can be used for other programmes and learning materials.

Burden suggests that it is reasonable to assume that dyslexic children have difficulty at the input stage of the information-processing cycle because they do not have the 'cognitive deficiencies' which can characterise general learning difficulties. Evidence for this view can be inferred from studies which suggest that the listening comprehension of diagnosed dyslexics is significantly in advance of their measured reading comprehension (Bedford-Feuell *et al.* 1995). Burden therefore comments that the application of metacognitive strategies is likely to offer a profitable means of 'remedial intervention'.

Burden also states that, in his view, the area of self-concept has been relatively unexplored in relation to dyslexia. He argues that, while there has tended to be an assumption that all aspects of an individual's self-esteem are likely to be affected by being faced with learning difficulties of a dyslexic nature (Edwards 1994), this may not always be the case. Although some may well show signs of a negative self-concept, others can display extraordinary determination and application to overcome their difficulties. Attribution theory can be used to understand these contrasting experiences. Some people with dyslexic difficulties might attribute those difficulties to lack of ability on their part, which they might also see as unchangeable and outside their control. On the other hand, Burden suggests they might equally interpret their difficulties as due to lack of effort or appropriate strategy use, which they might see as changeable and within their control. Therefore it is too simplistic to suggest that all dyslexic people will benefit from counselling.

Burden notes that because there are many different interactive aspects to learning it is important to consider holistic viewpoints, and this particularly applies to dyslexia, as thinking and learning are not isolated activities and effective learning needs to be contextualised. He therefore argues that 'dyslexia must be seen as one aspect of a discursive process within which the dynamic interaction of learners, their teachers, the valued learning activities and the learning contexts shapes the meaning of the term'.

Responses at the level of the community and family

At the level of community and family, responses to the issue of dyslexia have been in two directions. From families have come concerns that dyslexic children are inadequately provided for because there has been a lack of recognition of the difficulties they face in schools. From researchers investigating dyslexia has come the issue that students with inadequate access to literacy as a result of family background and circumstances may display problems with literacy similar to students whose difficulties have an identifiable cognitive basis. The first issue has clear implications for equity and resourcing and is discussed elsewhere in this book. With regard to the second, the British

Pyschological Society (BPS), in the working party report on *Dyslexia, Literacy and Psychological Assessment* (1999), provided a number of different hypotheses which can be associated with dyslexia. One such hypothesis is the learning opportunities and social context hypothesis, which is outlined below:

> [S]ome of the individual differences that are ascribed casual signif-icance in other theories of dyslexia may simply be indicators of consistent and important differences in different social contexts. Solity (1996) suggests that potential sources of learning opportuni-ties (e.g. parental input) might account both for pre-school differences in phonological awareness and for differences in progress with learning to read. ... it is always important to consider the availability of learning opportunities outside the school.
>
> (British Psychological Society 1999, p. 42)

In considering the implications of this hypothesis for practice, teachers often find themselves in a dilemma about the sensitivities associated with family background, which makes it difficult for them to engage with the issues. The easier option may be to view dyslexia as 'neutral' and separate from social context. However, in doing this there is a further problem of closing off possible avenues for addressing difficul-ties in literacy at the social level.

Responses at school level

The question of responses at school level is dealt with in other chap-ters in this book. However, it is appropriate at this stage to consider, first, the views expressed by Fawcett (2002) in relation to the response from the research and how this can impact on teaching.

Fawcett suggests that literacy and life support skills are crucial for the dyslexic child. Life skills can often be overlooked because of the obvious difficulties in literacy, but, as McLoughlin *et al.* (1994) argue, a failure to understand one's own strengths and weaknesses – and in particular to predict the effects that dyslexia will have on one's perfor-mance – could be the most basic problem.

In addition, McLoughlin feels that problems in dynamic working memory make it difficult for adults with dyslexia to hold information in mind whilst they manipulate it, thus leading to a further range of difficulties. A key requirement for life support according to Fawcett is therefore to establish the major goals for each individual and draw up an individual support plan tuned to these specific goals.

Fawcett suggests that a similar requirement holds for dyslexic children. It is not enough to provide literacy support alone because many children are scarred by their difficulties, which may have had devastating consequences – emotional trauma, loss of self-esteem and family problems. In her experience, it is important to take a number of broader factors into account when conceptualising ways to support the learning of dyslexic children. New technology can be harnessed, particularly to develop skills of automaticity, and children's strengths should be identified and exploited. The recent policy momentum needs to be maintained to ensure the development of learning in the pre-school years, in terms of a series of targets for nursery provision similar to the English National Curriculum. Policies relating to the inclusion of pupils with special educational needs should clearly address issues of difficulties in literacy. Particularly important, in Fawcett's opinion, are:

* 'overlearning' and reinforcement of new learning;
* particular attention paid to pupil motivation, given general slow progress in learning;
* reconsideration of whole-class teaching such as is evidenced in the English Literacy Hour;
* use of appropriate techniques to evaluate different teaching approaches and compare pupil improvement in learning in order to address the issue of cost-effectiveness of provision of additional support for dyslexic pupils as well as effectiveness;
* emphasis on early intervention in the first few years of a child's formal education.

Taking account of 'dyslexia' in the classroom

Crombie (2002) has set out some generic principles to take into account when considering how to respond to the learning needs of dyslexic pupils. She puts forward the view that teachers are often hesitant to label a child dyslexic. She suggests, however, that good communication with parents and an understanding of dyslexia will enable teachers to discuss with parents the reasons for their reluctance to label before the child has had the chance to make a real effort to learn to read. She suggests that appropriate intervention strategies for struggling readers are vital if children are to have an effective opportunity for success in spite of a slow start.

Class teachers are therefore in a key position, according to Crombie, and have to be able to access a range of knowledge, on, for example, information and communications technology (ICT) support, such as the hardware and software which is available to support individual needs, as well as having a knowledge of how the appropriate materials can be accessed.

Paying attention to students' learning styles is also an important area according to Crombie, who suggests that the notion of adapting teaching to the learning style of the child is a relatively new model. Focusing on learning styles can help children take responsibility for their own learning and facilitate a metacognitive approach. Although Crombie acknowledges that to accommodate to the whole range of learning styles within one classroom is not easy, this type of approach, using observable criteria to identify learning styles, can pay dividends. For some children the approach may not make an observable difference, but children who are dyslexic are likely to be more apparent and the approach will equip them with tools for 'life-long learning' (Given and Reid, 2001, p. 143) Crombie also highlights aspects such as student choice of subjects, and notes that it may not always be easy to adapt a pupil's timetable to accommodate their particular difficulties. She suggests, however, that curricular exemptions should be possible in a truly inclusive school where for reasons of special educational needs the pupil is gaining no benefit from taking a particular subject. Nevertheless, she acknowledges that this can only be established after full consultation with all concerned: pupil, parents, teachers, educational psychologist and school management.

Crombie also refers to the notion of dyslexia-friendly schools as a model of good practice which is likely to improve attainment and achievement for all. She suggests, however, that being dyslexia friendly and being effective are closely linked, and that leadership, staff development and quality teaching and learning, together with respect for the abilities and difficulties of all are essential ingredients of the effective school. Crombie appears to have taken account of research which points to genetic factors which suggest genetic inheritance within families, cognitive factors related to both phonological awareness and memory, issues of self-esteem and motivation, and theories of labelling. Any intervention strategy is bound to carry both advantages and disadvantages, and these need to be recognised in order to maximise the one whilst simultaneously minimising the other. On the one hand, notions of family inheritance risk stereotyping and 'sticky' labels. On the other, these notions can encourage educators to focus on games for young children which can help to develop phonological awareness, motor skills and mnemonic strategies to reinforce memory, and which will help to address difficulties in these areas and stand children in good stead in later years. In addition, working from the principle that prevention is better than cure, some children may never subsequently need additional identification and assessment.

Crombie notes that 'multisensory' approaches are commonly advocated to support the development of cognitive processing. What this means in effect is that students should be encouraged to use every sense simultaneously in quick succession to reinforce their learning of new skills. For example, when learning new spellings students might look at a word, say it out loud, say the letters in the word out loud whilst simultaneously writing them down, draw the letters on a rough surface whilst saying them out loud, etc.

The use of additional in-class support might well be an issue for school policy, not least because introducing visitors to classrooms on a regular basis raises important issues such as pupils' safety, confidentiality and ethics, and may have to be negotiated with the senior management team, and/or the whole staff. Nevertheless, there are schools which make a great deal of use of voluntary help in the classroom and/or help from other pupils as well as classroom assistants. The issue of training for all those involved in classroom support is clearly of the essence here.

Many teachers in the UK have undergone professional development in the area of the use of information and communications technology in the classroom. Suffice it to say, and this is supported by Crombie's work, that the use of ICT for 'special' purposes must relate to clearly identified learning needs. There is a very wide range of software on the market which can support different approaches to literacy development. For example, programmes are available to encourage the acquisition of 'basic skills' such as phonics if a bottom-up approach to reading is seen as appropriate. On the other hand, taped books and 'talking word processors' can support a top-down, meaning-based approach to reading. 'Metacognitive' strategies are also an important element of training programmes, and these include strategies designed to enable students to think about their own cognitive processes so that those who experience difficulty in particular areas of learning can develop alternative routes to accessing these areas. 'Mind-mapping' is an example of one way to develop a structure for producing extended text. It assumes that the structure and content of the text will be of higher quality if the learner is encouraged first to produce a visual representation of all those areas to be covered in the text before beginning on the written task. Those who experience difficulties in writing are likely to benefit by being able to separate out content from the technical aspects of producing the text by focusing on one before the other. Of course, there is considerable overlap between the first process and the second. 'Mind-mapping' is becoming an increasingly commonly used technique in classrooms. One might feel that it is appropriate to many other learners, in addition to those identified as 'dyslexic'.

Wray (2002) has summarised research on metacognition and considered ways in which metacognitive factors can be important for developing the reading skills of children with literacy difficulties. He has also offered suggestions for developing metacognitive skills. He feels that children need to consider the 'how' aspects of learning and to ask themselves how they tackled particular problems. He proposes that those children who are able successfully to complete complex learning tasks are those who have considered their learning strategies and the 'how' aspect of learning. Wray suggests that this is important for reading and that children who can monitor their self-understanding of reading are more successful readers and accomplished learners. The deliberate conscious control of one's actions and thought is called metacognition. This term is, according to Wray, associated with comprehension monitoring and has implications for reading comprehension. Wray also relates this to writing from the perspectives of knowledge of the person, knowledge of the task and knowledge of the process. Each of these can be influenced by the learner's metacognitive awareness. Wray also suggests that it is important that strategies are taught at an early age to help children develop metacognitive skills. Some of these include thinking aloud, teacher modelling and reciprocal teaching.

For pupils at the secondary stage who have experienced many years of failure in school as a result of dyslexia there may be a particular challenge in addressing literacy difficulties.

Peer and Reid (2002) suggest that when planning for a dyslexia-friendly school a number of questions need to be addressed. These include the following:

- Are the needs of dyslexic students recognised across the curriculum and within the social structure of the school?
- Who is responsible for provision?
- Who monitors and measures progress?
- Who liaises with parents, examination boards, careers and further education?

Peer and Reid suggest that without such fundamental questioning provision cannot be fully and effectively met. Furthermore, they argue that there needs to be provision for those who fall outside the categories which have traditionally been placed within the dyslexic group, such as children with hyperactivity, children whose first language is other than English and those with overlapping specific learning difficulties.

According to Peer and Reid, one of the key issues in successful outcomes in secondary school concerns the notion of responsibility. It is important to ensure that provision is firmly in place and that all members of staff become fully involved. It is important, for example, that the ethos of the school is supportive and that all staff should be encouraged to explore the range of routes to help children access the full curriculum through differentiation. They must be shown that, even though written literacy may be poor, dyslexic children need to have information given to them at the appropriate intellectual level. They feel that to be effective in addressing the needs of all dyslexic students schools need to focus on issues relating to the subject content, how the subjects are taught, the assessment, cross-curricular aspects to ensure transfer of learning from one subject area to another, metacognitive factors which can facilitate thinking and problem-solving skills, acknowledgement of individual learning styles and, importantly, staff development.

Peer and Reid suggest that if the subject materials and teaching are developed and implemented in a manner which is compatible with the dyslexic student the student should be able to perform on the same terms as his/her peers. Although much of the subject content is determined by examination considerations and the National Curriculum, much can still be done to identify the potential areas of the curriculum which may present difficulties for dyslexic students. Subjects such as modern foreign languages, English, art and drama, which can prove challenging in terms of the amount of reading, can lend themselves quite easily to kinaesthetic approaches by focusing on experiential learning activities. This acknowledges that the dyslexic student may have difficulty with written instructions and written responses.

Traditional forms of assessment, according to Peer and Reid, can disadvantage the dyslexic student because usually there is a discrepancy between their understanding of a topic and how they are able to display that understanding in written form. This can be overcome through continuous and portfolio assessment in most subject areas, although schools need to consider the importance of public examinations – many of which are set without any awareness of the needs of dyslexic students. Metacognitive assessment holds considerable promise, as it can provide information about children's true potential and can be used to develop teaching approaches, thereby strengthening the link between assessment and teaching.

Peer and Reid also suggest that cross-curricular aspects are important and that one should view dyslexia not as the responsibility of one teacher, or even one specialist teacher, but from a whole-school perspective. Tod and Fairman (2001) maintain that much of this can be achieved through skilful use of individual education programmes (IEPs), which need to be contextualised to identify the nature of the differentiation required. They also identify the need for flexible arrangements that would support individual provision for all students, including dyslexic students. This emphasises the need to take a holistic whole-school approach in relation to provision and practice in order to benefit all dyslexic students. This also emphasises the importance of staff development to ensure that all subject teachers are aware of the characteristics of dyslexia and the implications of this for their own subject. Peer and Reid suggest that in a subject-orientated – perhaps even examination-driven – education system it is difficult for teachers to manage the juggling act between meeting the needs of all and of each individual, and particularly those with special needs.

In many ways we might argue that good practice in addressing the needs of dyslexic pupils is good practice in teaching every student. Schools are required to have structures and processes in place to ensure that individual students' difficulties in learning are identified, assessed and met. There are times when every individual student may benefit from individual attention. However, offering appropriate support assumes a willingness to get to know students as individuals with their own idiosyncrasies.

The extent to which an emphasis on addressing the special needs of individuals permeates the whole school may depend to a large extent on the head teacher, as well as on the history and social context of the school itself. The School Development Plan drawn up or approved by the head and governors, for example, may include a priority given to addressing difficulties in literacy development and offer the opportunity to raise staff awareness of this issue in staff development sessions.

Although one might identify general indicators of 'dyslexia', above all the students concerned are individuals. It is a mistake to assume that general characteristics of any group automatically apply to every individual who, in broad terms, might be seen as a group member.

Social and emotional consequences of dyslexia

Among clinicians and educationalists there is general agreement about the 'devastating effects' that serious difficulties in literacy development can have on pupils and their families (Riddick 1996, p. 32). However, there is little formal research on the social and emotional consequences of dyslexia. Given that there is a whole body of research on what motivates learners in the context of schoolwork, including those who experience difficulties, this is somewhat surprising.

Much of the research that exists in the area of social and emotional consequences of dyslexia relates to individual accounts of personal experience. Below is an extract from an interview transcript in which a young adult, 'Katherine', who has been identified as 'dyslexic', describes her current feelings about her difficulties in the area of literacy acquisition and her recollections of school experiences.

Interview with 'Katherine'

Interviewer: What, then, do you want to do all this (learning to read, basic number work, etc.) for?

Katherine: To better myself.

Interviewer: What do you mean by that?

Katherine: To prove to myself that I'm as good as anybody else, to get better grades, to be able to stand there and write things down, to write letters – and also, for people in the same situation as myself, to say to them: 'Why don't you go and do something?' Everybody's got a talent. Everybody should have a chance. Dad told me once that you're never too old to stop learning.

Interviewer: Did you believe that at the time?

Katherine: I thought when you're 16 you walk out of school and that's that, but now I totally believe it.

Interviewer: Can you think of one thing that happened that made you suddenly stop and turn round and say to yourself: 'Right, I'm going to do something about this'?

Katherine: Yes. I was standing in Halford's and I wrote out a cheque three times. It was last September time, last year (1994 – seven months before the interview), and I was totally embarrassed. It was in front of a queue of people and the shop assistant. In the end I just gave her my Switch card and walked out. I felt everyone was looking at me and

	thinking: 'What's going on here.' I thought they were all saying behind my back: 'Oh, she's thick.'
Interviewer:	How old were you then?
Katherine:	I was 20.
Interviewer:	How old were you when you realised that you had a problem with reading?
Katherine:	It must have been when I was about 11, when the teacher used to come and take me off for extra spelling. But it never worked. It was not enough. They just used to give me spellings to go away and learn, and then I had a spelling test.
Interviewer:	Were there other people in the group?
Katherine:	Yes.
Interviewer:	And was it always at the same time during the week?
Katherine:	No. It was when the teacher had time, and we never used to know when it was going to be.
Interviewer:	So did you miss chunks of other people's lessons?
Katherine:	Yes, absolutely. I was always behind.
Interviewer:	Were the spellings words that you needed to use?
Katherine:	As much as I remember, they just seemed to be any old words that they thought we should have been able to spell.
Interviewer:	Did anyone ever talk to you about the problem, or what was going on, or how you could help yourself?
Katherine:	No, not at all.
Interviewer:	What about your parents? Were they ever consulted about this?
Katherine:	No, mum and dad didn't know anything unless I told them. Sometimes it was discussed, but not to a great degree. I was very embarrassed about it, so I wanted to keep quiet about it all.
Interviewer:	I was going to ask you – what did all this mean to you?
Katherine:	I felt really upset, as if there was something wrong. I felt really downhearted. My friends had no problem at all, and there was me having to be taken out. It was heart-breaking at times.
Interviewer:	Do you mean you cried sometimes?
Katherine:	Yes. I remember one time – I must have been about 6 – I got no spellings right at all, and I just sat there and cried.
Interviewer:	So this must have started at lower school then?
Katherine:	Yes. Everybody else knew about it as well because she read the spellings out. Then I got people taking the mickey because they thought it was really funny.

Interviewer: What did people say to you, then, when you were little?

Katherine: Oh, she's thick, she's stupid. She doesn't know what she's doing. Really cruel things like children say to one another.

Interviewer: You mentioned spellings. Did it affect your reading as well?

Katherine: Oh, yes. I wouldn't read anything. I used to do anything to get out of reading aloud. When we used to choose books from the library, I used to pretend that I'd read them. I'd read the back cover, and then make the rest up. If I was made to read aloud, I'd read really quietly and then the teacher would get really annoyed. She'd say she couldn't hear, and tell me to stop reading.

Interviewer: Were you aware of doing this deliberately at the time?

Katherine: Absolutely. Oh, yes. I didn't want people laughing at me, so whatever I could do to protect myself I would do. I'd make her get fed up, and then she wouldn't ask me to read. That was the way of it.

Interviewer: What does reading mean to you now?

Katherine: I've missed out so much by not reading books. Some of the children's books – I've really missed out by not being able to read them. I suppose to read a book you need to use your imagination, but I never. My mind has not been trained to imagine things, so I can't do it. That's just my little theory.

Interviewer: What does spelling mean to you now?

Katherine: Spelling to me now is very, very important. When you first leave school, if you can't spell you con your way through it somehow. But when you get to my age, you get to thinking that there's not always going to be someone around to help you.

Interviewer: Can you give me some examples of where you've really had to spell a word recently.

Katherine: Obviously, writing letters to friends, applying for jobs, writing cheques, quite a varied range of stuff.

Interviewer: And you're going to be able to in the near future?

Katherine: I certainly am, yes!

Interviewer: Looking back at school, did it affect how you were taught, not being able to read?

Katherine: Yes, absolutely. By the age of 13, at upper school I totally and utterly gave up – on school, on teachers. I just thought they were there to give you a hard time. Everyone seemed to be against me, whatever I was doing, and in the end I just mucked around. To get a bit of attention. I never did any homework. I got into trouble,

but I just gave up – and they gave up. They just put me in the group of other kids who just mucked around.

Interviewer: And do you think yourself this was simply due to the fact that you couldn't read and spell, nothing else?

Katherine: I think if I had had the proper help with reading and spelling I would not have dropped back as much as I did.

Interviewer: If we go on a bit from there – what are you doing now?

Katherine: A nanny.

Interviewer: Is this what you really want to do?

Katherine: No. I want to do some work with children with learning difficulties. I want to visit homes and see what parents want and need for the child.

Interviewer: If you could read better, how would it help you to get into that area?

Katherine: I need more college training. I need to be able to write reports. I need more independence.

Interviewer: So is learning to read and spell now a part of an overall plan for what you are trying to do for yourself?

Katherine: Yes.

Interviewer: Looking back at school, what sort of things could teachers have done with you that would have helped? Would it have been better to have helped you in class or taken you out?

Katherine: They did the best thing by taking me out. I would not have done the work with other children watching me. It would have been worse. What should have happened is that the teachers should have found out what the problems were properly, sat down and listened to me, talked to my parents, and got everybody involved – for me and other children like me. I knew what I was doing, but trying to write it down on paper was totally different.

Interviewer: If you had a geography or history book, could you read it?

Katherine: It was bigger words, and I never found it interesting. I would read all the sentences wrong. It never made sense.

Interviewer: So you just sat there in this world of semi-nonsense?

Katherine: Yes. Obviously, you've always got people in the class who want to muck around. You're blaming the teacher, so if you can wind them up enough … I used to write all over the tables because they hated it. I'd take the mickey out of them by calling them names out loud in class. We knew one teacher's Christian name, so we called it out loud. Whatever you could do to disrupt the class, you'd do it. The French teacher used to go out of the class, so we'd get hairspray and set light to it as it sprayed out. One French lesson, my friend got this little bottle of gin and we just sat there drinking it under the table. I don't think it's right that some teachers just used to come in, set the work and then go off for forty-five minutes. If you've left a bunch of 15-year-olds they're not going to do the work, are they?

(Wearmouth, unpublished ms.)

Katherine's is an individual account and we cannot generalise from it. However, her comments serve to reinforce some of the assumptions that one might hypothesise about the potential long-term consequences and effects on life chances of not addressing children's difficulties in literacy at an early stage. As an adult she felt humiliated at the public display of her poor literacy skills. She also felt cheated of opportunities that she might have had if she was competent in reading and writing. Her recollections of school experiences also reflect many of the comments recorded in Riddick's (1996) study of the personal experiences of twenty-two children aged from 8 to 14 years and identified as 'dyslexic', and their families. Here, for example, children reflected on similar feelings of disaffection and of dread of 'visible public indicators' (*ibid.*, p. 124) of their difficulties in literacy, such as reading aloud and always being the last to finish work.

The research that exists in the area of the relationship between difficulties in literacy development and self-esteem has resulted in somewhat mixed and apparently contradictory findings. The net result of this, for practitioners, is that research projects must be scrutinised very thoroughly before any generalisation of their findings can be assumed. For example, Riddick refers to work by D. Lawrence (1971), the results of which were used in some schools in the early 1970s to justify the use of counselling rather than individual reading programmes to raise the level of literacy of pupils with difficulties in literacy acquisition. Lawrence's study investigated the effects on reading attainment of individual personal counselling from a 'responsible, sympathetic' adult with 'status' in the child's eyes (1971, p. 120), and compared them with the results obtained by a traditional 'remedial' reading programme administered by a specialist remedial reading teacher. After six months the pupils in the counselled group showed a significant rise in reading attainment on a test of word recognition compared with all other groups, together with 'improved self-images' (*ibid.*, p 119). However, different adults carried out the counselling and the specialist teaching. We know nothing about the relationship that existed between the specialist remedial reading teacher and the pupils, or about the teacher's status in the eyes of the pupil group. Whilst the results of Lawrence's study clearly indicate the importance for pupil learning of the relationship between pupils and teachers, it does not disprove the need for good, well-structured teaching programmes in literacy.

Riddick (1996) concludes that:

- Clear definition of both dyslexia and social and emotional difficulties is problematic, so that comparing like with like is very difficult.
- Second, much research compares groups of pupils with and without difficulties in literacy development. Such studies mask individual differences between children. Those who experience difficulties in literacy but are well supported at home may have higher self-esteem than those with very difficult home circumstances but no literacy difficulties, for example.
- Furthermore, it is likely that social and emotional experiences fluctuate over time and that the child's home and school context may change, all of which can affect the outcome. In addition, it is not clear if difficulties in literacy lead to poor self-esteem, or whether poor self-esteem leads to poor literacy acquisition.
- Finally, what constitutes 'self-esteem' and also how to measure 'self-esteem' are highly problematic.

Early researchers (Rosenthal and Jacobson 1968) appeared to attribute overriding importance to teacher expectations on pupil performance. However, later researchers were much more circumspect in their conclusions, and believed that there was a great deal of individual difference in the significance attributed by pupils to particular teachers' attitudes and, therefore, much difference between the effects of such attitudes. In addition, teachers' expectations operate in interaction with other factors, all of which must be taken into account in their effect on pupils.

Results of earlier work into effective classroom practice for dyslexic students indicates that classroom teachers should interact evenly with all pupils, talk to all pupils, offer realistic praise and find a balance between being overcritical or over-commendatory, and, finally, match tasks to individuals. However, Riddick notes some of the challenges in putting these principles into practice in the busy classroom situation and advises seeking additional support where appropriate.

In Riddick's study the children had very strong views about which teachers were best able to support them in ways which were positive and productive: 'People jump to the wrong conclusions and they should be educated about what dyslexia means, It's just been one of my dreams to tell them all what it means' (interview, Riddick 1996, back cover). From her research Riddick identifies the key qualities of the 'best' teachers as a propensity to offer praise and encouragement, linked with understanding of the difficulties experienced by the child. The 'best' teachers:

- encourage and praise;
- help pupils, adapt work and explain clearly;
- understand pupils and do not attempt to humiliate them;
- do not shout;
- have a sense of humour;
- know if children are dyslexic;
- treat all children as if they are intelligent.

(Riddick 1996, p. 133)

The worst teachers, on the other hand:

- are cross, impatient and shout;
- criticise and humiliate pupils;
- are not helpful, and are negative about pupils' efforts;
- ignore some pupils and show they consider some pupils 'useless';
- do not understand the problems faced by pupils with difficulties in literacy and are insensitive;
- blame pupils for their problems and call them 'lazy';
- puts red lines through pupils' work.

(*ibid.*)

In a further study into dyslexic individuals' views of their educational experiences (interview for Open University E801 course materials, 2002) these and similar factors were identified as important in supporting the learning of students identified as dyslexic. It was recognised that teachers should attempt to understand students, never humiliate them, make an effort to investigate dyslexia, know about the cognitive difficulties involved and know appropriate strategies to employ to address these, be positive about students' efforts and treat them as if they are intelligent.

One of the issues raised by the dyslexic individuals in the Open University study is the extent to which labelling is a significant factor in contributing to emotional distress.

Labelling and stigmatisation

Pumfrey (2002) suggests that the label 'specific developmental dyslexia' leads to a 'pathologizing of normality'. He feels that there is an inevitable progression from the recognition of such differences to the identification of defects. 'Differentiation and labelling' leads to 'differences – deviations

– difficulties – disabilities – deficits – defects'. Pumfrey portrays this as an example of 'the slippery path from differences to defects [which] can lead to the pathologizing of normality' (2002, p. 48).

Riddick examines the relationship between labelling and stigmatisation and quotes from J.J. Gallagher (1976) in discussing the positive and negative aspects of labelling. These are:

Positive:

- diagnosis and appropriate treatment and alteration to the environment.
- to enable further research which may lead to better understanding, prevention and treatment.
- to act as a positive way to call attention to a particular difficulty and obtaining better resources through funding and legislation.

Negative:

- the professionals labelling for its own sake, without suggesting any form of treatment or support.
- as a way of maintaining the status quo by keeping minority groups at the bottom of the social hierarchy.

(Riddick 2000, p. 653)

It can, however, be suggested that the label 'dyslexia' carries less stigmatisation than most other special educational needs labels. In addition, there are other issues relating to gender differences in the amount of support provided – with boys generally outnumbering girls; class issues; as well as ethnic-minority issues.

Reed (2002) discusses more fully the issues that arise from using the dyslexia label to describe difficulties in literacy experienced by students for whom English is an additional language. She considers that dyslexia offers too restricted a view for bilingual learners and risks ignoring the range of factors significant to their learning, which is dependent on many contexts, for example the family, institution and society, and the interactional effects of, for example, physical or psychological problems, socio-economic and/or refugee status, degree of acculturation. One might argue that these factors potentially apply to all other students who experience difficulties in literacy development. Reed advocates a learning environment that is free from racism, and aims at motivating student achievement by means of a 'co-operative learning' culture where community mentors are used as role models.

She suggests that there has been a history of misassessment and misplacement which has not been helped by 'the "ignorance" and "thoughtlessness" displayed by western psychologists' (Reed 2002, p. 204), for example in extending the application of psychometric tests before considering the question of their validity for Black and Asian groups. She suggests that professionals are thoughtless if they gloss over the inherent cultural-linguistic bias that invalidates the use of such tools and the resultant discriminatory data. Reed also suggests that the indiscriminate classification that results from dyslexia research encourages overgeneralisation and a lack of real understanding of the complex needs of Black and Asian groups. Such indiscriminate classification, according to Reed, can confuse and mislead people and blur the distinction between English as an additional language (EAL) and special needs. She suggests that the results of cultural-bias assessment procedures can lead to professional misjudgement and to 'institutional racism'. Reed suggests that professionals would do well to heed the wisdom gained in the field of bilingual research:

> [C]hildren learning to read in their home language ... are not just developing home language skills. They are also developing higher order cognitive and linguistic skills that will help with their future development of reading in the majority language as well as with general intellectual development.
>
> (Reed, quoting Baker 1996, p. 155)

Reed therefore concludes that 'professionals have to accept that an anti racist perspective demands a clear vision that focuses exclusively on the interests of the Black and Asian communities which cannot sit with other self-serving agendas' (Reed 2002, p. 209).

Conclusion

Often responses to dyslexia focus on the need to improve literacy attainments. This can be a shortsighted approach if it attempts to achieve this from too narrow a perspective. This chapter has attempted to highlight elements such as metacognitive factors, thinking skills, differentiation, and social and emotional considerations which essentially broaden the perspectives from which we understand and respond to dyslexia at all levels – class, school, family and community. It is important to consider the individual needs of dyslexic children, and the cultural and contextual background, as this will make assessment and teaching more relevant, effective and meaningful to individual students.

Chapter 4

Socio-cultural models and approaches

Introduction

The previous two chapters have critically examined the notion of dyslexia, which, as we have seen, focuses upon individual cognitive difficulties that can be associated with information processing. This chapter will move beyond a cognitive perspective to explore wider disciplinary and interdisciplinary views and conceptualisations of literacy. In this chapter we will draw upon understandings of literacy derived from social psychology, social linguistics and sociological perspectives to explore the social and cultural factors that might contribute to particular groups of students experiencing difficulties in literacy. As we have seen, understanding literacy and the barriers to literacy acquisition is a complex project and one fraught with tensions and conflicts between differing viewpoints and their related teaching practices. These tensions and conflicts exist within socio-cultural views of literacy as well as between socio-cultural conceptualisations of literacy and the concepts, models and approaches examined in the previous three chapters.

Definitions of 'literacy' are many and various. In common parlance, literacy is often defined as the ability to read and write. Sometimes this definition might be extended to include the ability to calculate numbers, or having a basic knowledge of mathematics and calculation. In line with these definitions, a child or adult who has difficulties with literacy might be described as a child or adult who has difficulties with basic reading and writing. While this can include being competent in mathematics, many people might agree that they would see difficulties in reading and writing as the main barrier to being a literate citizen.

This definition of what constitutes literacy leads us to see literacy as a set of technical skills involving the decoding of written text and the on reading and writing as separate skills which can be evaluated and measured. While this may seem a straightforward and uncomplicated view of literacy, if we look more closely even this apparently simple view of literacy implies that there are different levels and expectations of what being literate might entail. Within this view of literacy it is possible to define being literate as achieving 'basic literacy', 'functional literacy', and having difficulties with literacy as 'functional illiteracy'.

Basic and functional literacy

Christie and Misson (2002) point out that the concept of literacy is a relatively recent one and that the emphasis in the past has been on reading and writing as separate skills:

> Until very recent times, the custom in educational theory and discussion was to talk of the teaching of reading and writing, rather than the teaching of literacy. Reading and writing were seen as separate skills. Time-honoured practice, going back some centuries, required that students learn to read first, moving on to learn writing much later on. In practice, in the nineteenth century and even in the early years of this century, many educational programmes for children, particularly at the elementary level, concentrated on the teaching of reading only, requiring no more than that the children also learned to pen their names. There was a sense in which, in much educational practice, reading was often seen as the more significant skill. Writing gained more significance for those students fortunate to stay on at school for the secondary years.
>
> From the fifteenth century on, a 'literate person' has been one who was acquainted with letters or with literature. The juxtaposition of the two terms is interesting: to be familiar with literature, one needed to know the alphabet, and this was a measure of one's status as an educated person.
>
> One who was 'illiterate' was necessarily ignorant of letters, and hence also of literature. But though the terms 'literate' and 'illiterate' were known and in use for several centuries, the term 'literacy' was not widely used. Teaching was understood to be about reading and writing, where these were seen as somewhat separate skills. Teacher education dates from the second half of the nineteenth century, and the first teacher training programmes in the English-speaking world attached a great deal of importance to

preparing their trainee teachers for instructing the young in their letters. Instruction in one's letters for the greater majority of children in the elementary schools of the nineteenth century was about learning to recognise the alphabet, to be able to read improving works, including religious tracts, and perhaps to write one's name. But the term 'literacy' was not a term much in use, nor was it widely used in educational discussions for much of the first half of this century.

(Christie and Misson 2002, p. 48)

The notion of functional literacy has also only recently come into common usage and is largely a post-war phenomenon:

After the second world war, a great many former colonies around the world became newly launched independent nations, and a priority for such nations very early on was to provide adequate educational opportunity for their children. Education was closely linked to the building of economic security. Bodies like the United Nations, and related agencies such as UNICEF [United Nations Children's Fund] and UNESCO [United Nations Educational, Scientific and Cultural Organisation] have, in the postwar period, devoted large amounts of resources to educational provision in the developing countries. After the 1960s, international agencies began to develop programmes in 'functional literacy' – a term intended to capture a sense of a basic competence in reading and writing of a kind held to be sufficient for fostering efficient and informed workers.

(*ibid.*, pp. 48–9)

In their attempts to conceptualise and evaluate mass literacy programmes UNESCO used the notion of 'basic literacy' to refer to the acquisition of 'technical skills involving the decoding of written text and the writing of simple statements in every day life' (Rassool 1999, p. 7). Basic literacy tended to focus on the acquisition of technical skills involving the decoding of text. Functional literacy was referred to as 'the process and content of learning to read and write to the preparation for work and vocational training' (UNESCO; quoted in Rassool 1999, pp. 6–7). However, as Rassool points out, these distinctions are not straightforward. The notion of 'basic literacy' can range from the acquisition of basic technical skills to include the gaining of broader socially based skills that enable an individual to relate to and interact with their community. This definition can therefore overlap with the notion of 'functional literacy', with its emphasis on work-based, vocationally orientated skills that are designed to increase the employee's productivity. Rassool argues that, despite this overlap, basic literacy and functional illiteracy have been used in ways which suggest that they are located in the individual, whereas functional literacy has evolved to focus on the external requirements of producing a literate and productive workforce (Rassool 1999, p. 7).

If one takes these definitions of functional and basic literacy and uses them to try to conceptualise possible barriers to the acquisition of literacy, it can be argued that this conceptualisation of literacy embodies different notions of the location of barriers to literacy. As Rassool points out, this notion of literacy suggests different locations for conceptualising literacy, so it follows that it is possible to devise programmes which focus on different strategies for removing barriers to the acquisition of literacy. This tension, between different conceptualisations of barriers to literacy acquisition and their different locations, and its tendency to create a diversity of approaches and programmes designed to address literacy development, is a key theme and focus within this course.

If the barriers to literacy are seen as existing within the individual, then it follows that we must develop programmes to cater for individual differences and work at overcoming these barriers through individual tuition. If, however, the barriers to literacy are seen to exist beyond the individual, it is possible to argue that they can be reduced by policies to change pedagogies in order to promote vocational education and training. This tension between addressing barriers to literacy through programmes aimed at catering for individuals and their particular needs, or through implementing programmes aimed at changing the pedagogical structures of teaching literacy, is therefore unavoidable even if we define literacy as functional and basic literacy. The tensions and complexities of addressing barriers to literacy expand if one attempts to view literacy as a more complex cultural and social process.

Cultural literacy

The skills of decoding print are clearly key aspects of literacy. However, there is considerable evidence that programmes designed to address literacy difficulties also need to take into account the fact that literacy is more than a set of skills and practical activities.

While the notions of functional literacy and basic literacy dominate the media, parliamentary debates and the average person's notion of literacy, they are a very narrow conceptualisation of literacy. Embodied in the concept of literacy are complex meanings and assumptions. Teachers and researchers writing in the field of literacy education have come to see literacy as being grounded in wider cultural, social and political contexts. Historically, educationalists spoke of reading and writing instruction rather than teaching literacy. Literacy was not usually associated with skills, as a literate person was someone who was familiar with English literature rather than a person who could effectively decode print (see, for example, Mathieson 1975; Williams 1965; Graff 1987).

The field of literacy research, as well as the term itself, reveals a complex and rich phenomenon that can be viewed from multiple disciplinary perspectives. These differing perspectives, viewpoints, frameworks and strands of interpretations are obviously going to have an impact on literacy teaching and interpretations of how to interpret and implement best research-based practice. It is against this complex, contradictory and multifaceted understanding of literacy that this book seeks to explore the different frameworks and programmes which one might draw upon to develop practices and programmes designed to help those who have difficulties in literacy over the barriers they may face.

Literacy is increasingly being recognised as a complex process which is part of a potent symbolic system related to the specific cultural environment in which it is being utilised. One of the authors of this book has experience of teaching ethnic minorities in New Zealand as well as England. She has also researched the historical exclusion of Maori as a language in New Zealand primary schools. This has made her aware that national language programmes, the existence of a dominant language such as English, and the privileging of certain literacies and literary traditions over others has led to the systematised exclusion of literacies in different cultures and languages through the dominance and insistence that being a literate individual implied literacy in English language and culture in New Zealand and other English colonies (Soler and Smith 2000).

Literacy practices of the dominant culture have had an impact not only on ex-colonial countries. They can also have an impact within the colonial power itself, through the proliferation of a 'selective tradition' which has intentionally given precedence to cultural traditions and meanings associated with specific dominant social groupings and classes (see, for example, Williams 1989). This selective tradition in the UK influences what is chosen in formal education as the particular values, knowledge and content which should be transmitted to future generations. It can lead to the discarding of whole areas of significant oral and recorded traditions, histories and practices which are relevant to other groups and ethnic cultures.

Critical literacy

The notions of functional and basic literacy imply that literacy is essentially a neutral, value-free collection of skills which are not influenced by surrounding societal and cultural influences. This is particularly evident if one examines the UNESCO framework within which they were conceived in the 1970s. As noted above, in the UNESCO framework functional and basic literacy represented a set of technical decoding and functional writing skills. This views literacy as neutral because it is characterised as a set of generic technical skills which exist outside, and unaffected by, the culture and society within which they are learned and practised. From this viewpoint acquiring literacy is merely a matter of learning a technique and then applying it. Any barriers to literacy are then seen to be barriers to the individual acquiring the techniques to read and write.

The emphasis upon the individual as the focal point for conceptualising literacy in the notion of functional and basic literacy has an important implication for literacy teachers. In terms of this definition of literacy, it can be seen to be beneficial and powerful because of its usefulness to the individual. It follows that schools must teach literacy and overcome barriers for those who may not acquire the technical skills of decoding print and writing simple text because it will have an impact on an individual's life chances and future in the labour market. Inability to become literate will disadvantage learners from becoming employable, good workers.

There is, however, another view of literacy which stands in stark contrast to the view and outcomes associated with the notion of functional and basic literacy. It is also possible to espouse a critical view of literacy. If one adopts this view, literacy is seen as an essential element in the development of, involvement in and transformation of society, and a crucial element in the development of cultural and political awareness. Christie and Misson point out that a critical-literacy perspective tends to emphasise text and aims to make the belief systems embedded in text explicit:

The main thrust of much work in critical literacy is towards analysing representations to make apparent the inherent ideology. Its aim is to render explicit the belief systems inscribed in the text and so negate their power. Since it is thought that ideology is at its most powerful when the representations through which it is being transmitted seem most natural, to denaturalise the naturalised image and show its constructedness and its tendentiousness is thought to defuse the ideology and make the student safe from its imposition. This does undoubtedly genuinely happen in some cases, but there must be some considerable doubt that the process is usually quite as simply effective as that. Ideology infiltrates our minds in particularly subtle and multifarious ways, and making explicit some of its workings does not necessarily free us from its multiplicitous grasp.

People are seen as being largely defined by their positioning in terms of class, ethnicity and gender. Much of the work in the classroom therefore is concerned to teach against limitations imposed on people in terms of one or other of these systems. This is done through analysis of the ideological implications of texts, examining how disadvantage is reproduced by constructing images that assume that certain qualities or ways of life are 'natural' to a certain group, or by looking at what is excluded from, or not acknowledged in, the way that a text is talking about a particular phenomenon. Excellent work has been done on teaching against discrimination, although it is worth noting that this, like anything else in the classroom, can become a rather empty routine. The students can produce the expected answer and mouth the appropriate sentiments without any notable impact on their actual attitudes.

(Christie and Misson 2002, p. 57)

Writers who adopt this viewpoint usually draw upon the work of Freire (1996), who stressed the importance of developing literacy programmes which recognised the cultural power dynamics implicit in literacy instruction. This view enables literacy to be used as a tool to transform self-identity and self-definition, and promote cultural transformation by encouraging critical thinking and social critique. Freire critiqued the idea of the neutrality of print and highlighted the power and patterns of interest both within the practice of teaching literacy and in the wider society. He opposed the traditional approaches adopted in programmes designed to promote functional and basic literacy.

Freire argued for programmes that can counteract the lack of power and social isolation, and that comes from 'banking' education where students are expected to learn supposedly neutral skills and knowledge without engaging in dialogue with the teacher or the material with which they are presented. He saw this form of literacy education as increasing the alienation and barriers to acquiring literacy, especially for groups who are not from the dominant culture or class. The supposedly neutral content of these literacy programmes was not removing the barriers to literacy for those from disadvantaged groups and non-dominant cultures. Rather than being neutral, these programmes were actually promoting selective traditions which privileged the dominant group over their own cultural and social traditions.

The principles which underpin Freire's notion of critical literacy are clearly expressed in his autobiographical letters to his niece Cristina, where he set out his ideas in a manner which she could understand as an adolescent and young adult. Freire summarises the basic principles of literacy teaching and the removal of barriers for disadvantaged groups as follows:

> [E]ducational practice cannot be neutral, however, [and it] must not lead educators to impose, subliminally or not, their taste on learners, whatever those tastes may be. This is the ethical dimension of educational practice ...
> ... a fundamental starting point is respect for the learner's cultural identity and the aspects of class that mark this identity: the learner's language, syntax, prosody, semantics and informal knowledge, realised through the experiences the learner brings to school.
>
> (Freire 1996, p. 127)

Embedded within the notion of critical literacy is also the notion that literacy can play an important role in enabling participation in democratic citizenship by providing skills and knowledge development that extend beyond the decoding of print. Thus critical-literacy theorists argue that literacy programmes should actively work to remove the 'culture of silence' that functional-literacy and basic-literacy programmes may unwittingly impose by developing skills and knowledge related to the multiple literacy demands of democratic citizenship. From this viewpoint, literacy programmes should enable students to engage in dialogue and social critique through the development of argumentation, and the formulation and expression of ideas, as well as enabling them to decode text and write simple communications.

Rassool (1999) also indicates the difficulties associated with the reconceptualisation of literacy that has arisen out of the influence of critical literacy and its emphasis on literacy as 'a social process' and 'cultural activity' that is 'multidimensional' and 'suited to a range of context-related situations'. This multidimensional view of literacy sees it as being 'integrally linked with ideology, culture, knowledge and power'. As he points out, this view of literacy counters the traditional functional view of literacy as 'an autonomous set of technical skills' and shifts the emphasis away from 'concerns about process, or individual behaviours during reading, to that of agency, or active involvement within a defined context' (Rassool 2002, p. 17).

Rassool draws attention to the ongoing debate and exploration of the ways in which different disciplinary frameworks – drawing upon, for example, social psychology, socio-linguistics, social anthropology and critical theory – have resulted in the conceptualisation of literacy as a multidimensional culturally related process. While researchers from these disciplinary groups explore the multifaceted nature of literacy, experimental, behavioural and psychometric-based psychologists view literacy as a cognitive, skills-based and less socially complex process.

Rassool points out that the analysis of literacy from the perspective of experimental, behavioural psychology tends to emphasise cognitive processes associated with how individuals construct meaning from text. He states that '[e]xperimental psychology provides a view of literacy that is primarily concerned with the de-coding of texts involving the perceptual process (phonological and graphic), word structure (morphological) and technical writing (spelling)'. He also notes that, from this perspective, it is the 'cognitive processes that underlie skilled reading and learning how to read that underpins this perspective of literacy skills' (Rassool 1999, p. 26). Perspectives that are informed by experimental psychology, therefore, tend to conceptualise literacy as a process rather than a result of agency and active involvement, as is the view of Freire and other critical theorists.

The 'Models of reading' section of Chapter 1 contains outlines of various conceptualisations of the reading process that have been derived from psychological perspectives, in particular experimental, behavioural psychology and psycholinguistics. Most literacy educators will find these psychologically derived interpretations of literacy and the associated notions of what might constitute barriers to literacy more familiar than the notions of cultural and critical literacy introduced earlier in this chapter.

Discussion of the models of reading indicates that perspectives derived from a psychological discipline base tend to focus on the individual's engagement with learning and utilising the skills of literacy. Frameworks which have been derived from sociological and historical perspectives draw attention to social structures, such as political, ethnic and socio-economic practices.

Rassool (1999), however, raises awareness of the fact that, even within psychologically related fields of study, individual and cultural-social perspectives of literacy have begun to merge through the development of paradigms such as 'New Literacy Studies'. This group of literacy theorists draws upon conceptual-analytic frameworks that bridge the gap between concerns over understanding and teaching specific skills and the social and cultural practices within which they take place.

It is possible to place the models and frameworks currently available for understanding and conceptualising literacy along a continuum. This continuum ranges from experimental, behavioural and psychometric-based models which view literacy as teaching the individual the neutral skills of reading and writing, to psycholinguistically inspired frameworks such as whole-language/real-book approaches, and then on to New Literacy Studies, which embodies an even more dynamic, interactive and social context-based view of literacy. At the end most distant from the neutral, skills-based views of literacy, critical cultural theorists move entirely away from individual cognitive processes and focus on literacy as a product of social organisation, wider conceptual systems, political structures and economic processes. These different perspectives, models and frameworks for understanding literacy suggest different notions of how schools might teach literacy, and therefore where they might locate the barriers to literacy.

Multi-literacies and new literacies

The 'Great Debate' and the 'Literacy Wars' resulted in a focus on methods of reading instruction that resulted from conflicts between behavioural, experimental psychology and psycholinguistics. The 1970s also saw the development of New Literacy Studies, which drew upon even broader social-science disciplinary influences than the whole-language and real-book approaches. New Literacy Studies arose from the influences of social anthropology, social and cultural psychology, and psycholinguistics (Rassool 1999, p. 31; Gregory 2002, p. 248).

In drawing upon these perspectives, New Literacy Studies began to incorporate a stronger emphasis on social and cultural practices and the contexts in which literacy could promote social change. In the 1980s and 1990s in England, New Literacy Studies approaches were adopted to address issues associated with the cultural and socio-economic environment of the home. Researchers and educators have drawn upon this paradigm in order to understand and overcome the barriers to literacy acquisition thrown up by power structures and cultural differences that influence literacy acquisition in out-of-school as well as in-school contexts.

Gregory's (2002) study reveals the ways in which literacy practices exist beyond the school and are linked to community and home environments. In this study she draws upon New Literacy Studies to investigate power and cultural structures, as well as cultural psychology and cultural anthropology. She argues against the accepted link that assumes poverty will necessarily produce low literacy interests and achievements.

> The theoretical framework informing this research synthesises perspectives from the 'New Literacy Studies,' cultural psychology, and cultural anthropology. The New Literacy Studies support an ideological model of literacy which signals explicitly that literacy practices are aspects not only of culture but also of power structures (Street 1995, Baynham 1995). Viewed in this way, school-sanctioned literacy – or 'Literacy,' as referred to by Street (1995: 14) – is just one of a multiplicity of literacies which take place in peoples' lives, in different domains, for a variety of purposes and in different languages. Within this model, children and adults draw upon a number of 'mediators of literacy'; such a mediator is defined as a person who makes his or her skills available to others, on a formal or informal basis, for them to accomplish specific literacy purposes' (Baynham 1995: 39). They may be teachers at out-of-school community language classes, clubs, drama activities etc.; or they may be 'guiding lights' – mediators of literacy who are especially inspiring as mentors or role models, such as grandparents (Padmore 1994) or siblings (Gregory 1998).
>
> (Gregory 2002, pp. 248–9)

Gregory draws upon the notion that literacy is multifaceted and implies that there are 'multi-literacies'. She argues that this should lead to an educational provision of literacy where children and adults can develop literacy skills through a number of 'mediators of literacy'. This would enable different members of the community and family to make their skills available to others in different formal and informal contexts to enable the development of different literacies for different situations (Gregory 2002). In this conception of literacy instruction and associated frameworks for addressing difficulties in literacy, the responsibility for developing literacy could reside in different community and family members, not just parents and teachers. These might include grandparents, siblings, leaders of clubs and other community activities.

Gregory examined the home, school and reading practices of current and past generations of teachers and pupils in two Spitalfields schools, in London, with the aim of examining the experiences of pupils who had succeeded at school while not appearing to fulfil accepted notions of what counts as a successful reader. Gregory (2002) reports on two groups of participants from this study. Her participants insisted that 'invisible' or 'unofficial' home and community literacy practices were a factor in their school reading success. She argues that her findings supported and helped give further insight into theories of literacy as a social and cultural practice, and she indicates that educators should not expect to find a single practice that will ensure success in literacy development:

> [A]n important argument of this paper is that young people are not trapped within any single practice of early childhood literacy. The families in all phases of this study reveal a complex heterogeneity of traditions whereby reading practices from different domains are blended, resulting in a form of reinterpretation which is both new and dynamic. Duranti & Ochs 1996 refer to this type of blending as SYNCRETIC LITERACY, which merges not simply linguistic codes or texts, but different ACTIVITIES. Their example is the activity of doing homework by Samoan Americans, and they provide a finetuned analysis of the way in which Samoan and American traditions, languages, teaching and child-rearing strategies are blended. In the present study, I argue that CONTRASTING home and school strategies and practices may provide children with an enlarged treasure trove, upon which they can draw in the official English school.
>
> (Gregory 2002, p. 249)

Gregory's study indicates, along with the findings from a growing body of research, that 'literacies are embedded in activities that are carried out for purposes other than reading instruction' (Gregory 2002, p. 262). This research also indicates that parents and families have a crucial role to play in providing opportunities for children to participate in literacy-promoting activities. Moreover, her study supports the assertions of critical theorists that literacy can be a transformative experience which changes people's lives.

While Gregory's paper gives us notions about the people who might be involved in literacy development if schools are to adopt a New Literacy Studies framework, it does not indicate how 'mediators of literacy' might plan and develop pedagogies to achieve multi-literacies. Nor does it give guidance on how teachers and school-based practitioners might adopt a New Literacy Studies perspective to develop their literacy programmes.

Willinsky's work fills this gap, as he gives a clear description and definition of the pedagogical implications of New Literacy Studies for teachers and educational institutions in his book *The New Literacy: Redefining Reading and Writing in the Schools* (1990). Like Gregory, he argues that New Literacy Studies provides a different way of thinking about, and a different form of practice in the area of, about teaching and literacy. He argues that adopting the New Literacy Studies framework within an educational institution also sets new goals for educational institutions, implies new dimensions for teaching practice, and must result in new ways of evaluating the acquisition of literacy.

It is clear that there are differences and conflicts between the behaviourist experimental psychological perspective of literacy and literacy instruction and the New Literacy Studies' view. As Rassool points out, strategies and programmes that are developed within the behaviourist experimental paradigm stress a 'primary involvement with the diagnosis of reading ability and the remediation of specific literacy skills amongst children in schools' (Rassool 1999, p. 31).

As noted above, perspectives that take account of cultural, societal and socio-economic factors, unlike experimental psychology-based frameworks, see literacy as a multifaceted phenomenon. There are also clear links with theories and pedagogical programmes developed by critical-literacy theorists such as Freire, as these theorists are also primarily concerned with educational and cultural practices. Like Gregory and Willinsky, critical theorists such as Lankshear (see, for example, Lankshear 1994; Lankshear and Knobel 1997; Lankshear *et al.* 1998) are aware of the way in which learning environments can be reorganised to prevent a lack of cultural capital, traditional power structures and differing cultural practices from becoming a barrier to literacy development.

Since critical theorists like Freire have contested the idea that literacy is a neutral set of technical skills, it has become much more widely accepted that literacy is related to culture, power, knowledge and selective traditions. Some critical theorists are now suggesting that, since literacy can be seen to vary between cultures and may be specific to certain groups and classes, there may be many 'literacies', all related to specific situations. This concept has direct implications for literacy educators and those who are implementing barriers to overcome difficulties with literacy.

Conclusion: the implications for practitioners who seek to help students experiencing difficulties in literacy

If educators view literacy as a complex social and culturally related process rather than a technological skill, it follows that literacy programmes need to be designed to address a range of context-related situations. This is particularly evident for educators working in multicultural and multilingual contexts, as was highlighted in a recent interview with Fernando Diniz, a senior lecturer at Moray House Faculty of Education, University of Edinburgh. Diniz is himself of a multilingual, multi-ethnic background, as he is Black, born in Portuguese Africa. His mother was of Indian origin and is married to a Brazilian. In this interview Diniz draws upon his own experiences as a practising educational psychologist and academic researcher working in areas related to pupils' special needs. He identifies some of the major socio-cultural factors that contribute to barriers to literacy acquisition and points out their importance for teachers:

> [O]ne of the things I've learned from research is that the connections (between race, ethnicity, culture, family and literacy) are not acknowledged. That's the first point and I think for practitioners that that is key, that they acknowledge that there are connections and the purpose of a professional is to try to discover what the connections might be ... if one believes in child centeredness of learning and if we believe that we start from where the children are, then we're starting from the home, the home in the sense of the child's environment. So the first thing one wants to know about that is what is the cultural context within which the child is

learning. Those might be articulated in terms of the language, or languages very often, that are used in the home.

(interview with Fernando Diniz for Open University E801 course materials, 2002)

Diniz also argues that teachers need to be aware of the notion of power, which, as we have seen in this chapter, is implicit in notions of 'critical' and 'new literacies'. Diniz's views of issues related to socio-cultural factors such as race, gender, ethnicity, bilingualism and multilingualism reflect the need to analyse power relationships in society:

> I think teachers might think of power in terms of the policy makers who have the power to do things to them. But there is a lot of power operating in the normal classroom. Perhaps the way that teachers have interpreted that is that they are professionals, they would conceive themselves as working in the interests of children. I think what they perhaps minimise is the power that is operating when they make decisions about which children do what. So every act that any of us is engaged in has an element of power although we may not call it that, we may call it our duty, our role, or our ability to influence something. I'm using the term power in a very operation way as a class teacher in the dynamics of the classroom, in decisions about who is valued and about the teacher's own values, and that the teacher's own values can in fact determine the way power is exercised in the classroom.
>
> (interview with Fernando Diniz for Open University E801 course materials, 2002)

Diniz draws our attention to the need to consider language and culture and our 'common sense assumptions' that surround notions of other cultures when considering access, outcomes, and achievement in literacy education. For example, he notes that many of the 'debates about standards and about underachievement are very much centred around performance in the English language from an English language perspective'. He also notes that teachers' judgements can be affected by misinterpretations of cultural behaviours:

> [An Asian] girl who is apparently a quiet, well behaved, hard working person, usually at the back of the classroom, doesn't attract the attention of anybody. But her learning is given some

cause for concern. The questions that might be asked could be to do with the girl's performance in the classroom and at home. But there may be other issues as well and they may be issues to do with gender and the perception of Asian girls as always being well behaved.

(interview with Fernando Diniz for Open University E801 course materials, 2002)

Earlier discussion in this chapter focused on potential barriers to literacy at both the cultural/societal and individual psychological levels. Diniz agrees that barriers can arise at both of these levels and warns that cognitive-literacy difficulties such as dyslexia may be masked by teachers' assumptions about culture. He feels that teachers need to be able to differentiate between cognitive and cultural issues in relation to difficulties in literacy development at the classroom level in order to support students' literacy learning in the most appropriate ways.

Finally, viewing literacy as a social and cultural phenomenon also raises particular ethical and social issues for educators working with students who experience difficulties in learning. These issues are evident when we consider bi-cultural and bilingual children who experience difficulties with literacy:

[T]he field of special educational needs has its own problems in terms of the way that special educational needs have been defined and so on. When you relate that to issues of bi-culturalism and bi-lingualism ... the international research literature now ... points to three, three major problems. One is what is called the over representation of children from these particular backgrounds in special education provision. I certainly think we've got that in Britain, although the statistical evidence is poor. But it's not purely a question of how many children are mis-categorised for example in relation to having severe and profound learning difficulties, rather than say in having more general learning difficulties.

... There's also the issue of under representation which ... is misdiagnosis. For example, rarely are children of bi-lingual background diagnosed as dyslexic. There is research evidence ... as well on that. And a question might be why? Most probably those children are being diagnosed as having learning difficulties because they are slow learners or have intellectual impairments rather than the higher status diagnosis of being a dyslexic ... the question of course then goes down to the practice in the classroom and that's where curriculum assessment comes into operation. I would say that there is a kind of conceptual ambiguity in teachers' understandings of the power of language ... in learning. They're not sure whether in fact difficulties arise from the child's first language, by which I mean the language of the home, the second language, by which I mean the language of instruction, or a combination of both of those two, ... teachers tend to think that if you have the two, you have [been] accorded the status of a bilingual person, which I think could be challenged. Or in fact where it's none of those, and it is something called special educational needs.

(interview with Fernando Diniz for Open University E801 course materials, 2002)

If one accepts the notion of multi-literacies it is no longer possible to develop one universal rigid and overarching programme to address the range of barriers to literacy. It also implies that schools need to adopt a multidisciplinary approach to investigating and teaching literacy in order to move beyond conceptualising one key approach to addressing these barriers. Accepting the notion of multi-literacies also implies the adoption of multifaceted approaches to literacy and a move away from an emphasis on developing one nationwide universal programme. It will also necessitate traditional linear, decontextualised, skills-orientated programmes.

Hannon comments on the difficulties that practitioners face in conceptualising literacy as a multifaceted process in his book *Literacy, Home and School*:

The suggestion that there could be many literacies is a disturbing one for educators. Teacher training courses and text books rarely acknowledge it as a possibility or a problem. This is especially so perhaps in early childhood education where teachers have been drawn to individual psychological models of development more than have teachers of older students. Which literacy should we teach, and why? What if the child's home literacy is different from the school's literacy?

There is certainly a problem here for teachers who wish to respect families' language and literacy and who do not want uncritically to impose school literacy on them. However, teachers' business is school literacy and it would be self-deceiving to imagine that under current schooling arrangements all families' literacies can be accepted as a substitute for school literacy. For many families, involvement in the teaching of literacy is bound to mean being involved in new and different forms of literacy.

(Hannon 1995, pp. 34–5)

In Chapter 5 we will continue to explore these issues and their implications for literacy and special needs educators. In particular we will be examining social and cultural factors – such as gender, ethnicity and socio-economic status – that can impact upon families and socio-cultural groups who experience difficulties in literacy. We will also examine the implications for practitioners arising from socio-cultural views of literacy related to social justice and inclusive practices in literacy programmes and schooling.

Chapter 5

Gender, ethnicity and experiences of difficulties in literacy development

Introduction

Public education systems such as those in the UK and Eire have been built on the belief that they will provide equality of opportunity for all. Yet these systems must also cater for differing abilities in literacy and literacy development. National education systems have tended to expect children to have reasonably similar abilities and often assume children enter education on a 'level playing field'; that is, they come into the system with similar resources and backgrounds. It can be argued that schools have historically defined acceptable literacy practices and competencies in a way which served the interests of the more powerful dominant groups and classes (Green and Kostogriz 2002; Luke 1993). This tendency for schooling and literacy programmes to privilege certain groups takes place against increasing concerns over the 'gender gap' and 'linguistic minority learners'.

Social justice implies that 'some basic level of material and psychological well-being (that is, income) should not be withheld from individuals by society for arbitrary or capricious reasons' (Gerber 1996, p. 62). One argument for compulsory schooling is that access to schooling and literacy would foster an environment which will create equal opportunities and increased access to psychological and material well-being by fostering children's 'natural abilities' and catering for their individual needs. This argument assumes that becoming literate and having access to schooling would provide the opportunity to compete according to ability, so that children's occupational and future life chances would not be hindered by socio-economic disadvantage or other restrictions. It also implies that differences in students' ability and the school environment are independent of wider social and cultural processes.

There are, however, particular groups of students who may be perceived as experiencing barriers to literacy development which are associated with their cultural or socio-economic background or their gender. For example, the issues associated with students who are labelled with severe cognitive or individual difficulties are different from the issues relating to students who face socially constructed barriers to literacy development (Gerber 1996). The latter are seen to have an 'underlying average ability', whereas the former group are not seen as being able to achieve at this level. This implies that there can be different ethical issues and pedagogical approaches associated with 'severely disabled individuals' from those associated with socially/culturally disadvantaged groups. An understanding of the social processes which underpin these barriers that socially disadvantaged groups face can lead to these groups achieving at the level of more privileged groups, whereas this may not be achievable for severely disabled students. The implication of this is that there are particular concerns that schools need to address:

- how much emphasis should be placed on catering for individual differences and personal literacy needs versus recognising the community need for a national schooling system to produce highly literate citizens to participate in vocational and democratic processes;
- ways to acknowledge and cater for the barriers to literacy development created by different social status, beliefs, languages and cultural backgrounds;
- consideration of the gender gap in literacy achievement and ways that teachers and educators might address this;
- ethical and social issues associated with current teachers' beliefs, professional practice, literacy policies and programmes regarding the development of literacy with linguistic minority learners;
- ways in which home–school links can most appropriately support the literacy development of students from a diverse range of backgrounds.

Differential access to literacy

For a number of years the belief that access to literacy, and greater levels of literacy through education and schooling will in turn lead to increased economic and social progress, personal enlightenment and cognitive development has been questioned (see, for example, Scribner and Cole 1981). It can be argued that schools act to exclude as well as include. This applies not only to literacy skills, but also to resources and cultural practices. Within schools a selective tradition operates, ensuring that texts, language and literacy genres are more widely distributed and accessible to some social groups than others. This can create a cyclical process. Children's differing levels of literacy achievement can be influenced by the cultural capital they bring to the classroom from their particular social and cultural settings, and these different levels of achievement are, in turn, key factors in subsequent educational and occupational outcomes.

Luke (1993) explores the links between differential access to literacy in schooling and socio-economic and cultural factors. He concludes that particular procedures (for example streaming and testing) and choice of texts in the school environment can interact with children's varying linguistic, socio-economic, gender and cultural backgrounds to heighten differential patterns of success and failure in literacy achievement:

> [D]ifferent literacies continue to be distributed unequally through schooling. School students from minority groups, lower socioeconomic groups and demographically isolated areas do not gain access as readily to, or mastery of, the same kinds of literacies as those from economically privileged groups within Australian society. Literacy achievement in this country – and with it access to tertiary education, better-paying and high-status jobs – continues to fall along distinctive fault lines of urban/rural location, ethnicity and class. Further, recent research has begun to specify the patterns of differential access to kinds of texts, and social power, by gender.

> There is an ongoing debate over the causes of children's differential achievement and access. It is popularly attributed to mass media and popular culture, purported decay in morality and family structure, and deficit socialisation among client groups. As we will see in further examples here, children come to schools with different world-views and values, beliefs and practices – among which are schemata for and about literacy. For now, suffice to say that there is a century-long history across English-speaking countries of trying to defer 'blame' for differing educational access and outcomes to 'fault' in children and parents. Who gets what kinds of literacy, and thereby who is positioned to be able to demonstrate competence with texts in which contexts, is in part the

product of schooling. Further, problems children encounter with primary school literacy are linked closely to failure in other aspects of schooling and to unequal credential outcomes.

To return to our starting point, literacy refers to a range of possible reading and writing practices. Some such practices have evolved for criticism, others not; some for the conserving of extant cultural values and knowledges, others for the critique and transformation of those same values and knowledges; some are active, some passive; some, rightly or wrongly, are seen as signs of virtue and power in the society, others not. All literate practices are not of equivalent power in terms of the socio-economic benefits and cultural knowledges they yield. Nor do schools successfully impart to all socially powerful or critical literacies. This should not come as news to teachers, policy makers, or teacher educators. But what the definition offered here suggests is that the question is not one of 'more or less' literacy, but of 'what kinds of literate practices' are and should be disbursed to children.

(Luke 1993, p. 17)

A consideration of the link between literacy and disadvantage entails grappling with and rethinking some of the common assumptions about the barriers to literacy development for children who come from disadvantaged backgrounds. Luke's work draws attention to the need also to consider the contexts and purposes for literacy in the wider classroom and school environment, including the choice of texts, resources and programmes, as well as focusing upon particular techniques with individual children.

Making appropriate links between the experiences and backgrounds which children bring to school and specific programmes that can support the literacy development of individual learners can be challenging. Lankshear and Knobel (2002) offer a conceptual framework for literacy intervention and critique of specific programmes that may be useful for the construction and choice of literacy intervention strategies and programmes in professional contexts. Their work draws upon a socio-cultural perspective which focuses on what it means to read and be a reader in terms of social interactions with others and the wider socio-cultural environment. Taking this perspective leads them to consider ways in which pupils' difficulties with reading and writing need to be addressed through an understanding of the wider social and cultural contexts and social practices, and students' backgrounds and experiences in relation to mastering literacy. They argue that literacy programmes need to go beyond an emphasis on the mastery of skills associated with decoding print in the classroom. Early intervention programmes such as Reading Recovery, they point out, focus on mechanics and code breaking, which diverts attention from the mastery of other aspects of literacy, particularly text use and text analysis. These programmes can therefore only make a limited contribution for students who have difficulties with literacy, as they are not aiming to extend students' abilities to mastering the richness, fullness and depth of that demanded of a literate person. This argument is all the more interesting in the light of the phonics versus real books whole-language debate explored earlier in this book, where critics of Reading Recovery have argued that it does not have enough emphasis on specific – that is, phonemic skills – essential to decoding print.

Lankshear and Knobel outline the possibilities of devising two very different approaches in literacy programmes, using tape recorders as tools for literacy in the excerpt below. Skills-based, decoding-skills-based programmes, such as Reading Recovery and other Australasian-based approaches described in this excerpt, teach students to break the code.

> The sorts of issues we have been trying to get at so far can be neatly illustrated by reference to two very different approaches to using tape recorders in literacy enhancement activities. One approach is outlined in *Intervention Strategies: Reading and Writing* (Department of Education, Queensland, 1995a). Here the tape recorder is used in conjunction with written texts as an aid to helping readers identify words and follow the text – i.e. break the code – and perhaps to get better access to the meaning of a test they might otherwise find difficult to make meaningful. The procedure is augmented by use of oral cloze exercises, where the person making the tape leaves a generous pause so that the learner can fill in the gap.
>
> (Lankshear and Knobel 2002, p. 275)

The alternative, they argue is to take socioculturally based approaches such as that devised by Heath (1983), which enables students to gain better access to the meaning of a text which they find difficult:

> A very different approach is evident in the rich examples provided by Heath (1983; see also Heath and Mangiola 1991). Heath describes tape recorders being used by teachers and learners to tape

real-life transactions, conversations and participation in other literacy events – such as constructing narratives and other generic forms. These are then exchanged – at times among different year levels and different schools (from different kinds of community) – and used as opportunities for making differences in kind and quality among various texts explicit; for editing purposes; for accessing different cultures; and for expanding the range of text types over which learners gain mastery. In one example, Heath (1983: 297–8) reports how a previously low achieving African American child learned to produce written stories which obeyed the conventions of mainstream print narratives through a process of 'augmenting' tape-recorded oral texts, thereby accessing modes of school discourse which are more highly rewarded than those she had available to her via her 'primary discourse' (Gee et al. 1996). Over a two-year period this child moved from being a very low performer to acting two-year editor of collaborative text productions. In other cases, teachers who transcribed their students' recorded oral stories found some children rejecting these oral versions upon seeing them in print, and developing new sensitivities to the kinds of accounts other classmates liked to read (and why). In such cases we find rich and real approximations to the kinds of outcomes Freebody sees as integral to successful reading. We also find learners attaining the kinds of 'higher order literacy' outcomes espoused in a range of education reform statements: outcomes which are put at risk by emergent narrow and one-dimensional regimes of assessment and validation. Not surprisingly, reports of teachers teaching to the validation tests from Year 1 began to surface in Queensland shortly after literacy validation was announced. This is a perfectly understandable and predictable response on the part of 'accountable teachers'. It is, however, bad news for successful reading.

How do we get out of such messes? One way is by paying less homage to psychology-based approaches to reading, and directing greater attention instead to what James Gee calls 'a sociocultural approach to literacies'.

(Lankshear and Knobel 2002, pp. 275–6)

Gender issues

Boys 'underachievement' in literacy has been documented for some time and there is reliable evidence that boys have dominated literacy remediation classes. Until recently educators and school administrators appeared unconcerned about gender imbalance in remediation resourcing and the gendered difference in children's literacy performance at school. During the 1980s and early 1990s most of the concern related to 'gender gaps' in achievement was targeted at girls' lower achievement in maths- and science-based subjects. In the late 1990s, however, boys' underachievement in education became a recognisable topic for educational debate and discussion. Policy-makers and politicians are now focusing on boys' poor performance and achievement in literacy, as boys are seen to trail behind the girls in reading and writing assessments:

> Boys in their final primary year are rapidly catching up with girls at reading, but more than half are still not able to write at the level expected of 11-year-olds.
>
> The latest analysis of national test results shows that in the last year the reading scores of boys have shot up by 14 percentage points, narrowing the gender gap.
>
> While girls are now only six percentage points ahead in reading, they retain their substantial lead in writing – almost two-thirds of them achieve the required level, compared with 49 per cent of boys. Boys' writing score is up four percentage points and girls' three points. In maths, the boys' one percentage point lead has disappeared at level 4, but a higher proportion of them are achieving level 5.
>
> Ministers are likely to point to the success of the English and maths strategies, particularly in tough inner-city areas. The fastest rates of progress in maths are in the London boroughs of Tower Hamlets and Lambeth, where standards are low. English results are rising fastest in areas such as Wakefield and Rotherham.
>
> However, ministers recognise that to reach English targets set for 2002, standards in writing among boys will have to improve. Funds are being provided to train all teachers of 10 and 11-year-olds in the teaching of writing.
>
> John Stannard, director of the national literacy strategy, said boys seemed to have benefited from the concentration on guided reading during the literacy hour but the biggest challenge was raising standards in writing.
>
> Results at key stage 2 have improved nationwide, but the gender gap in English ranges from 21 percentage points in Hackney, London, where only 43 per cent boys reach the required

standard, to five percentage points in Sutton. In Barking and Dagenham, which is improving faster, there is still a gap of 14 percentage points.

(Hackett 1999, p. 2)

The debate over boys failing to achieve in reading and writing compared to girls is not confined to the United Kingdom. The issue has also received attention in academic publications in the US, Canada and Australasia. For example, there is evidence in Australia (Alloway and Gilbert 1997), New Zealand (Wilkinson 1998) and Canada (Gambell and Hunter 2002) that girls outperform boys in literacy-based tasks.

In order to answer the question of how to address this gender gap, researchers in the field are taking a number of perspectives and there- fore arriving at diverse explanations of how parents and teachers might bring about change and address this issue. These researchers draw upon differing disciplinary influences and orientations and approaches to research, but most presume that gender differences in literacy achieve- ment are socially constructed rather than innate and biologically constructed. Implicit in these approaches is the belief that educators and parents can actively construct and shape environments which can foster childhood and adolescent literacy development. Because they take this socio-constructionist view rather than draw upon biological explanations, they are not forced to be resigned to the notion that biology is destiny in literacy. Below are examples of recent researchers seeking to provide explanations and suggestions for educators on possible curricula and pedagogical approaches to address this issue.

Gambell and Hunter (2002) provide five hypothetical models to explain gender differences in literacy, where literacy is defined as a measurable contextualised and communicative act which encompasses both reading and writing. These five models locate the widening of the gender gap in literacy achievement in different locations and the gendering processes that may take place in those locations – that is, in the home, within the student, in the classroom, within the assessment instruments, and in identification with the text.

One way in which language practices within our schools might be reinforcing the 'textual construction of femininity and masculinity' is through the choice of fact or fiction text. It has been argued that the dominance of female teachers in primary schools has led to a domi- nance of narrative- and fiction-based text in the primary curriculum. This is seen to be to the detriment of boys, who express a preference for non-fiction. In a study called the 'Fact and Fiction project', Moss (2002) set out to look in detail at what the current school curriculum does with fact and fiction texts, in order to look at the impact that these genres might have on the different development of boys and girls as readers. This study, like the Lankshear and Knobel critique of reading programmes which we examined above, draws upon the socio-cultural approaches to literacy.

The Moss research project focused on 'literacy events', which are the particular 'situated moments' when reading is achieved within the school curriculum during the course of a school day. In considering each literacy event the researchers looked at three dimensions: 'the context in which it took place; the readers who were involved and their relationship to the process; and the texts that were incorporated into the literacy event' (Moss 2002, p. 188). They identified and documented the different kinds of literacy events that were orchestrated and marked out through the teachers' designation of the use of space, time and resources. From this data they identified three different ways of conducting reading which were routinely used in the classrooms observed across a number of schools:

> There were regularities in how this happened which ran across all four case study sites. Focusing in on these patterns led to the identification of three different ways of doing reading routinely invoked in the classrooms the project observed: procedural reading; reading for proficiency; and reading for choice. Each of these was underpinned by a distinct set of principles, which produced fundamentally different orientations to the business of reading. In each case there were different ground rules about who will read what, where, and how the business of reading will be conducted. These ground rules would be spelt out through the specific mobilisation of texts, readers and contexts, as the teacher orchestrated the particular curricular activity in which reading played a part.
>
> (Moss 2002, p. 189)

The researchers found that there are strong gender-differentiated genre choices that can be linked to these categories of literacy events:

> Approaching the genre preferences children make through the range of social contexts for reading which frame texts in school suggests a new way of understanding their choices. In the project

data, weaker girl readers were quite happy to go along with teacher judgements about their proficiency as readers, many of the weaker boy readers were not. During quiet reading time, weaker girl readers often chose to spend time on fiction texts which were well within or even below, their competence, turning this kind of reading into a collaborative exercise in which they helped each other through the pages. Weaker boy readers often did everything they could to avoid spending time on text, and thus disguising their status as readers from their peers. Low proficiency rankings seemed to conflict more with their sense of self-esteem. Weaker boy readers were in flight from negative proficiency judgements in ways in which girls were not. Non-fiction texts give them somewhere to go. Indeed, precisely because of the role of visual rather than verbal text, they provide one of the few arenas where more and less able boys can meet on a level, as it were. Weaker boys can muster their expertise in response to such a text, without having to stumble through the print to identify what is going on. This is an advantage in relation to boys' status politics. It works less well in terms of making progress with their reading. One net result of the strategies they employ is that they spend less time on verbal text. The kind of visual competences some of the weaker boy readers showed in steering their way round non-fiction texts have their place. But alone, they are not enough.

(Moss 2002, p. 198)

Moss points out that the project findings had direct implications for the delivery of the National Literacy Hour in English schools, even though the study was conducted before the hour was introduced. These findings imply that there is a need to consider how the literacy events and their impact on gender differentiation might occur within the pedagogies and approaches advocated by the literacy hour, for example how texts might be shared during the twenty minutes of teacher time given to group reading. They also indicate that there is a need to work within the pedagogies of the literacy hour to address gender differentiation in reading and encourage children to read more widely, when there is a de-emphasis on silent reading and the management of small-group activities encourages a greater emphasis on setting comprehension exercises.

This research project also raises an issue which is common to other socio-culturally based approaches to reading and literacy difficulties. Socio-cultural approaches to literacy may not fit that easily with prescribed approaches such as the literacy hour as they place a more progressive emphasis on process, context and interaction and flexibility rather than documented prescribed approaches and pedagogies for decoding print. As Moss reminds us in her conclusion:

> [T]his research shows us that supporting reading is always more than providing children with resources; it is also about closely observing the relationship with text, context and reader and the ways in which they work together to establish what reading is.
>
> (Moss 2002, p. 200)

The assessment of pupils' attainment in literacy raised by the research reported by Moss also emphasises that such testing had a much greater impact on practice in the current drive to increase literacy standards and norms. The newspaper article below highlights how gendering processes related to the chosen texts can impact on the assessment of reading achievement. It also highlights the need for caution in interpreting the results of standardised tests in relation to factors such as gender.

National curriculum reading tests sat by 600,000 11-year-olds last week were biased towards boys, headteachers say.

Labour is desperate to raise the academic performance of boys as it tries to reach its targets for literacy and numeracy next year. Last year, 86 per cent of girls reached the expected level in reading compared with 80 per cent of boys. Teachers say this year's fact-filled, non-fiction text in magazine format, chopped into bite-sized chunks, was better suited to boys.

Their criticisms echo those made two years ago when a dramatic jump in the scores of boys was put down to a 'biased' reading test about spiders, illustrated with cartoons.

The number of boys reaching the expected level for their age group rose by 11 percentage points. Girls made a three-point gain but remained ahead.

Last week's key stage 2 English paper consisted of non-fiction text about saving the whale. It was laid out in a 13-page mock-up magazine, with an editor's introduction and a double-page spread containing facts about the blue whale.

Research by booksellers and a survey of more than 2,000 primary children by the Hornchurch Curriculum Centre has shown that boys prefer magazines, comics and non-fiction to the stories and novels beloved of girls.

Peter Downes, former secondary head and member of the Rose inquiry into test standards, said: 'We are clearly moving away from the literary genre, which boys do not seem to deal with as well.'

Barry Dawson, chairman of the National Primary Heads Association, described this year's test as 'undoubtedly boy-biased' ...

Elaine Millard, director of literacy research at Sheffield University, said the national literacy strategy and national year of reading had broadened the concept of reading. Tests in the past failed to consider boys' different tastes in reading matter ...

Tim Cornford, head of the assessment division at the QCA [Qualifications and Curriculum Authority], said: 'National curriculum tests have to assess a wide range of achievement – the KS2 tests cover three different levels of ability. They must be fair to both girls and boys. All the pre-test evidence we have is that this year's tests are fair on all these counts.'

A Department for Education and Employment spokeswoman said this year's test was developed to criteria endorsed by the independent Rose inquiry two years ago.

(Henry 2001, p. 3)

Despite the concern over boys' underachievement and female superiority in literacy tests, there is continued male dominance in the workplace. Ultimately, even in the language-based professions such as law and journalism, men not women tend to dominate the positions of power. This raises a number of questions about how this can happen despite the fact that girls have a clear academic superiority in school-assessed literacy tasks, how concerned schools should become over the gender gap in literacy achievement, and what happens in high-school literacy curricula in relation to the differential achievement of boys and girls.

Alloway and Gilbert argue that 'Despite rhetoric to the contrary, literacy competence seems not to be highly valued in the economic world of work, and school success at literacy is not a valued or prized competence' (1997, p. 50). In order to address this issue, they focus on the secondary-school environment and adolescent students, and the implications of the gender gap in literacy achievement for secondary teachers. In their view schools produce a 'domain of knowledge' and a 'set of technologies' in school-based literacy skills which are associated with humanities-based subjects such as English. These subject areas are 'feminised' and therefore do not fit 'dominant constructions of masculinity'. They argue that locating and defining literacy skills in this way excludes a consideration of literacy skills to include electronic and visually based skills, which are more readily accessible for boys.

Alloway and Gilbert's suggestions for how teachers can address the issue of a gender gap in literacy assessments while considering the complex issue of which gender is ultimately advantaged and disadvantaged is reproduced below:

> While, for instance, groups of girls may achieve well at school-based literacy, many school literacy practices have not been advantageous for girls (see Gilbert, 1989a). The compatibility of the 'literate' self with a 'feminine' self has not necessarily served girls well in terms of introducing them to a range of other ways of taking up social positions as girls and women (Walkerdine, 1990). In addition, as we have argued earlier, there is little social valuation of school literacy competence. Being good at reading and writing has not necessarily led to careers in language-based professions – or even to well-paid jobs. It is still predominantly girls who become secretaries and typists for male managers and bosses; it is still predominantly women who do the word-processing while men write software programs.
>
> But teachers who pick up these issues should be wary of falling prey to the 'competing victims syndrome' (Cox, 1995) whereby girls' interests and boys' interests are pitted against one another. A basic tenet of working on the boys and literacy agenda should be that both girls' and boys' interests in improved literacy performance are promoted; boys' gains in literacy should not be promoted at the expense of girls' gains; efforts to enfranchise the boys should not disenfranchise the girls. Rather than developing programmes that are 'good for girls', or 'good for boys', we need instead to focus on a critique of school literacy practices and the assumptions upon which they rely, and to widen our understanding of literacy and literate practice. We need a critique of the 'literate self' in terms of how such a construct affects both girls and boys. We also need an understanding of the social, textual construction of femininity and masculinity, and how language practices within the school reinforce such constructions. And we need access to a range of skills and technologies that will help in such critiques and understandings.
>
> (Alloway and Gilbert 1997, p. 57)

Bilingual/biliteracy issues

Issues arising from bilingualism/biliteracy and associated difficulties in literacy development have produced a large field of research and professional literature which often raises different concerns in relation to different contexts. The discussion below focuses on recent research literature and public debates over bilingualism and literacy in England and Scotland, in order to consider the related key equity and professional issues for the professional development of teachers working with pupils from linguistic minorities and bilingual backgrounds in these regions.

Bilingualism and professional beliefs about literacy development

When English is used as the main medium of discourse, as it is in the majority of English and Scottish educational institutions, it will incorporate particular linguistic and cultural assumptions, with which students who do not have English as their first language will be unfamiliar. These students will therefore be at a disadvantage compared to students who are familiar with English and its particular specialist uses in the classroom and curriculum. To compound this difficulty, teachers who have had very little experience of working with bilingual children often also bring with them their own 'taken-for-granted' beliefs, which shape the ways they think about and interact with their bilingual pupils (Gee, cited in Smyth 2000). These beliefs also influence how teachers perceive the barriers to literacy development faced by bilingual and linguistic minority students.

Below is a summary of the beliefs of a group of Scottish teachers who were monolingual English speakers and worked in monolingual school and classroom environments. This summary is taken from an analysis of the teachers' 'commonsense thinking' about bilingual students, as expressed in a series of interviews (see Smyth 2000).

Main assumption: Bilingual pupils need to become monolingual in order to succeed.

(This assumption helps to shape and organise the teachers' beliefs and leads to a number of related beliefs, listed below.)

Related beliefs:

> - Parents who do not speak English hinder the child's academic
>   progress, by definition their ability to become monolingual.
> - The role of schools and literacy events is to promote monolin-
>   gualism.
> - There are two types of bilingual learner – those who can
>   operate monolingually in the dominant language and those
>   who do not.
> - Those bilingual learners who do not become monolingual are
>   problematic and require learning support.

Martin argues that such assumptions form part of a 'widely held
deficit thesis' because 'becoming bilingual is perceived as a problem
and a disadvantage to learning' (2002, p. 211). She argues that this
is in effect 'linguistic racism' and demands language 'assimilation'
because this view assumes that '[i]f you live in England you should
speak English' (*ibid.*). She also argues that professionals need to
think about bilingualism differently and develop different frameworks for their understanding of its implications for literacy
development, and that this poses challenges for teachers working
with linguistic minorities.

Martin's work has a number of key implications for professional
practice in schools:

- *The need to think carefully about links between community, home
  and school.* Martin argues that viewing bilingualism as a deficit
  and primarily as a group of technical skills can exclude a consideration of the home and community environment. If bilingual
  development of literacy is perceived merely as a set of skills and
  only to be addressed in the classroom, valuable resources and
  contexts for developing literacy with these students may be
  ignored and neglected.
- *The need to think carefully about the implementation of current
  literacy policies and programmes.* This applies particularly to those
  who tend to view literacy as a technical skill, for example the
  National Literacy Strategy. Martin's work alerts educators to the
  problems associated with viewing literacy purely as a collection
  of technical skills and ignoring the social and cultural contexts
  for literacy development. She argues that this creates problems
  when working with students from bilingual and multilingual
  backgrounds, because linguistic minority pupils draw upon
  multiple meanings across a wide range of cultural and social

events through their knowledge of different languages. Martin gives the example of 'holy books', which illustrates the impact of the home and community environment on the child and the possible tensions that can be created between the school and home environment. She also discusses the issues associated with working with parents and communities of linguistic minority students.

- *Being aware of the possibilities of differing relationship between spoken and written language.* Martin points out that other cultures and languages have implicitly different relationships between the spoken and written language. She notes that this has implications for how we approach the teaching of literacy with bilingual and multilingual students and colleagues. If spoken and written forms are perceived as different and non-interchangeable we may need to think about how to approach the teaching of reading and writing in a literacy programme. Martin also draws attention to the need to be aware that language and literacy skills must also be applied in situations of communicative need and competence. This implies that, as well as teaching psycho-linguistically based literacy skills, teachers need to offer linguistically diverse classes the opportunity to practice spoken and written literacy in socially appropriate situations.
- *The negative consequences of applying the deficit hypothesis to 'becoming and being bilingual'.* Martin highlights the potentially negative impact of a deficit hypothesis in relation to the literacy development of bilingual and multilingual students. Yet, while this model is prevalent amongst many professionals, there is mounting research evidence that to be bi- or multilingual is much more of an advantage than a disadvantage.

One issue that is hotly debated by educators is whether minority language learners are advantaged or disadvantaged by being educated in special classes and separate units. It is crucially important for local education authorities (LEAs) and schools to consider the consequences and subsequent limitations of adopting one approach rather than another, and to take parents'/carers' and students' views into account in any decision-making process. John Landon, a senior lecturer in bilingualism and education at Moray House Institute of Education, has particularly strong views about the inadvisability of setting up special units:

We shouldn't discriminate against learners of English as a second language by placing them in separate units, argues John Landon

If a black child were placed in a school where he was harassed because of his skin colour by uncaring teachers and pupils, what would the response be? To put him in a special class with other black children with similar experiences where their confidence could be boosted, and then send them back into their schools unsupported?

No, the response would be to intervene in the school where the harassment is taking place, to ensure that a more accepting environment is created for the child. Yet, in Seonag MacKinnon's article, 'A strange language a long way from home' ([*Times Educational Supplement*], Scotland, May 15), it is the first response that is advocated for learners of English as a second language who are unhappy with the lack of understanding they receive in mainstream classrooms.

This is the solution advanced by the Bilingual Support Unit based in North Ayrshire. If the same solution were applied to other children who experience difficulties in mainstream classes – children with behavioural problems, or with dyslexia, for example – there would be an outcry. And yet this policy of extraction is, we are told, praised and rewarded.

What does provision in North Ayrshire tell us? First, that lack of understanding of the linguistic and cultural needs of ESL [English as a second language] learners is widespread in schools. North Ayrshire recognises that this is the case, particularly in schools in rural areas where the ethnic minority population is scattered. This is one justification that the staff of the Bilingual Support Unit gives for separate provision.

(Landon 1998)

Issues facing refugee children

There are particular issues facing refugee students as they acquire literacy which are not necessarily pertinent to other bilingual and multilingual literacy learners. In a recent interview for Open University course materials (Open University 2002) an LEA officer with responsibility for the education of refugee children outlined what he saw as the most significant of these issues, and how schools and other professionals might address them. He draws attention to a number of equity issues at various levels, from individual relationships to wider cultural and societal structures. They highlight the dynamic and complex nature of literacy and its relationship to culture, race, ethnicity and resources. In particular, they highlight the practical consequences arising from the way in which educators can conceptualise bilingualism and multiculturalism, and embed these conceptions in the micro-politics of our teaching life. They also raise awareness of the wider social and cultural politics, and the consequences of cultural oppression and injustice on refugee children and children from ethnic minorities.

This interview highlights the need to acknowledge a complex and close interrelationship between race, ethnicity, family and literacy in schools' teaching practices, as well as to address these issues in educational research. He asserts that teachers should start from the perspective of the student, so that the first issue that needs to be addressed is the cultural context within which the student is learning. The officer recounts the difficulties that arise when there is a lack of knowledge in the school about the cultural background of the student, and when the student has a lack of cultural knowledge about school life.

The LEA officer's experiences also highlight the need for teachers to relegate some of their power in the classroom to the students themselves, particularly when decisions have to be made about which students should engage in which activity. His interview offers specific examples of when it is important to be aware of this; for example, he notes that teachers need to make decisions about when refugee students need to be supported in small groups in order to build their confidence. This interview also alerts teachers to the power dynamics implicit within intercultural and social relations in the wider society as well as in the classroom. For example, he provides a moving account of the cultural dislocation, marginalisation and social injustice with which minority groups and refugee children may have had to contend in their schooled lives.

He also provides examples of ways in which difficulties in language, literacy or communication can be put down to the student's bi- or multilingualism, so that cognitive difficulties in learning can be missed.

Conclusion

This chapter has considered the difficulties students can experience in literacy development through factors related to socio-economic status, ethnicity, cultural and linguistic background and gender. In our discussion of these factors it has become apparent that there is a complex dynamic interaction between socially located influences on literacy development. In addition to the complexities related to social-cultural factors, there is also the need to account for individual differences and levels of disability. The discussion has also highlighted the additional complexities created between interactions between these factors and differences, and cognitive difficulties related to individual students. Literacy educators and the school system therefore have to address the equity and social-justice issues against a complicated and varied background of social and individual differences. This chapter has illustrated some of the various debates related to social justice and equity that surround attempts to include and exclude particular social groups in relation to class, gender, ethnicity and language.

Chapter 6

Equity, inclusion and the law

Introduction

Developing curriculum practices and policies for students who may experience difficulties in literacy development in order to take account of the equity and social-justice issues we have raised so far presents a major challenge for any universal, national education system. In addition, historical and current developments in literacy policy and practices raise a number of ethical issues, which also need to be critically examined in order to make informed decisions on school-based policies and individual pedagogical practices.

Currently, the law across the UK and in the Republic of Ireland supports an individualised view of 'learning difficulties', including difficulties in the area of literacy development. Within the current system, from a legal perspective in England, Wales, Northern Ireland and Scotland learning needs arising from difficulties in literacy acquisition are 'special' only if they require 'special' provision to be made. A child has special educational needs if he or she has 'a learning difficulty which calls for special educational provision to be made for him or her' (Department of Education and Skills 2001, para. 1:3; Department for Education Northern Ireland 1998, para. 1.4; Education Act (Scotland) 1980, section 1(5)(d)). In the Republic of Ireland 'special educational needs' means 'the educational needs of students who have a disability and the educational needs of exceptionally able students' (Education Act, 1998, Part 1, 2(1); quoted in Open University 2001a, p. 17).

Implicit in any discussion of the law in relation to provision in schools for pupils who experience difficulties in literacy development are issues of equality of opportunity in education, fairness in allocation of resources and the question of whether individual learning programmes for students or a whole-school approach to learning support are more likely to encourage all learners to reach their potential.

Catering for those who have 'special' difficulties in literacy is all the more challenging given a historical development of systematised national education systems, and, within this, recent developments in special educational provision and the current move towards including all pupils in mainstream schools.

Exploring principles of ethics and social justice in relation to disabilities in literacy

Attempts to provide efficient compulsory mass education systems have historically tended to focus on the need to cater for children who can be considered to fit in the range of 'normal development' (Gerber 1996). This historical background has made it particularly difficult to address extreme individual differences and maintain equity and equal opportunities. The need to cater for extreme individual differences has become all the more urgent as many national education systems adopt inclusion policies and attempt to accommodate those with extreme literacy disabilities within the mainstream facilities of national education systems. The conflict between legislating for equal access to mainstream national education systems for those with literacy difficulties and putting in place equal opportunities initiatives through mass, systematised curriculum policies such as the literacy hour creates huge dilemmas and tensions for national education systems.

From segregation to inclusion

The principle of universal access to education is now enshrined in public policy in many countries. To put this principle into operation policy-makers are faced with the fundamental dilemma of how to make educational provision for all pupils which takes full account of 'sameness' and, at the same time, pays due regard to 'difference' and 'diversity' amongst individuals.

There are many different ways in which a national education system might be designed to address the learning needs of all children. Recent years have witnessed a developing international movement towards the inclusion of all pupils in mainstream schools wherever possible. Inclusion in mainstream has not always been the case. In England and Wales, for example, the Elementary Education Act of 1870 marked the beginning of compulsory state education, and subsequent education laws improved and expanded the system of state education, increasing access for the next hundred years. This continually evolving and expanded notion of who was entitled to schooling put pressure on schools. The question of what to do with children who made little or no progress and whose presence in the classroom was felt to be holding others back now became important. Categorisation of pupils was a major element of developing legislation. One solution was to categorise pupils who were not achieving at the same level as peers under one of three headings, 'feeble minded', 'imbeciles' and 'idiots'. The last group was not thought to be educable. Admission to asylums was considered suitable for 'imbeciles', whilst the 'feeble-minded' were educated in special schools or classes. Warnock notes the difference in status and respect given to the various groups of pupils seen as 'different' from the rest (Department for Education and Science 1978). 'Idiots', the 'feeble minded' and 'imbeciles' should be separated off from the rest for the good of the majority. The deaf and blind, however, were to be educated in separate institutions to receive the specialised form of education which teachers should be specially qualified to deliver.

However, the changing social and historical context of provision during the twentieth century meant that many labels once attached to pupils ('imbeciles', 'feeble minded') became unacceptable. Wearmouth (2000) notes that, in seeking to develop a common national framework for the education of (nearly) all children, the creators of the 1944 Act were faced with decisions about how to construct an educational framework that would support the learning of a diverse pupil population. The legislators formalised a system of selection and segregation based on the results of assessment tests – largely of literacy, numeracy and 'reasoning skills – that, they believed, could differentiate between different 'types' of learners. Different curricula could then be designed for different learning 'types' to be educated in separate sectors of the system. Selection on the basis of the results of the eleven-plus examination operated between types of secondary school in mainstream: grammar, technical and secondary modern. Within individual schools pupils were selected into ability 'streams' and academic or work-related programmes according to measured 'ability'. Many pupils were segregated into special schools as a result of tests of 'intelligence'. Many commentators viewed the educational hierarchy that developed as equitable, both because pupils appeared to be able to rise to a level which reflected their ability and also because it was based on psychometric testing, considered largely reliable and valid at that time.

However, as Clark et al. (1997) comment, a number of factors conspired to undermine the credibility of the system:

- differing proportions of pupils were selected for each type of school in different local education authority areas;
- considerable doubt was increasingly thrown on the reliability and validity of the psychometric tests being used;
- there was obvious overlap between the learning needs of pupils in mainstream and special schools;
- movement between school types was very difficult indeed, regardless of the amount of progress made by individual pupils.

(Clark *et al.*; summarised in Wearmouth 2000, p. 11)

In addition, there were other factors that militated against the stability of the selective system, for example a growing concern for equality of opportunity and social cohesion in society at large. The result was the establishment of comprehensive schools in the mainstream, the introduction of methods and curricula into mainstream from special school through the addition of special classes and 'remedial' provision, and the integration of some children from special into mainstream schools.

The 1978 Warnock Report reviewed educational provision in Great Britain for children and young people who, up to that time, were considered 'handicapped by disabilities of body or mind'. It introduced the concept of 'special educational needs', recommending that it should replace the categorisation of handicap. The 1981 Education Act attempted to translate the Warnock Report into action underpinned by legislation and reaffirmed the principle of integration. All children should be educated in mainstream schools but with certain provisos: that their needs could be met there, and that it was compatible with the education of other children and with the 'efficient use of resources'.

Recent years have witnessed an increase in pressure at government level towards inclusion in mainstream schools as a matter of 'human rights'. For example, in June 1994 representatives of ninety-two governments and twenty-five international organisations formed the World Conference on Special Needs Education, held in Salamanca, Spain. They agreed a Statement (UNESCO 1994) on the education of all disabled children and adopted a new Framework for Action:

> The guiding principle that informs this Framework is that schools should accommodate all children regardless of their physical, intellectual, social, emotional, linguistic or other conditions. ... Many children experience learning difficulties and thus have special educational needs at some time during their schooling.

Schools have to find ways of successfully educating all children, including those who have serious disadvantages and disabilities. There is an emerging consensus that children and youth with special educational needs should be included in the educational arrangements made for the majority of children. This has led to the concept of the inclusive school.

(UNESCO 1994, p. 6)

Inclusion and equity

As noted above, in many countries there is currently an increasing move towards including all pupils in mainstream schools. However, 'inclusion' itself is a highly problematic concept. Hornby (1999) attributes these problems to a number of confusions about inclusion. Among these are confusions over definitions, rights, aetiology and curriculum. Inclusion is variously defined as an increase in the numbers of pupils in mainstream schools whilst maintaining the special sector for those pupils with more serious needs (Department for Education and Employment 1997), an end-state of 'full inclusion' of all children in mainstream classes (CSIE 1986), a process involving whole-school restructuring (Ainscow 1999), or a process of increasing the learning and participation of the diversity of pupils within a school and its local community (Booth et al. 2000).

There are a number of different ways of conceptualising the root causes of pupils' difficulties in learning: factors within the child, within the environment or the interaction between all of them. In the midst of this confusion it is difficult to see how pupils' needs can be met adequately in every mainstream school when there is often disagreement about their cause.

A powerful argument that is often made in favour of inclusion is that every child has the right to be educated in his/her neighbourhood school together with peers. However, a 'right' to be in a school does not necessarily mean that the resources will be available there to meet any particular learning need. In addition, not every parent wishes his/her child to attend the neighbourhood school, and not every child wishes to go there.

Gerber (1996) points out that there is a key difference between socially reproduced disadvantage related to factors such as socioeconomic status, class and gender, and individuals who experience severe difficulties in learning. This latter group faces individual serious and chronic barriers to learning and the potential, over their entire life span, to fail to reach 'normal' or typically acceptable standards in literacy attainment that are required and increasingly being demanded from most national education systems. Gerber's work raises questions about the way educators define and construct the rhetoric surrounding notions of 'inclusion' by drawing attention to the ethical and social-justice issues that accompany common notions of inclusion as participation in current reform movements in special education.

The issues that Gerber raises become even more pertinent when they are applied to literacy development. As unskilled jobs disappear and skilled jobs increase, becoming literate is increasingly seen as essential to gaining employment and becoming a functional member of society. This implies it will be difficult for students who are labelled 'disabled' in a national educational system to become literate citizens when they differ so much in their natural ability that it may be impossible to achieve what are considered 'normal levels of literacy', even when they are allowed to participate in mainstream national education systems. As well as these increasingly difficult external demands, there are also growing pressures from within the education system to reach 'normal' literacy attainment. Given the current stress on the majority of students achieving accepted 'literacy standards' and 'effective whole-class teaching', it is difficult to see how participation in mainstream education will lead to inclusion rather than exclusion and alienation for this particular group.

Gerber's work highlights the tensions and ethical issues that occur when inclusion is interpreted as the right to participate in mainstream education if the mainstream system stresses 'normality' and the increasingly perceived need for all participating students to attain similar levels of literacy achievement. This raises questions concerning the ethical and equity issues associated with including disabled students in a system where they will be defined as failing because they can never hope to attain what is considered 'normal' literacy achievement.

Gerber also raises issues of how the social-justice and equal-opportunities issues associated with providing additional funding and resourcing for national education to address individual needs in literacy can be reconciled if 'equal opportunities' is defined as participation in all aspects of national education. It is difficult to see how the barriers to literacy development can be addressed and participation in mainstream schooling achieved if participation is not accompanied by funding and resourcing of individual needs in literacy development. Yet, if schools provide funding and resourcing for individual programmes to address these individual literacy needs, it is not possible to reconcile the provision of different resources and programmes with the inclusion rhetoric that demands that there needs to be equal participation in all aspects of national education.

In Chapter 1, one way of defining 'literacy' was as a dynamic, evolving, social and historical process. When one considers the historical evolution of schooling it can also be seen that the institutions, ideologies and interest groups which operate to shape the possibilities and limits of literacy acquisition interact in complex and selective ways rather than as straightforward conduits of literacy skills to all students. Schools, teachers and national education policies interact to control factors which define and identify who is competent in literacy, by determining factors such as access, participation, assessment and recognition of achievements. These processes are complex and at times contradictory, so that it can be seen 'as much as a system of exclusion as of inclusion' (Foucault, cited in Luke 1993 p. 14). If schooling is seen in this light it also calls into question the assumption that merely assuring the participation of any particular group in a national school system will lead to inclusion and cater for equal opportunities.

Issues of labelling pupils by category to access additional provision

One issue that often evokes a great deal of controversy is the kind of categorising and labelling of pupils who experience difficulties in literacy that is often used to justify a request for additional provision. There is evidence from studies of individual pupils' experience that the 'dyslexia' label is acceptable to many individuals so identified because it clearly indicates that this particular difficulty in learning is associated with a particular cognitive difference rather than an indication of overall lack of intelligence and ability (Riddick 1996). This issue is discussed further in later chapters in this book. Sometimes, ensuring that a pupil is identified as 'having a special educational need' such as dyslexia could be the best way to protect a mainstream placement for a child experiencing difficulties. Paradoxically, 'inclusion' in a mainstream school might need to be accompanied by more labelling and categorising of individual pupils than would be the case if the same learner attended a special school (Wearmouth 2000).

In the education system operating in England, Wales and Northern Ireland all students of school age have a legal entitlement to access to the National Curriculum. There is a duty for local education authorities (LEAs) to make special provision at the level of the school for those students identified as needing it, because students have the statutory right to have their 'special educational needs' assessed and met. Identification labels the student as different, with the possibility that s/he may feel stigmatised. Lack of identification, however, means that s/he may be denied access to additional support. A similar dilemma accompanies the choice of appropriate curricula. Young people sharing identical learning aims may be deprived of the opportunity to develop competencies appropriate to their needs, yet may be made to feel inferior if their curriculum is different.

Current curriculum contexts for inclusion and literacy difficulties

The current UK national context is one which attempts to reconcile principles of individuality, distinctiveness and diversity with inclusion and equal opportunities, and it is therefore bound to be characterised by tensions and contradictions (Norwich 1996). As was noted by Wearmouth and Soler (2001), these tensions and contradictions permeate policy and practice throughout the whole education system in England and Wales. On the one hand, there is a drive to raise the standards of learning of all pupils through whole-class and whole-group teaching, standardised forms of assessment (Broadfoot 1996) and the encouragement of competition between schools by means of a focus on league tables of academic performance. On the other, there is a statutory requirement to pay due regard to the principle of inclusion of pupils, and, within this, to address the identified learning needs of individuals who experience difficulties in learning. Ultimately, the dilemmas created in schools by what often appear to be somewhat fragmented and contradictory government policies may be insoluble without a reconceptualisation of current policies at national level.

One clear example of a situation where individuals have been driven to seek redress against perceived injustice in the formal curriculum is the system for seeking special dispensation for formal examinations for individual pupils who experience certain types of difficulties in learning, including literacy difficulties. Peacey (2002) explains that in granting any special arrangements for students who experience difficulties in literacy development two dimensions must be considered:

- the assessment demands of the test or examination in question;
- the needs of the candidate in that assessment.

He reports the guidance offered by the Joint Council for General Qualifications, which points out that any provision for special arrangements and special consideration must not change the assessment requirements of the qualifications. Special arrangements and special consideration are given for the purpose of enabling recognition of attainment in a particular area, with the requirement that 'valid' and 'reliable' examinations or assessments can be given. Clearly, if the assessment was a test of spelling it would be inappropriate to allow a student with literacy difficulties to use a spellchecker.

Peacey notes the difficulty of creating fair assessments in general terms, and quotes Stobart (2000) in pointing out that in recent years, for a variety of reasons, there has been less confidence generally in the fairness of examinations. The undermining of confidence is the result, partly, of challenges, particularly in the United States, which have forced a reappraisal of formal assessment in a multicultural society. For example, school or college curricula may marginalise important cultural knowledge in particular ethnic groups. Peacey further notes Stobart's comments that any study of equity and assessment in education needs to take account of the whole system. He goes on to set out four principles that those taking decisions about formal assessment might be expected to follow:

- They are guided by an awareness of the relationship between curriculum (what is to be learnt and how it is learnt) and assessment discussed above;
- They monitor a formal assessment's effects on different groups;
- They build the results of such monitoring into the preparation of future examinations and assessments (including the special arrangements);
- All decisions are taken within a commitment to inclusive principles.

(Peacey 2002, p. 211)

Legal issues

The current position

In principle, the law is based on individually defined need. However, in practice resource limitations have meant that only a proportion of individuals have been covered by the legislation. In Britain, a study by Rutter, Tizard and Whitmore (1970) enquired into the incidence of difficulties in learning in the school population. The report from this study showed that teachers' perceptions are that, on average, 20 per cent of their pupils were experiencing difficulty of some kind. Since that time the figure of 20 per cent has been used in the UK to estimate the number of children nationally who might experience difficulties. Of the total number of pupils, approximately 2 per cent are seen by policy-makers as likely to have difficulties which require additional or extra resources to be provided. This figure of 2 per cent is an arbitrary one, drawn from a count of pupils in special schools in 1944. The law, focusing as it does on individual need, gives no such figures for the incidence of children likely to have 'special educational needs'. However, LEAs, whose duty it is to implement legislation, have used such Department for Education and Employment (DfEE) guidance to establish general criteria for assessment.

In the British education system all students of school age have a legal entitlement to access to the National Curriculum. There is a duty for LEAs and Library Boards to make special provision at the level of the school for those students identified as needing it, because students have the statutory right to have their 'special educational needs' assessed and met. In the education system in the Republic of Ireland all students have a legal entitlement to an education appropriate to their needs. School Boards have the duty to make special provision at school level for identified pupils. Identification labels the student as different, with the possibility that they may feel stigmatised. Lack of identification, however, means that they may be denied access to additional support.

The law relating to special needs in England and Wales

By law, decisions about the issuing of individual statements of special educational needs should be based on individual need, not on externally imposed criteria. Prior to the introduction of the new Code of Practice (Department of Education and Skills 2001) the DfEE commissioned a study aimed at national guidance criteria for statements. However, this did not result in any national 'benchmark' for their issue. The code of practice has attempted to introduce some consistency into judgements of whether a child needs a statement. Judgements on whether a child needs a statement or not could vary considerably from school to school, depending on the level of resources in each school and how those resources are deployed. In one school a child with a high level of additional need could have those needs met as part of the general provision within the school. In another school which is less well geared to individual need or less well resourced, the same child would need to have his/her provision arranged by the LEA through the statementing process.

Children with an 'obvious' difficulty would only need a statement if their needs could not be met within the resources generally available to their school. There are LEAs, with a clear commitment to inclusion, which have put enough resources into schools so that children with Down's Syndrome, for example, do not necessarily need a statement. During the consultation period on the 1997 Green Paper, some respondents argued that such arrangements are to be preferred, since they avoid the 'stigma' of a statement.

The option of the statement remains, of course, if the level of school-based resourcing falls. Many parents seek a statement simply because it is the only guarantee they have that a level of support will be maintained.

Children with special educational needs are entitled, in law, to have those needs identified, assessed and then met, with appropriate provision guaranteed by their LEA. Uniquely in English law, in principle students who have a statement of needs are not subject to the vagaries of local 'discretion' or cuts in funding, though parents may have to struggle to secure their child's individual entitlement. The law is based on individual need, which means that individual parents must act on their child's behalf. Sometimes this leads to charges that the law as it stands is 'unfair' to those children whose parents cannot promote their child's interests. The voluntary sector has rejected this view, arguing instead that it is important that less articulate and energetic parents be supported in securing their child's entitlement. The programme for action (Department for Education and Employment 1998), which followed the 1997 Green Paper, stated that the government intended to expand local parent partnership services and to give guidance on a new service to parents through independent parental supporters schemes.

Testing the law

The House of Lords has recently given judgement in a number of cases concerning allegations of negligence against LEAs in relation to special provision made for students who experience difficulties in literacy. One of these, Phelps v. London Borough of Hillingdon, is particularly pertinent because it concerns the issue of dyslexia. An outline of this case appears on the website of the Independent Panel for Special Education Advice:

> Prior to 1995, it had not been thought possible to bring court cases against LEAs for the negligent failure to provide appropriate education. Then, in June 1995, the House of Lords gave judgement in three test cases (known as E v Dorset County Council and Others), concerning this question. Although the judgement did not determine that there was negligence in any of those particular cases, the Court established the principle that educational psychologists, teachers and other similar staff may be held liable in negligence to the children for whom they are responsible. The Court also held that a LEA or school may be 'vicariously' liable for the negligent actions of their staff. This means that an individual could sue an LEA or school if one or more of its staff had been negligent.
>
> (http://www.ipsea.org.uk/phelps.htm)

David Ruebain, the author of this article, defines three conditions which must be met to establish 'negligence':

- The person who is being held responsible for the negligence (such as the educational psychologist or teacher) must owe the victim a 'duty of care'.
- That duty of care must have been breached. This means that the person responsible failed to provide a standard of education that would have been expected of him or her.
- As a result of that breach, the victim has suffered identifiable loss.

Ruebain goes on to discuss the case itself:

> In September 1997, the first substantive education negligence case was decided: Phelps v London Borough of Hillingdon. Ms Phelps has dyslexia and argued that, when she was at school, an educational psychologist employed by Hillingdon LEA should have diagnosed her dyslexia. Because this did not happen, Ms Phelps said that she failed to receive necessary educational provision for her dyslexia and did not learn to read and write as well as she could have done.

The High Court determined that the educational psychologist owed Ms Phelps a duty of care which was breached and that Ms Phelps suffered as a result. The Court also held that Hillingdon LEA, which employed the educational psychologist, was vicariously liable and ordered them to pay compensation to Ms Phelps.

However, Hillingdon LEA then appealed this decision to the Court of Appeal, who gave their judgement on 4 November 1998. That judgement reversed the decision of the High Court and held that, in fact, an individual educational psychologist does not owe a duty of care to a child. The Court considered that such a psychologist is part of a multi-disciplinary team whose function is to provide information to the LEA, rather than owing a direct duty of care to the child concerned. This meant that the first requirement for bringing a negligence case was not satisfied. Ms Phelps appealed to the House of Lords.

The House of Lords decision of 27 July, 2000

... In summary, the House of Lords reversed the decision of the Court of Appeal in Phelps and has made it more possible for individuals to bring claims for compensation. The judgement is long but it is possible to extract key principles:

The law does not, at the moment, allow actions for compensation for straightforward breaches of statutory duty. In other words, duties given to LEAs by legislation which are not carried out may not allow for compensation.

However, there is what is known as a common law duty of care (in other words, separate from duties given to LEAs by legislation) to undertake duties correctly. If they fail in this duty so that there is negligence resulting in loss, then compensation may be sought.

If, however, a LEA makes a decision on grounds of a policy, it may not be possible to bring a claim for compensation, even if that policy is found to have been wrong. Alternatively, if the negligent action was not directly as a result of a policy decision, a claim may be brought.

Local authorities and schools can be held vicariously liable for the negligent actions of staff members including educational psychologists, teachers, education officers etc.

In establishing negligence, it must be shown that the professional concerned went beyond the alternatives available to a competent person exercising that professional skill. A person will not be guilty of negligence if he has acted in accordance with a practice accepted as proper by a responsible body of that profession, skilled in that particular art. Negligence will not arise simply because somebody else disagrees with the steps taken, even if those steps are found to have been the wrong ones.

Claims in education negligence are likely to be considered as personal injury claims.

In the light of these decisions, ... it will be very important to ensure that as many school and other educational records are kept, to assist in proving claims of negligence.

(David Ruebain, http://www.ipsea.org.uk/phelps.htm)

In a recent interview (for Open University E801 course materials, 2002) parents were asked their views on the kind of literacy provision that they saw as necessary to meet the needs of their child, who was experiencing difficulties in literacy acquisition of a dyslexic nature and who was educated in a bilingual, Welsh/English, educational context. Among the legal issues raised in this interview was the statutory requirement to show that a school has taken parents' views into account whilst at the same time maintaining the coherence of their particular school policies. This is a difficult dilemma for educationalists because it highlights the tension between matters of professional judgement and parents' knowledge and awareness and understanding of their own child. The law in this area is complex. Many professionals may be faced with a similar situation when asked to make a professional judgement in relation to a student's entitlement to have his or her special educational needs identified, assessed and met. Professional, possibly legal, advice may need to be sought from outside the school in order to resolve difficult issues.

The Code of Practice in England

In 2001 a revised Code of Practice was issued by the Secretary of State for Education, giving guidance to local authorities and school governing boards on their duties in making special provision for pupils. Legally, local authorities, school governors and their employees must 'have regard to' the provisions of the code.

The 'fundamental principles' of the code include entitlement to a broad curriculum, integration, pupil self-advocacy and parental involvement:

- A child with special educational needs should have their needs met.
- The special educational needs of children will normally be met in mainstream schools or settings.
- The views of the child should be sought and taken into account.
- Parents have a vital role to play in supporting their child's education.
- Children with special educational needs should be offered full access to a broad, balanced and relevant education, including an appropriate curriculum for the foundation stage and the National Curriculum.

(Department of Education and Skills 2001, 1:5)

In the code, specific requirements are made of LEAs regarding assessment and provision, which schools and parents need to be aware of:

There are four main legal duties, which form the cornerstones of the law and consequently create entitlements for children. As with all legislation, these cornerstones have been elaborated and developed by case law arising out of the 1981 Act and this case law still holds good under the new legislation. …

The four cornerstones can be summarised as follows:

1   The duty to identify
An LEA must identify any child if 'he has special educational need' and 'it is necessary for the authority to determine the special educational provision which any learning difficulty he may have calls for' (s321, EA 1996).

The law identifies two kinds of children with special needs
- those whose needs can be met by their school;
- those for whom the LEA should take responsibility.

For children in the latter category, this duty creates for children with special needs an entitlement to have their needs identified.

2   The duty to assess
Once a child has been identified as having, or probably having, needs which require the LEA to make provision for him, then the child is entitled to an assessment. LEAs have the duty to assess children even when some doubt remains as to whether the child has needs greater than those that their school can meet (s323, EA 1996).

3   The duty to issue a statement

If, following an assessment under Section 323, it is necessary for the LEA to determine the special educational provision which the child needs, the authority shall 'make and maintain a statement of his special educational needs' (s324(1), EA 1996).

This part of the legislation entitles the child to specified and detailed provision to match clearly identified needs. For more details of the legislation see pages 37–40.

4   The duty to arrange the special education provision

LEAs must 'arrange that the special educational provision specified in the statement is made for the child' (s324(5), EA 1996).

This section of the law creates an entitlement for the child to have what is set out on the statement. Even if LEAs do not meet the child's needs directly, they must ensure that provision is delivered as specified in Part 3 of the statement. If such provision is not delivered then it is enforceable in law.

The law as it is currently framed is thus based on the notion of identification of need. Children are entitled to have their needs identified, have them met with appropriate provision and to have guarantees that that provision will not arbitrarily be removed but will be in place until review shows that it is no longer necessary. Once a need is identified, it must be met. There is no 'if we can afford it' clause attached to entitlement: LEAs cannot argue that they have no money. They cannot be absolved of their legal responsibility nor can they give that responsibility away to schools. There is only one occasion in the decision-making process where an LEA can make a decision based on potential cost and that is at the point where a mainstream placement as opposed to a special school placement is at issue. At no other point should cost be a determining factor.

(Open University E801 course materials, 2002, Legal Supplement)

In addition, guidance is offered on the content of 'individual education plans' (IEPs). The outline of content asks schools to specify what the pupil's learning need is and then state clearly how that need will be met and monitored:

- short-term targets set for or by the child
- the teaching strategies to be used
- the provision to be put in place

- when the plan is to be reviewed
- success and/or exit criteria
- outcomes (to be recorded when IEP is reviewed)
  (Department of Education and Skills 2001, 5:60 and 6: 58)

Ways of conceptualising IEPs for students who experience difficulties in literacy development are discussed in Chapter 9.

The issue of time limits on the statutory assessment process has assumed an added significance as a result of their omission in Northern Ireland. There, Education Boards do not have to work to the same time limits as their English and Welsh counterparts. Schools in England need to keep themselves informed of the stage the process has reached, though the legal responsibility to conform to time limits lies with the LEA.

Parents and the law

Throughout the 1980s and 1990s there was a series of initiatives designed to support parents in exercising their rights. However, exercising rights requires a high level of motivation and determination as well as, sometimes, access to legal representation and financial resources. The inevitable consequence of this is that some parents will be better able to exercise their rights than others. The law in relation to 'special educational needs' is concerned with meeting an individual need that has been assessed, not with what local authorities decide they can afford or what they and/or schools think is desirable. The basis of special education legislation is that of entitlement for individual learners. Gross (1996) concludes that resources are unfairly allocated to children whose parents are more literate, persistent and articulate and supports the notion of formula funding in the interests of 'fairness' for all children. Making the same point about unfairness, the Audit Commission observed:

> LEAs admitted that factors which had no bearing on the level of need of a child were influential in the decision to issue a statement. The most significant factors were the level of determination of the school or the parent and whether the parent was represented by a lawyer or voluntary organisation.
> (Audit Commission 1992, para. 22)

However, as Simmons points out:

Those who support the case for formula funding in the interests of 'fairness' must be prepared to acknowledge that they support the dismantling of entitlement. Seen in that light, how many professionals or voluntary agencies would say publicly that they were in favour of removing entitlement from the most vulnerable sector of the educational community? Are they really willing to support restructuring which would give disabled children only what local politicians had determined was available rather than what was needed?

(Simmons 1996, p. 107)

She concludes that the solution to the problem is not to remove entitlement from learners, but to persuade local authorities to fulfil their obligations towards every child. Even if the local authority does meet its resource obligations, however, there is still no guarantee that the child will be accepted by the school as a fully participant member and his/her needs met appropriately across the curriculum. Marsh summarises the dilemmas inherent in the question of the fairness of funding as follows:

The funding of SEN [special educational needs] is at the cross-roads. Since the implementation of the Education Acts 1981 and 1988, LEAs have seen significant increases in the SEN budget. LEAs are now faced with the choice of attempting to control the amount of resources designated for supporting pupils with statements of SEN or accepting a 'demand led' budget. The bulk of the 'additional' money is being used to support pupils with statements in mainstream primary and secondary schools, where the numbers have more than doubled from 62,000 (0.8%) in January 1991 to 134,000 (1.6%) in January 1997. However the evidence suggests that the number of pupils educated in special schools (1.2%) has remained virtually constant during the same period ([Department for Education and Employment 1997]). The continuing growth in the number of statements would appear, then, not only to draw disproportionate amounts from the general schools budget but also to divert attention away from inclusive policies aimed at reducing the special school population. The impact of LMS [local management of schools] has meant that many mainstream schools have accrued additional resources from statements for 'their own' pupils perhaps at the expense of reviewing and adapting their approaches in order to achieve greater inclusion of pupils who would normally have been educated in a special school.

(Marsh 1998, pp. 74–5)

Marsh feels that, although a rigorously designed and transparent formula for funding additional or special learning needs can be a useful method for allocating resources, nevertheless the current system of individualised funding requires radical reconceptualisation:

[I]t is still apparent that a radical rethink is needed about the system of statementing which is becoming too confrontational and adversarial. The system may even be restricting the prospects for improved inclusion practice by a concentration of attention on the 'increasing 2 per cent' in mainstream schools rather than on reducing the 'static 1 per cent' in special schools. The resources delivered by statements are becoming an inequitable method of ensuring that a child's special educational needs are met or whether the child has a greater chance of being educated in a mainstream school. Parental pressure groups are increasingly getting an unfair share of the limited resources available and perhaps damaging inclusive education options for other groups of parents who are not so articulate. The Independent Panel for Special Education Advice (IPSEA) have made a vigorous attack upon *The SEN Initiative* (Coopers and Lybrand /Society of Education Officers, 1996) and have viewed the issue from a children's rights standpoint. IPSEA claim that more resources should be found in order to ensure the protection of the child's special educational needs. It is not clear however why such a formal promise and contract, in the form of a statement, should be required only at a point where an LEA becomes involved in directing the provision (and often providing directly). Children have SEN at all stages of the *Code of Practice* and the argument is that they (or their parents) are entitled to as much reassurance as any others.

... The challenge for LEAs and governing bodies as we approach the turn of the century is to develop inclusive education policies and formula funding arrangements for SEN which fully encompass the needs of all pupils with SEN, with and without a statement.

(Marsh 1998, pp. 74–5)

The Code of Practice in Northern Ireland

The responsibility of the Department of Education, Northern Ireland (DENI), for educational provision is devolved to the five education and library boards. Membership of these boards is at the discretion of DENI.

There is a clear division between schools along religious lines. 'Controlled' schools tend to be Protestant, maintained schools are Catholic and integrated schools are interdenominational. The selective system makes the grammar schools the preferred choice at secondary level for most parents. The system of special schools is seen as separate and distinct. The number and type of special schools vary across boards. The policy of each board determines the special system in each area.

The Northern Ireland code is a more succinct version of that in England. An important difference is that of time limits within which local authorities have to assess pupils whose needs may require a statement. In England and Wales the law relating to time limits for the various stages in the process is made clear. However, there is only one time limit underpinned by law in Northern Ireland. The rest are given as guidance in the code, which does not carry the force of law. This means that where the process is delayed parents have no recourse to the tribunal because they have not received full notice of the proposed provision. The 'named person' in the code in England and Wales is the 'named Board officer' in Northern Ireland. The importance of education plans in Northern Ireland, rather than individual education plans as in England and Wales, is that teachers in the province have the chance to consider group education plans rather than solely plans for individuals.

Overriding everything, however, is the fact that the system is driven by the selection procedure at 11-plus. Children are therefore coached; many primary schools are streamed, as are many secondary. Quite frequently there is a 'special needs' stream, or pupils are withdrawn from classes. There is still little sense in educating all pupils as members of the mainstream class.

However, there is evidence that the code in Northern Ireland has proved the impetus for new initiatives. In some schools there is targeted support to meet specific needs. Nevertheless, the paperwork associated with the code is burdensome and detracts from the time available to work with other staff and pupils. The code has highlighted the need for additional professional development for teachers, some of whom appear to be funding their own training.

The law relating to special educational needs in Scotland

As noted above in the context of England and Wales, decisions should be based on individual need, not on externally imposed criteria. Circular 4/96 (SOEID 1996) comments that, in general terms, pupils have a 'learning difficulty' if they require additional arrangements to be made for them in order to have full access to the school curriculum. Therefore, whether a child needs a record or not could vary considerably, depending on the individual school's level of resources in and the deployment of those resources. Children only need a record if their learning needs cannot be met within the resources generally available to their school.

Children with special educational needs in Scotland are legally entitled to have those needs identified, assessed and then met with appropriate provision guaranteed by their local education authority.

In Scotland, the equivalent of the IEP in England is known as a Record of Needs. Circular 4/96 outlines the process of formalising a record:

111. There are 2 stages in the preparation of a Record of Needs. These are:
(a) setting out of the terms on which it is proposed to open a Record, on which the parents' or young person's comments, as appropriate, must be invited. (NB In practice, this is usually done by sending a completed, but unsigned, draft Record, the draft status of which should be clearly explained, to the parents or the young person, as appropriate);
(b) finalising the Record, which is then signed by the authority and may thereafter only be altered or modified in accordance with statute.

It also advises on the form of the record:

115. The language used in the Record needs to be clear, concise and jargon free. It should include precise reference to a child's or young person's known educational attainments and general development, to enable his or her progress to be monitored, reviewed and reassessed against specific aims and objectives which themselves may be subject to modification in the light of that progress.
116. Section 651 (2) of the 1980 Act, and regulation 3 of the Education (Record of Needs) (Scotland) Regulations 1982, prescribe the information the Record must contain and the

Schedule to the Regulations prescribes the form in which this information is to be set out (a copy of the Schedule is attached at Annex 3 to this Circular). Within the prescribed structure, a common and consistent format for writing Records, using the same headings and numbering, is desirable.

Official guidance relating to 'good practice' in drawing up records has been summarised by SEED (2001, pp. 3–4) and is quoted in Chapter 9, 'Framework for planning'.

A number of researchers have expressed views about the likely direction of developments in the area of special educational provision for students in Scotland. Mackay and McLarty note the difficulty in predicting the future in relation to students who experience difficulty in learning of any kind in Scotland because of the political changes instigated by the change to single-tier local authorities in 1996, and the change of government and the pro-devolution vote in 1997:

> Lack of finance may constrain some developments. Others may be essential, irrespective of cost. For example, litigation has begun against a Scottish education authority concerning the support of a former pupil with dyslexia. This may have far-reaching consequences. There are still others where changes of perspective are essential: parents' involvement in their children's education is one example. The following points also seem significant.
>
> It is time to revisit the vast literature on curriculum development and re-assess current demands in the light of principles such as the structure of subjects, and the actual worth of the curriculum. Scotland does not yet have a curricular framework that is suitable for all pupils. Perhaps it cannot or should not exist. That debate has still to take place.
>
> Children and young people from ethnic minorities should have access to any support they may need. Their special needs may be difficult to discern if the first language at home is not English.
>
> There should be continued development of specialisms which have only recently been addressed as areas of priority for the provision of services across Scotland. This applies particularly to the education of children and young people who have difficulty communicating. They include those with autistic behaviour, which makes exceptional demands on themselves, their families and the education system.

The pre-service and in-service training of teachers in SEN is still a priority. In some cases, this could be facilitated by joint in-service exercises with other professionals such as speech and language therapists. Some models of practice are emerging.

More broadly, there must be respect for the different ways of understanding SEN. For more than a decade, the support-for-learning movement has advocated moves away from what it calls 'deficit' and 'medical' models which describe people with reference to their disabilities. Instead, that movement advocates different models, for example, focusing on experiences offered to learners in schools and other services. This preoccupation with models is old-fashioned modernism. No model of response is right or wrong intrinsically. They are all legitimate ways of knowing, appropriate in some circumstances and not so in others. Pupils, families, teachers and the general community are done a disservice when the diversity that is normality is treated as a philosophical, political or fiscal inconvenience.

(Mackay and McLarty 1999, p. 804)

Comparisons between Scotland, and England and Wales

Mackay and McLarty note a number of differences between the system of supporting the learning needs of pupils identified as experiencing 'special' difficulties in learning, and that operating in England and Wales:

The differences between the education systems of Scotland and England & Wales have been relatively slight in respect of pupils with SEN, but some are worth noting.

In 1970, England and Wales were four years ahead of Scotland in ensuring that all children were entitled to education. The 1970 Act also entitled pupils with disabilities to integrated education whenever possible. This does not apply in Scotland. The Record of Needs is the 'Statement' in England and Wales, and uses less paper than the Record. However, the time needed to complete Records and Statements is a problem on both sides of the border.

The mandatory nature of the National Curriculum in England and Wales has worried many special educationists (though an important exception was made for deaf–blind pupils). Officially, the current 5–14 Scottish curriculum is not mandatory, but its adoption is close to universal in education authority schools, and there is pressure at central and local level to ensure that all pupils are 'doing 5–14'. Earlier, concern was expressed about the 'elaborated curriculum' that has emerged from 5–14 for pupils with the most severe disabilities. Both educational systems can do better than persist with current curriculum models, because they have done better in the past.

In 1994, the English and Welsh system adopted the Code of Practice, a set of required standards [which have the status of 'advisory' only] for services for those with SEN. Scotland has no Code, though EPSEN fulfils a similar function. The critical difference between EPSEN and the Code is the … nature of the latter because of its roots in the English and Welsh Education Act, 1993. It will be interesting to assess the extent to which practices in the two systems diverge.

(Mackay and McLarty 1999, pp. 803–4)

The law relating to special educational needs in the Republic of Ireland

In the Republic of Ireland Education Act 1998 every person in the state is legally entitled to an education appropriate to meeting his or her needs. As Swan (2002) notes, according to Section 2(1) of the Act, special educational needs means the educational needs of students who have a disability and the educational needs of exceptionally able children. This is based on the definition of disability given in Section 2(1) of that Act. This is a category-based approach, which seems to be predicated on the assumption that special educational needs and learning-support (formerly 'remedial') needs can be validly treated as a dichotomy, with an IQ score of 70 as the dividing line on the continuum of general abilities between those who have a general intellectual disability and those who do not. Besides those who have a disability, the Act also refers to 'any person – who has other special educational needs' (Part 1, Section 6 (A)), and this is defined as referring to the educational needs of exceptionally able students (Part 1, Section 2).

The Act therefore does not directly refer to students who have learning-support ('remedial') needs, but the references in its preamble to 'every person in the State' and again (in Part 1, Section 7) to 'each person resident in the State' suggest, at least, that there is a responsibility on the minister to make appropriate education available to each one, including those deemed to have learning-support needs. According to the *Learning-Support Guidelines* (Ireland 2000, p. 55), priority should be given to pupils who achieve at or below the tenth percentile – seemingly on a norm-referenced, standardised test of reading achievement. There is no national criterion for having special educational needs, and therefore for having entitlement to support services other than that of having a disability or being 'exceptionally able'.

Swan, commenting on the terms of the 1998 Education Act, notes that:

> The preamble to the Act begins as follows:
> An Act to make provision, in the interests of the common good, for the education of every person in the State including any person with a disability or who has other special educational needs. ...
> In short, Special Needs education had moved from the periphery of national policy concerns right to the centre.
> The Education Act, 1998 sets out the updated statutory framework for the provision of most primary and post primary education in particular, in Ireland, and for Special Needs Education within it.
> Two relevant definitions are furnished in the Act. Disability means any one or more of the following:
>
> (a) the total or partial loss of bodily or mental function, or
> (b) the presence in the body of harmful organisms, or
> (c) malfunction, malformation or disfigurement, or
> (d) a condition ... which results in a person learning differently ..., or
> (e) a condition, illness or disease which affects a person's thinking, perception, emotions or judgment or which results in disturbed behaviour (Part 1, S2)
> 'Special educational needs' is defined as 'the educational needs of students who have a disability and the educational needs of exceptionally able students' (Part 1, S2). It is a stated objective of the Act to 'give practical effect to the constitutional rights of children, including children who have a disability or other special educational needs' (Part 1, Section 6(a)).
> Perhaps the most relevant achievements of the Act are to enshrine explicitly in law, for the first time, the entitlement of persons with disabilities to education appropriate to their needs,

and to require the Minister 'to ensure that there is made available to each person resident in the State, including a person with a disability or who has other special educational needs, support services and a level and quality of education appropriate to meeting the needs and abilities of that person' (Section 7(1)).

It also requires the Minister to 'provide support services to recognised schools and students who have a disability or ... other special educational needs' ... 'while having regard to the resources available' (Ibid.) – a very familiar phrase which some critics have seen as a 'cop-out', so to speak; indeed information material distributed by the Association for the Severely and Profoundly Mentally Handicapped claims that this restriction has rendered this Act unconstitutional.

Regarding obligations on schools, the Act requires that they (1) have an admissions policy that provides the maximum accessibility to the school, (2) ensure that the educational needs of all students, including those with a disability or other special educational needs are identified and provided for, and (3) 'provide education to students which is appropriate to their abilities and needs' (Part 11, Section 9).

The Act therefore moves the status of such education from availability to entitlement, thus incorporating a human rights perspective in an Irish education statute *for the first time*. It also seems to mark a transition in policy-making from the reactive to the proactive; policy is now seen to lead practice in many respects, whereas hitherto it had all too frequently followed after it.

(Swan 2002, pp. 45–6)

Conclusion

Given a historical development of national education systems and, within this, current moves towards including all pupils in mainstream schools, catering for students who experience 'special' difficulties in literacy development is seen as challenging in many schools. Across the UK and in the Republic of Ireland the courts continue to uphold the notion of individual need. Inherent in any discussion of the law in the area of difficulties in learning are issues of equality of opportunity, fairness in resource allocation, and the tension between a system that offers individual learning programmes for some students and one that provides a whole-school approach to learning in order to encourage all learners to reach their potential.

Chapter 7

National curricula frameworks for literacy development

Introduction

Both internationally and across the UK, teachers in classrooms have varying degrees of opportunity to make their own decisions about what to teach pupils and also how to teach it. Some countries have legally required national curricula, with close prescriptions of content, modes of teaching and forms of assessment. There may be less flexibility for decision-making at school or classroom level about how to implement the curriculum in such countries compared with the greater freedom elsewhere. However, as Wragg notes, even in those countries which have a prescriptive national curriculum it is impossible for central government to prescribe every detail of a school's curriculum (Wragg et al. 1998, p. 23). Teachers often still have the opportunity to make decisions which may have a profound effect on the quality of pupil learning. Schools' and teachers' autonomy over curricular decision-making is a particularly important issue where students experience difficulties in learning such as in the acquisition of literacy. It is crucial, therefore, that all those associated with the literacy learning of students of school age are fully conversant with the detail of requirements of their own national curriculum context and the room for manoeuvre there is within it to respond appropriately to individual students' learning needs:

> One important element of the craft skills of teaching ... is the ability to pick ways through a curriculum, even a prescribed one, via as imaginative and challenging routes as possible.
>
> (Wragg et al. 1998, p. 23)

The national curricula frameworks relating to Scotland, England and the Republic of Ireland, and the literacy curricula within them, vary in the detail of their prescription and the level of their flexibility. A comparison of these documents reveals differing emphases on issues significant to the education of students who experience difficulties in literacy development. For example, individual child-centred approaches are evident in the Scottish Curriculum Guideline Developments. However a uniform approach to all children is privileged in the whole-class approaches in the English National Literacy Strategy (NLS).

The National Curriculum in England and Wales

The organisation of education in England and Wales changed dramatically in 1988 with the introduction of the Education Reform Act, the most significant piece of legislation since 1944. It made wide-ranging changes to the organisation of education at primary, secondary and tertiary levels, including the introduction of a National Curriculum. Before 1988 the curriculum in schools was the responsibility of individual schools, departments and teachers, with, at the upper end of the secondary sector, the content of the curriculum effectively controlled by examination boards. Prior to this time the English Plowden Report (Central Advisory Council for Education (England) 1967) had been seen to offer exemplary guidance on a child-centred philosophy of education in the primary years. However, in England and Wales, as in Scotland (see below), the political context enabled a Conservative government, coping with the aftermath of a teachers' strike in the mid-1980s, to seek central control over the school curriculum. For the government, political priorities entailed:

> an increase in parental choice and in the provision of information on schools. The frequent expression of traditional concerns about alleged falling standards and the ideological distrust of so-called 'progressive' methods created the context for the introduction of a programme to provide a centralised initiative on the curriculum which would simultaneously limit teacher autonomy, promise clearer definition of the curriculum and better communication with parents, and exercise greater control over standards through national testing, thus creating a comprehensive, appropriate political response.
>
> (F.R. Adams 1999, p. 349)

The change to centralised control over the content and assessment of the curriculum occurred after only a minimal consultation with educational professionals. This change was accompanied by an emphasis on quantifiable measures in order to show anticipated improvement in the standard of pupil learning, and it led to the formulation of an assessment-based curriculum (Lawton and Chitty 1988). Norwich explains what is meant by this:

> [C]urricular targets are defined with a primary focus on how attainment can be assessed. There is less emphasis on the complex process of curriculum development and design, with the careful linking and translating of broad, general into increasingly specific and more concrete intentions at different levels in the education system. ... The focus on attainment targets and assessment derives mainly from the government's wish to raise national educational attainment levels. It is based on the belief that the wider use of assessment information by those with a stake in schools will increase accountability and raise standards.
>
> (Norwich 1990, p. 160)

The English NLS

The 1997 preliminary report of the Literacy Task Force

The English NLS was introduced against a background of increasing external government control exercised over the curriculum and teaching styles. The emphasis of the newly introduced National Literacy Project's (NLP) was on the management of literacy at whole-school level through monitoring by senior staff and National Foundation for Education Research (NFER)-based researchers. After the election of a Labour government in 1997, as Labour's education policy evolved it became clear that many of the objectives and structures of the NLP would be kept and further developed. During the late 1980s and 1990s England revised the National Curriculum first introduced in the 1988 Education Reform Act. This Act introduced a prescriptive and detailed curriculum with statutory national testing in the primary school at ages 7 and 11. It also initiated an inspection system which was controlled by the Office for Standards in Education (OFSTED).

The 1990s were a decade where, once again, the adoption of ability-setting and whole-class teaching directly impacted upon policies related to literacy instruction. This marked a significant move away from teacher-devised strategies to address literacy difficulties. For example, in May 1996 the Labour Party announced a back-to-basics drive to improve literacy standards if it was elected the following year. David Blunkett, the Shadow Education Secretary, noted that a recently published OFSTED report on the teaching of reading in forty-five inner-London primary schools found that 40 per cent of Year 6 pupils had reading ages two or more years below their chronological ages. The Labour Party announced that it planned to raise standards through the introduction of a new literacy task force and wanted to examine ways of ensuring 'that every child leaving primary school does so with a reading age of 11 by the end of the second term of office' (Rafferty 1996). In the same announcement David Blunkett stated that teachers were to 'use teaching methods which work and are not just the latest fashion' (*ibid.*). The Labour Party's dissatisfaction with the quality of newly trained teachers also resulted in a pledge to place greater emphasis on basic skills, classroom discipline and whole-class teaching. Blunkett also stressed the use of phonics.

The need to raise standards and skills was a key point in the 'New Life for Britain' document announced in July to lay the foundations for the Labour Party's election campaign. The document promised a 'radical improvement in primary standards through focussing on the basics, better testing and assessment with target-setting of results; value-added performance tables; the reform of teacher training and the sacking of inadequate staff' (quoted in Rafferty 1996b). It also announced that the newly formed task force on literacy would have its report and recommendations ready for an incoming government.

On 28 February 1997 the preliminary report of the English Literacy Task Force was released by the Labour Party (Literacy Task Force 1997). Drawing upon international and local data and understandings of 'best practice', the Literacy Task Force report argued for a national literacy strategy for England. In Sections 1 and 2 of the document the English Literacy Task Force set out the evidence which they saw as supporting the introduction of a national strategy. They argued that '[t]he strategy we set out in the remainder of this document combines what we now know about best practice in the teaching of reading with an appreciation of the lessons of ten years of educational reform' (*ibid.*, s. 1 and 2). They also claimed that 'a constant national strategic approach over five to ten years' is the only possible way to 'bring about a dramatic improvement in literacy standards' (*ibid.*, para. 38). The strategy was presented in Sections 3 and 4 of the document. In Section 3 they laid out the details of phase one of the strategy, which would be implemented from 1997 to 2001. Finally, in Section 4 they provided some indication of the nature of phase two, which would cover the years 2001–6.

In Sections 2 and 3 the 1997 preliminary report of the Literacy Task Force pays particular attention to 'children with special educational needs'. However, the entire document raises a number of issues of particular importance to the themes discussed in this book:

- The location of the failure in learning to read.
- The advocacy of phonics in particular, with some reference to the whole-book/whole-language approach to the reading process.
- A coherent strategy utilising predominantly whole-class teaching, with some provision for the individual needs of students who experience difficulties in literacy.
- A recognition of particular reading programmes aimed at addressing difficulties in literacy such as Reading Recovery.
- The management and evaluation of the strategy.

Allocation of responsibility for the failure in learning to read and how we address it

There appears to be an emphasis in the preliminary report of the Literacy Task Force on the education system rather than home or environmental factors. The cause of failure to learn to read and a perceived drop in 'literacy standards' is located in the education system. For example, paragraph 21 of the document states:

> International comparisons of children's achievements in reading suggest Britain is not performing well, with a slightly below average position in international literacy league tables. Most studies show also a long 'tail' of underachievement in Britain and a relatively poor performance from lower ability students. Whilst general societal factors (such as the status given to school learning or the prevalence of television viewing amongst adolescents) may be responsible for some of the poor British performance, most are agreed that the educational system bears the main responsibility.
> (Literacy Task Force 1997, para. 21)

Paragraph 32 further highlighted the seriousness of the issue for British schools by pointing out that in 'British schools' the 'performance of lower ability pupils is substantially below that of other countries'. Overall the document tends to stress addressing literacy difficulties within the education system through a 'coherent strategy' rather than 'fleeting and unconnected initiatives such as Reading Recovery'.

Beard's (1999) subsequent account of the 'influences on the Literacy Hour' reinforces an emphasis in the report on the need for the school rather than society or family to address literacy development, and indicates that this emphasis on the school as the main agent for improving literacy 'performance' is derived from the school effectiveness research. Beard argued that the influences from the 'international school effective evidence' have 'consistently challenged earlier assumptions that pupils' social background largely determines their school performance', and argued that 'once pupils begin school, then the school itself can have a significantly greater influence on pupil progress' (Beard, 1999, p. 8).

Advocacy of different models of reading

In the section of the report on 'The Teaching of Reading: What Works', paragraph 46 (entitled 'The successful teaching of reading in particular') mentions both 'reading for meaning' – that is, the whole-language/real-book approach – and phonic knowledge. It emphasises the development of skills and reading techniques, as well as the development of a literacy-rich environment:

The successful teaching of reading in particular: equips pupils at the earliest stage to draw upon the sources of knowledge needed when reading for meaning, including phonic knowledge (simple and complex sound/symbol relationships), graphic knowledge (patterns within words), word recognition (a sight vocabulary which includes common features of words), grammatical knowledge (checking for sense through the ways words are organised) and contextual information (meaning derived from the text as a whole); continues the direct teaching of reading techniques through both key stages, building systematically on the skills pupils have learnt earlier in, for example, tackling unfamiliar words, deduction and using texts to find information; provides a range of reading material, usually based around a core reading programme, but substantially enriched with other good quality material, including information texts used selectively to deepen reading experience and to provide choice at each level; encourages library usage; extends pupils' reading by focused work on challenging texts with the whole class or in groups, and involves frequent opportunities for pupils to hear, read and discuss texts and to think about the content and the language used; gives time for

productive individual reading at school and at home, and opportunities for pupils to share their response with others.

(Literacy Task Force 1997, para. 46)

Adoption of whole-class, group-based and individual approaches to teaching reading

The document appears to be ambiguous regarding its support for
whole-class and/or individual approaches to teaching reading. For
example, at the beginning of the introduction the New Zealand
strategy for addressing reading difficulties, which at the time focused
upon Reading Recovery, was praised as the way forward for English
literacy policy. Yet, as noted above, in paragraph 36, at the conclusion
of the section, Reading Recovery was rejected as part of 'fleeting and
unconnected initiatives' which are difficult to implement across the
range of English schools.

In Section 3, the subsection on the 'Teaching of Reading', both
whole-class and individual tuition appeared to be suggested for the
proposed literacy strategy. For example, paragraph 45 suggests that the
emphasis will be upon whole-class as well as individual tuition. It
stresses 'carefully sequenced whole-class, group and individual work to focus
upon strategies and skills, with the teacher combining instruction,
demonstration, questioning and discussion, providing the structure for
subsequent tasks and giving help and constructive response'.

Particular reading programmes aimed at addressing 'children with special educational needs'

In the section of the document entitled 'Children with Special
Educational Needs', Reading Recovery was mentioned as providing a
model for these needs (Reading Recovery is discussed further below).
This section also noted the need for 'an individualised learning plan'
and the role of special educational needs co-ordinators (SENCOs) in
diagnosing children's particular needs (paras 105–6).

Management and evaluation of the strategy

The section on 'Management of the National Strategy' clearly spells this
out (paras 57–60). This section argues that it will be overseen by a senior
official in the 'enhanced standards and effectiveness group' which will be
created in the Department for Education and Employment (DfEE). The

overseeing of the strategy will also have input from OFSTED and other groups such as the School Curriculum and Assessment Authority (SCAA), Teacher Training Authority (TTA), British Dyslexia Association (BDA) and NLP. Evaluation was to be 'independent'. It is interesting to note that these paragraphs suggest that, at the point this document was written, the differences between emphasising a whole-class based strategy and implementing methods such as Reading Recovery, which targets individual children, are not clearly acknowledged. This can be seen in paragraph 58:

> The Literacy Strategy Group should commission an independent evaluation of the NLP as soon as possible after an election. It should involve comparison of the participating schools with a control group. It should be undertaken with the specific goal of showing how the model could be refined and built upon to form the basis of a national approach to the teaching of literacy in primary schools. It would need to examine not only the details of where the approach works well and where it needs improvement. It would also need to draw on other innovative primary school approaches such as target-grouping, the use of trained classroom assistants and effective home–school collaboration, Reading Recovery methods and the use of information technology, each of which, we believe, has a contribution to make. Above all, it should consider the strategic policy implications of spreading the approach from a relatively small number of volunteer schools to large numbers and ultimately to all schools.
>
> (Literacy Task Force 1997, para. 58)

This paragraph, like many of the statements made in the report, appears to be straightforward on the first reading. On closer examination, however, it is possible to identify underlying tensions that would need to be resolved to implement the national strategy being outlined in this report. For example, the document clearly locates the implementation of the strategy within schools, and its management within government-controlled bodies and targets. It also acknowledges a need to utilise 'effective home–school collaboration'. Yet there is no reference to how this is to take place or to the tensions that need to be resolved. Nor is there a recognition of the tensions that might arise from the implementation of programmes such as Reading Recovery, which stresses teacher expertise, and the use of 'trained classroom assistants' to implement 'innovative primary school approaches'.

The 1998 *Framework for Teaching* document and the literacy hour

The Framework for Teaching (Department for Education and Employment 1998) followed on from the release of the NLS, which was launched in August 1997. The Framework came into operation under a quasi-statutory status in all state primary schools in England in September 1998. This document set out the teaching objectives in literacy for pupils from Reception to Year 6. It was this document which set out the format of a literacy hour as a daily period of time throughout the school which would be dedicated to 'literacy teaching time for all pupils' (*ibid.*, p.8). The hour was intended to cover both reading and writing and was to take the form of an introduction of thirty minutes – twenty minutes independent work and a ten-minute plenary – which has been reproduced below:

What is The Literacy Hour?

1. Whole class (15 mins approx): KS1 and KS2 – Shared text work (a balance of reading and writing).
2. Whole class (15 mins approx): KS1 – Focused word work. KS2 – A balance over the term of focused word work or sentence work.
3. Group & independent work (20 mins): KS1 – Independent reading, writing or word work, while the teacher works with at least two ability groups each day on guided text work (reading or writing).
4. Whole class (10 mins approx): KS1 and KS2 – Reviewing, reflecting, consolidating teaching points, and presenting work covered in the lesson.

Approx 15 minutes shared reading and writing – whole class.
Shared reading is a class activity using a common text eg a 'big book', poetry poster or text extract. At Key Stage 1, teachers should use shared reading to read with the class, focusing on comprehension and on specific features eg word-building and spelling patterns, punctuation, the layout and purpose, the structure and organisation of sentences. Shared reading provides a context for applying and teaching word level skills and for teaching how to use other reading cues to check for meaning, and identify and self-correct errors. Shared reading, with shared writing, also provide the context for developing pupils' grammatical awareness, and their understanding of sentence construction and punctuation.

At Key Stage 2 shared reading is used to extend reading skills in line with the objectives in the text level column of the Framework. Teachers should also use this work as a context for teaching and reinforcing grammar, punctuation and vocabulary work.

At both Key Stages, because the teacher is supporting the reading, pupils can work from texts that are beyond their independent reading levels. This is particularly valuable for less able readers who gain access to texts of greater richness and complexity than they would otherwise be able to read. This builds confidence and teaches more advanced skills which feed into other independent reading.

Shared writing provides many opportunities for pupils to learn, apply and reinforce skills in the context of a larger group with careful guidance from the teacher. Teachers should use texts to provide ideas and structures for the writing and, in collaboration with the class, compose texts, teaching how they are planned and how ideas are sequenced and clarified and structured. Shared writing is also used to teach grammar and spelling skills, to demonstrate features of layout and presentation and to focus on editing and refining work. It should also be used as a starting point for subsequent independent writing. Wherever possible, shared reading and writing should be interlinked. For example, over a five-day period, a teacher may plan to (a) introduce a text, (b) work on it through shared reading and then (c) use the text as a 'frame' for writing or as a stimulus to extend, alter or comment on it.

Approx 15 minutes word level work – whole class.
There must be a systematic, regular and frequent teaching of phonological awareness, phonics and spelling throughout Key Stage 1. Teachers should follow the progression set out in the word level objectives carefully. It sets out both an order of teaching and the expectations for what pupils should achieve by the end of each term. Appendix List 3 summarises these objectives and can be used as a list of criteria for assessing progress. The work must be given a specific teaching focus in the Literacy Hour. Although it is essential that these decoding skills are practised and applied in shared reading, they also need to be taught through carefully structured activities, which help pupils to hear and discriminate regularities in speech and to see how these are related to letters and letter combinations in spelling and reading. The majority of pupils can learn these basic phonic skills rapidly and easily. Word recognition,

graphic knowledge, and vocabulary work should also have a teaching focus during this period of 15 minutes.

At Key Stage 2, this time should be used to cover spelling and vocabulary work and the teaching of grammar and punctuation from the sentence level objectives. For Key Stage 1 pupils, these sentence level objectives should be covered in the context of shared reading and writing and this remains an important context for teaching skills at Key Stage 2. Nevertheless, teachers will need to plan a balance of word and sentence level work for this second part of the Hour, across each half-term, to ensure that all these objectives are covered.

Approx 20 minutes guided group and independent work.
This section of the Literacy Hour has two complementary purposes:

- to enable the teacher to teach at least one group per day, differentiated by ability, for a sustained period through 'guided' reading or writing;
- to enable other pupils to work independently – individually, in pairs or in groups – without recourse to the teacher.

Guided reading is the counterpart to shared reading. The essential difference is that, in guided reading and writing, the teacher focuses on independent reading and writing, rather than modelling the processes for pupils. Guided reading should be a fundamental part of each school's literacy programme. In effect, it takes the place of an individualised reading programme and, as a carefully structured group activity, it significantly increases time for sustained teaching. In ability groups of four to six, pupils should have individual copies of the same text. The texts need to be carefully selected to match the reading level of the group. In the early stages pupils should meet texts of graded difficulty, as they progress these texts will often be selected from reading schemes or programmes and can usually be built up from existing book stocks with some careful supplementation.

At Key Stage 1, teachers should introduce the text to the group, to familiarise them with the overall context of the story and point out any key words they need to know. Pupils then read it independently, while the teacher assesses and supports each pupil in the group. The same principles apply at Key Stage 2. However, as pupils progress, the teaching should focus increasingly on guided silent reading with questions to direct or check up on the reading, points to note, problems to solve etc., to meet the text level objectives in the Framework.

Guided writing – as with guided reading, these writing sessions should be to teach pupils to write independently. The work will normally be linked to reading, and will often flow from work in the whole-class shared writing session. These sessions should also be used to meet specific objectives and focus on specific aspects of the writing process, rather than on the completion of a single piece of work. Often, these teaching inputs can be followed through during independent work in subsequent sessions. For example, pupils might focus on:

- planning a piece of writing to be continued independently later;
- composing a letter;
- expanding or contracting a text to elaborate, summarise, etc.;
- constructing complex sentences;
- connecting points together in an argument;
- editing work into paragraphs, headings, etc. for clarity and presentation.

Independent work – this happens at the same time as the guided group work. The class needs to be carefully managed and the pupils well trained so that they are clear about what they should be doing and do not interrupt the teacher. There are many forms of organisation ranging from a carousel of ability groups, with a rotation of activities for each group, to completely individual work eg a whole-class writing activity derived from an earlier shared writing session. Independent tasks should cover a wide range of objectives including:

- independent reading and writing;
- phonic and spelling investigations and practice;
- comprehension work;
- note-making;
- reviewing and evaluating;
- proofreading and editing;
- vocabulary extension and dictionary work;
- handwriting practice;
- practice and investigations in grammar, punctuation and sentence construction;
- preparing presentations for the class.

Pupils should be trained not to interrupt the teacher and there should be sufficient resources and alternative strategies for them to fall back on if they get stuck. They should also understand the importance of independence for literacy, and how to use their own resources to solve problems and bring tasks to successful conclusions.

Final 10 minutes – plenary session with the whole class.
The final plenary is at least as important as the other parts of the lesson. It is not a time for clearing up and should be clearly signalled as a separate session when the whole class is brought together. It should be used to:

- enable the teacher to spread ideas, re-emphasise teaching points, clarify misconceptions and develop new teaching points;
- enable pupils to reflect upon and explain what they have learned and to clarify their thinking;
- enable pupils to revise and practise new skills acquired in an earlier part of the lesson;
- develop an atmosphere of constructive criticism and provide feed back and encouragement to pupils;
- provide opportunities for the teacher to monitor and assess the work of some of the pupils;
- provide opportunities for pupils to present and discuss key issues in their work.

(Department for Education and Employment 1998, p. 9; available at http://www.standards.dfee.gov.uk/literacy/publications/ ?pub_id=135&atcl_id=2104&top_id=327)

It has been argued that this document emphasised 'interactive whole-class' teaching from the school-improvement literature which had been espoused by influential members of the Literacy Task Force (Mroz *et al.* 2000). This emphasis on a particular form of whole-class teaching also raises issues associated with the need for individualised teaching in order to address literacy difficulties, which, as we have seen, was recognised by the Literacy Task Force's 1997 report in the section related to children who have special needs in literacy (Literacy Task Force 1997, paras 105–6). It is not surprising, therefore, that *The Framework for Teaching* was criticised for its lack of acknowledgement of individualised instruction, and therefore a failure to cater successfully for children with special educational needs (Byers 1999).

Specific strategies for teaching reading

The Framework advocates the pedagogical approaches of 'guided reading', 'shared writing', 'guided writing', and 'the plenary' and 'independent work'. The detailed account of these approaches given on pages 11–13 indicates that all of these approaches are to be carried out as whole-class or group activities apart from the 'independent work' which students undertake on their own while the teacher is supervising the 'guided group work'. This emphasis on whole-class teaching and group activities is supported by Beard in his outline of the rationale underpinning the literacy hour:

> It stresses the importance of direct teaching by the use of the whole class teaching in the first half of the literacy hour and the maintenance of direct teaching with groups, and then with the class again in the second half. It also maximises effective learning time by ensuring that there is a dedicated literacy hour each day, with further suggestions on providing additional literacy learning time during the rest of the day, including extended writing, reading to the class and independent reading.
>
> (Beard 1999, p. 8–9)

Implications of an 'interactive whole-class teaching approach' for children with special needs

The lack of individualised programmes in the Framework has given rise to concerns about the ability of the Framework to address the particular, complex individual needs of those students who may experience severe difficulties in learning to read. Mroz *et al.* (2000) outline concerns about whether or not 'interactive whole-class teaching' differs from 'whole-class teaching'. This summary of the research surrounding interactive whole-class teaching appears to lend weight to Byers' (1999) concerns about the ability of this form of teaching to address the needs of all students, particularly those who may experience difficulties in their literacy development.

> Following criticism that there was little research-based evidence to support the strategy, particularly concerning the progression prescribed, the teaching methods advocated and the detailed format of the hour, a report was commissioned to review the evidence (Beard, 1999). In the report it is acknowledged that the emphasis

on direct, 'whole class interactive teaching', with termly objectives and dedicated literacy time, draws mainly upon the school effectiveness and school improvement literature. Citing the work of Reynolds & Farrell (1996) it suggests that 'interactive whole class teaching' will play a vital role in raising literacy standards. However, as Galton *et al.* (1999) argue, the concept of interactive whole class teaching is not well defined and little evidence has been presented to show it differs from traditional whole class teaching. Nor does it explicitly appear in the framework document ([Department for Education and Employment] 1998). According to Reynolds (1998) it encompasses rapid question and answer sessions when teachers are finding out what pupils know, followed by 'teacher-led discussion' involving slower paced, 'higher order' questioning designed to promote higher levels of pupil thinking.

Studies of classroom discourse from North America and the UK (see for example Mehan, 1979; Dillon, 1994; Edwards & Westgate, 1994; Hardman & Williamson, 1998), however, show that whole class teaching across all stages of schooling is dominated by what Tharp & Gallimore (1988) call the 'recitation script'. In its prototypical form teacher-led recitation consists of three moves: an initiation, usually in the form of a teacher question; a response, in which a student attempts to answer the question; a follow-up move, in which the teacher provides some form of feedback (very often in the form of an evaluation) to the pupil's response. This three part exchange structure, as revealed by Sinclair & Coulthard (1992), is therefore seen as a 'teaching technology' which is particularly prevalent in directive forms of teaching and consists of a series of unrelated teacher questions that require convergent factual answers and pupil display of (presumably) known information. Recitation questioning therefore seeks predictable correct answers and only rarely are teachers' questions used to assist pupils to more complete or elaborated ideas.

(Mroz *et al.* 2000, pp. 379–80)

Views of literacy and models of reading implicit in the English NLS

The NLS is underpinned by the notion of basic and functional literacy. The literacy hour, with its whole-class approach, focuses on raising standards through changing pedagogical approaches at the classroom, school and national level, rather than on providing a programme which adjusts to the needs of individual teachers. The NLS has arisen in the context of increasing public concern over declining standards in basic and functional literacy in England and other Western countries, such as Australasia and the United States. This concern over 'literacy standards' has led policy-makers to adopt 'literacy benchmarks' and led to the nationwide introduction of pedagogical approaches such as the literacy hour, which are designed to raise 'literacy'. These policies can, therefore, be seen to be underpinned by a concept of 'basic literacy', because they view literacy as a set of technical skills which can be quantified and evaluated.

The Literacy Task Force report, which gave rise to the NLS, and other policy documents produced since New Labour came to power in 1997 also argue that raising literacy benchmarks will enable a country to compete successfully with other nations and competitors in international markets. The emphasis here is on functional literacy, as the key concern is to meet vocational and occupational needs rather than the fulfilment and development of the individual. The emphasis is primarily on economic needs, and the failure to become literate is seen to imply the hindering of national as well as individual social development.

An examination of the Framework for the NLS reveals that its model for the teaching of reading as described in Section 1 of the NLS is 'a series of searchlights' each of which 'sheds light on the text', as outlined in this excerpt:

> All teachers know that pupils become successful readers by learning to use a range of strategies to get at the meaning of a text. This principle is at the heart of the National Curriculum for English and has formed the basis of successful literacy teaching for many years. The range of strategies can be depicted as a series of searchlights, each of which sheds light on the text. Successful readers use as many of these strategies as possible.
>
> Most teachers know about all these, but have often been over-cautious about the teaching of phonics – sounds and spelling. It is vital that pupils are taught to use these word level strategies effectively. Research evidence shows that pupils do not learn to distinguish between the different sounds of words simply by being exposed to books. They need to be taught to do this. When they begin to read, most pupils tend to see words as images, with a particular shape and pattern. They tend not to understand that words are made up of letters used in particular combinations that correspond with spoken sounds. It is essential that pupils are taught these basic decoding and spelling skills from the outset.

When pupils read familiar and predictable texts, they can easily become over-reliant on their knowledge of context and grammar. They may pay too little attention to how words sound and how they are spelt. But if pupils cannot decode individual words through their knowledge of sounds and spellings, they find it difficult to get at the meaning of more complex, less familiar texts. They are likely to have problems in dealing with more extended texts and information books used across the curriculum at Key Stage 2, and with spelling. As they learn these basic decoding skills they should also be taught to check their reading for sense by reference to the grammar and meaning of the text. This helps them to identify and correct their reading errors. At Key Stage 1, there should be a strong and systematic emphasis on the teaching of phonics and other word level skills.

Pupils should be taught to:

- discriminate between the separate sounds in words;
- learn the letters and letter combinations most commonly used to spell those sounds;
- read words by sounding out and blending their separate parts;
- write words by combining the spelling patterns of their sounds.

In the early stages, pupils should have a carefully balanced programme of guided reading from books of graded difficulty, matched to their independent reading levels. These guided reading books should have a cumulative vocabulary, sensible grammatical structure and a lively and interesting content. Through shared reading, pupils should also be given a rich experience of more challenging texts.

(Department for Education and Employment 1998, p. 3–4)

In the outline of the 'searchlight approach', and in the diagram given on page 4 of the document, there appears to be a recognition of the need to teach both skills to decode phonics and strategies to use the context to make sense of the text. In the two pages dedicated to explaining this approach, however, most of the space is given to explaining the need to teach phonics, as it was felt that 'most teachers know about these but have been over-cautious about the teaching of phonics – sounds and spellings'. Riley analyses this 'searchlight model' and its characteristics which attempt to combine and interrelate 'decoding skills' with 'meaning-making approaches':

Structure of the Framework for Teaching

The organizational basis of the Framework for Teaching adopts a subdivision of written language which reflects its visual features. The word/sentence/text level distinctions provide points of reference for teachers and pupils to use when talking about the processes and products of literacy experiences and learning. These organizational distinctions are compatible with models used by Crystal (1995) and Perera (1979). The teaching objectives of the content at the three levels encompass:

1   the word which is the smallest free-standing unit of linguistic description – the teaching at this level covers vocabulary which includes phonics and spelling and also morphology (the within-word rules, e.g. prefixes, roots, suffixes);
2   the sentence is the largest linguistic unit within which grammatical rules systematically operate – the teaching at this level covers between-word rules (syntax) and punctuation (the main function of punctuation being to separate units of grammar or to indicate contractions, e.g. Jeni's ...)
3   a text (or discourse) is a collection of one or more sentences that display a coherent theme and with the appropriate cohesion. The teaching at this level deals with the structures of discourse as well as with both the comprehension and composition of the meanings which texts can convey.

(Riley 2001, p. 33)

Implications of the NLS for pupils with special educational needs

Byers outlines what he considered to be the effectiveness and relevance of the NLS in the extract below. This is taken from a paper which was written in 1999, the year after the publication of the NLS:

On first acquaintance, The National Literacy Strategy Framework for Teaching ([Department for Education and Employment 1988]), launched ready for implementation in the autumn of 1998, did not seem tailor-made for pupils with special educational needs. In fact, eager readers were hard-pressed to find any references within the document to pupils experiencing difficulties with learning, despite the fact that the Government had made the following commitment a few months earlier in its Green Paper, Excellence for All

Children: Meeting Special Educational Needs ([Department for Education and Employment] 1997):
'We will ensure that all our policies and programmes for schools are explicit about their implications for children with special educational needs' (p. 12).
The authors of the Framework for Teaching ... did helpfully suggest that groups of pupils should be 'differentiated by ability' during the Literacy Hour and that individual pupils should be 'well-trained' so that they 'do not interrupt' (p. 12) during literacy-focused activities, but these ideas did not wholly satisfy anxious teachers working with pupils with a range of difficulties.

Requests for more detailed guidance on provision for pupils with special educational needs elicited a range of responses. It was emphasised that the full implementation of the National Literacy Strategy would not be a statutory requirement, but the clear expectation that all pupils should be included was expressed. Staff working with pupils with special educational needs were encouraged to use their professional judgement in approaching the teaching of the Literacy Hour but were not given any detailed sense of the flexibilities that were available and acceptable. Indeed, phrases such as 'equality of expectation' and the notion of 'a line drawn under low achievement' were bandied about and observers began to get a real sense of the tension that existed in the hearts and minds of the National Literacy Strategy's proponents, between the raising of standards for all (so that 80 per cent of 11-year-olds would indeed reach Level 4 or above in the Key Stage 2 English tests in 2002) and the desire to include all pupils, even those with the most complex needs.

(Byers, 1999, pp. 8–9)

The NLS approach for pupils with difficulties in literacy

After the NLS was introduced in England and Wales a number of initiatives were designed to support pupils who have difficulties in literacy. These initiatives are examples of what is seen to be the 'second wave' of strategies to address literacy standards and literacy provision. The first wave, the literacy hour/English lesson (KS3) is designed to meet the needs of 80 per cent of the pupil population, and strategies such as Additional Literacy Support (ALS) are aimed at supporting the next 15 per cent of the population via focused group teaching.

The ALS consists of a programmatic package of materials which was introduced 'to help pupils in Key Stage 2 who had not been taught the literacy hour from the beginning of primary school' and 'would now benefit from further support'. The materials, strategies and lesson plans provided in this package of materials were designed to 'be delivered during the group session of the Literacy Hour by teachers and classroom assistants' for these children 'who would not otherwise receive additional support in this area' (Michael Barber, writing in the Foreword, Department for Education and Employment 1999). This explanation, which was reprinted in all four of the ALS modules, indicated that the ALS was, initially, largely regarded as an interim measure.

The conception of ALS and associated booster programmes as being an interim measure while the NLS came into effect throughout the school system is reflected in the funding arrangements. This initial conception of a limited funding period appears to be supported by the statement that ALS was allocated to local education authorities (LEAs) in 1999–2000 by taking into account pupil's achievements in Key Stage 1 tests (see, for example, Department for Education and Employment 1999, p. 5), and the statement that the support for ALS was a £22.5 million Standards Fund grant to LEAs for the same two-year period (see for example DfEE, 1999, p. 5). A booster programme funded by an annual £42 million was introduced along with the ALS. This booster programme was designed to provide extra literacy and numeracy classes for Year 6 pupils in need of assistance, and provided extra training in writing. In 2000 an additional £9.5 million pilot was initiated in order to address the relative lack of progress in literacy development in the early years of secondary education. This pilot involved 200 schools which were aiming to raise literacy standards at Key Stage 3. Estelle Morris, Secretary of State for Education, argued that the pilot was to build on successful attainment at Key Stage 2, as they wanted all pupils to build on the benefits of the primary strategies from the moment they enter secondary schools (Department for Education and Employment 2000d). Such statements indicate that when they were initially introduced these initiatives were intended to support the NLS whole-class and group-based strategies and models of teaching literacy rather than implement specific individualised programmes for special needs children as had been outlined in the Literacy Task Force report.

Beard had noted that the NLS would enable schools to focus their energies on learning about, and then intelligently implementing, well-designed models rather than evolving their own strategies in a way that meant 'every school had to reinvent the wheel' (Beard

1999, p. 7). The ALS continued this philosophy of providing an externally developed programme of what Barber called a 'practical, high quality teaching programme' (Michael Barber, writing in Department for Education and Employment 2000c, p. 4). It was also noted that such a set of 'structured teaching materials' would enable the additional 2,000 full-time equivalent classroom assistants who would be in place by 2002 to deliver the ALS in schools in 'partnership with teachers'. As this set of ALS-structured materials only covered twenty-four weeks it was acknowledged that teachers would have to consider what needs to be revisited and what future support pupils may need in 'order to master literacy skills by the end of primary school' (*ibid.*, p. 13).

The ALS materials took the form of four separate modules and had components related to strategies identified in the Framework as the key components of the literacy hour. The modules covered phonics, reading (guided and supported) and writing (shared and supported).

During 2000 and 2001 training modules particularly related to supporting pupils who were achieving 'below expectations' and who had special needs were released. These included:

* *The National Literacy Strategy: Supporting Pupils with Special Educational Needs in the Literacy Hour* (Department for Education and Employment 2000b);
* *Supporting Pupils Working Significantly Below Age-related Expectations* (Department for Education and Employment 2000c).

As in the ALS materials discussed above, both of these publications examine 'issues and strategies' involving including pupils with special educational needs within the literacy hour. The first of these publications states that there will be a series of three publications in this area. These will look at the issues and strategies involved in including pupils with special needs in the literacy hour, and it is implied that the rationale for these publications is linked to the 'inclusion statement from the National Curriculum 2000'. The content of the first publication, as in the publications discussed earlier, is clearly linked to the format and strategies employed within the literacy hour. For example, the first sections covered in this publication are 'strategies for inclusion', 'transition points' and 'independent, group and guided work'.

The second publication aims to guide participants through a range of management issues, starting from the diagnosis of results and then moving through the stages of supporting change. This publication focuses on meeting curricular targets for literacy and its implementation in individual schools. Guidance for supporting head teachers and teachers running summer schools and literacy support programmes was also released. This included:

- *Making Links: Guidance for Summer Schools and Year 7 Catch-up Programmes* (Department for Education and Employment 2000a);
- *Making Links: Guidance for Summer Schools and Year 7 Support Programmes* (Department for Education and Employment 2001)

These documents give guidance on how to manage and successfully raise standards for children aged 11–14 through the additional support given in summer schools, which have been run since April 2001. The target group is '11 year olds who have reached Level 3 in the Key Stage 2 National Curriculum Tests and who have the potential, with the support of an intensive programme over two or three weeks, to raise their performance to (or towards) level 4'. Teachers are advised to 'use the features of the Literacy Hour' when teaching pupils in the summer school and also to use lessons from one of the six Literacy Progress Units, which form the basis of the Year 7 catch-up programme (Department for Education and Employment 2001, p. 26).

The curriculum guidelines in Scotland

In comparison with the English National Curriculum context, a number of commentators have noted that the following issues are particularly pertinent in relation to literacy policy in the Scottish context:

- child-centredness versus the need for conformity in response to concerns voiced over falling standards;
- the demands for focus and conformity from prescribed guidelines versus flexibility afforded to teachers and LEAs;
- reductionist, skills-based approaches versus whole-language meaning-based approaches.

Curriculum and Assessment 5–14 Programme: challenges to child-centredness

In Scotland, the Scottish Curriculum and Assessment 5–14 Programme is an essential part of the initiative that has been promoted by Her

Majesty's Inspectorate (HMI) as upholding and maintaining the standard of pupils' achievements in Scottish schools. A Scottish Education Department consultative paper enjoined the inspectorate to 'pay particular attention in their inspection of schools in the extent to which schools and education authorities have had regard to the national curricular policies' (SED 1987, p. 7).

F.R. Adams notes two 'linked but distinctive' origins of the Scottish Curriculum and Assessment 5–14 Programme (1999, p. 349). The first was the same political circumstances operating upon central government as in England and Wales. When the Secretary of State's Consultative Paper (SED 1987) was introduced it was described as 'a shift in policy-making style in Scotland from debate followed by consensus to consultation followed by imposition' (Roger, in Hartley and Roger 1990, p. 1). The other origin of the 5–14 programme was 'the professional imperatives which have led to the curriculum for the primary and early secondary stages being more explicitly formulated than in the previous forty years' (F.R. Adams 1999, p. 349).

Adams traces these imperatives back to the Scottish Education Department's policy document *The Primary School in Scotland* (SED 1965), commonly known as The Memorandum. This policy document set out principles of primary education which 'started with the needs and was responsive to the interests of the child, was appropriate to age, aptitude and ability and which saw pupils as active in their own learning' (F.R. Adams 1999, pp. 350–1). Adams comments that The Memorandum emphasised discussion and consultation, and did not prescribe teaching methods or subject material, privileging variety over conformity. Through its very lack of prescription it 'challenged teachers, and perhaps more significantly headteachers, to reconceptualise their approaches to the education of primary school age children. This is in stark contrast to the prescription of the present centralised arrangements' (*ibid.*, p. 351).

Provision of guidance to schools on the curriculum was left to the education authorities. However, a report (SED 1971) on progress made in advice given to teachers on implementing The Memorandum by education authorities, colleges of education and head teachers suggested wide variability in the quality and impact of that advice. There appeared to be evidence that 'few headteachers [had] done anything to formulate a policy for the planned implementation of the approaches suggested by the Primary Memorandum' (*ibid.*, p. 16, quoted in Adams 1999, p. 350).

A policy for the '90s: concern over falling standards

There followed a number of reports from the Scottish Education Office offering guidance to schools on developing particular aspects of the curriculum. These culminated in a consultative paper, *Curriculum and Assessment in Scotland. A Policy for the '90s* (SED 1987), which identified apparent poor practice in school curricular policy-making, lack of continuity in the school curriculum, lack of challenge for pupils in Years 6 and 7 of primary schools, lack of consistency in the practice of assessment of pupils' achievement, and poor communication with parents (F.R. Adams 1999, p. 352). The resultant detailed guidelines on the aims, objectives and content of each curriculum area for pupils aged from 5 to 14 years aimed at curriculum continuity and coherence in pupil assessment at national and school level.

However, these guidelines were presented as sets of instructions without any overt rationale or philosophy. This is particularly problematic if we consider the differences between the philosophies underpinning curricula in the primary and secondary sectors. The lack of rationale underlying time allocations in the guidelines has increased the overall lack of coherence between the primary and secondary sector. An example of this is the way in which the notion of balance and breadth of the curriculum at primary level, set against the existing structured timetable of the early years of secondary schooling, has been expressed in *Structure and Balance of the Curriculum 5–14* (SOED 1993) simply in terms of the percentages of time recommended for each curriculum area. For example, in the area of mathematics 15 per cent of time is recommended at primary level, and 10 per cent at secondary 1 and 2. In the area of language, the percentages of time are 15 per cent and 20 per cent, respectively, and in the expressive arts they are 15 per cent and 0 per cent. It is recommended that 20 per cent of time at both primary and secondary levels should be used to achieve flexibility.

Despite these centrally prescribed guidelines, there is evidence that as a result of the early-intervention initiative some LEAs have already chosen to be more flexible, and have emphasised early literacy acquisition and offered schools in their areas guidance which differs from the Scottish Office Education and Industry Department (SOEID) guidelines.

English Language 5–14 (SOEID 1991): flexibility versus conformity

Although 15 per cent of the primary timetable is allocated to the teaching and learning of the English language, as Ellis and Friel (1999) note, 'many schools allocate a proportion of the 20 per cent flexibility factor to English Language'. There are four overall attainment outcomes – listening, talking, reading and writing – while within each outcome 'strands' outline the specific aspects of learning and assume progression through a series of attainment targets. For example, the strands within the 'reading' outcome include 'reading for information', 'reading for enjoyment', 'reading to reflect the writer's ideas and craft', 'awareness of genre', 'reading aloud' and 'knowledge about language' (Ellis and Friel 1999, p. 360). The guidelines also include an emphasis on 'diversity of language and culture; knowledge about language, and Scottish culture' (*ibid.*).

Implementation of the guidelines and standards of attainment are monitored by HMI through inspection reports of individual schools. Parents and teachers opposed national tests for all children in Years 4 and 7 in primary schools when they were introduced in 1991. The programme was changed following the withdrawal by parents of two-thirds of the pupils who were eligible for the test trials (Ellis and Friel 1999). Currently all children take national tests in reading and writing when, in the opinion of their own teacher, they are ready to be tested at the next level of attainment. Reading tests are administered and marked by the teachers, and chosen from a given bank of items by the teacher who administers and marks them. Writing tests are designed to reflect classroom practice and marked against national criteria.

English Language 5–14: reductionist skills-based approach versus whole-language

Ellis and Friel identify a number of concerns in relation to the 5–14 guidelines for English:

> *English Language 5–14* presented a welcome return to a focus on the content of language teaching. However, unless sympathetically interpreted, it presents a skills-based and reductionist model of language which does not capture and promote the rich model that underpins best practice in Scottish schools. Although language as a vehicle for learning is recognised in the rationale of the

Guidelines, this is rarely exemplified in the strands, targets and programmes of study. In practice, the Guidelines promote the view that language is used to communicate and transmit knowledge but only rarely and incidentally to explore and re-frame ideas to create new understandings.

If the Guidelines were used merely to audit and highlight gaps in teachers' planning this would not be a serious problem. However, teachers are invited to use the 5–14 strands and targets as a basis for planning their teaching programmes. Thus, whilst the 5–14 framework undoubtedly supports weaker teachers, it can divert average teachers from developing more complex models and simply frustrate the best.

The pressure for accountability created in the wake of the Guidelines ensured that talking and listening was taken seriously and aspects of attainment have improved. However, it may also have led to an over-emphasis on forward planning and on schemes and worksheets to ensure coverage. This could encourage fragmentation of the curriculum and limit the opportunities for children (and teachers) to follow their interests and devote time to understanding things in depth. It is an approach which sits uneasily with the notion of a flexible curriculum in which teaching input is adapted to meet the children's needs and produce language work that is intellectually and emotionally satisfying. In reading, where teachers were already working to reasonably sophisticated models, this is less of a problem than in writing, where it militates against a shift in the teaching focus from the product to the writer.

The early intervention projects may encourage headteachers to see that promoting effective language teaching is a cornerstone of quality management and leadership. This would help to create a climate in which good management is seen as helping teachers acquire the knowledge to use the Guidelines appropriately and creatively rather than mechanistically. Staff development initiatives of the future may be driven by this need to develop a rich and broad understanding of language, teaching and learning.

(Ellis and Friel 1999, pp. 363–4)

Ellis and Friel report on initiatives currently being taken to address particular concerns:

AAP [Assessment of Achievement Programme] and HMI reports indicate that reading standards have remained stable over the past ten years and the debate about teaching reading is less politicised than in England. However, the proportion of children leaving school with unsatisfactory reading competence has not declined and the variable success rates of schools with apparently similar catchment areas hints at hidden under-achievement. In 1997, education authorities were given SOEID funding for 3-year early intervention projects. These should prompt healthy debate on literacy; baseline assessment; pedagogical knowledge; staff development and policy into practice. Most authorities appear to be targeting schools in social priority areas, which may limit the range of issues addressed and the projects' ability to promote wide reflection and change. ...

Traditionally, nurseries have not been associated with, and were frequently discouraged from, literacy teaching. Research showing the link between pre-school knowledge of literacy and school success has caused a re-examination of this policy and recent advice (SOEID, 1997) promotes knowledge of print, stories, phonological awareness and home–school links.

(Ellis and Friel 1999, pp. 362–3)

Comparison of flexibility within the national curricula in England, Wales, Northern Ireland and Scotland

In order to compare the literacy curricula operating in England and Scotland it is useful to return to an issue discussed above, that of flexibility. This issue is particularly significant because the flexibility of interpretation of literacy frameworks and guidelines by teachers, schools and LEAs may be seen as one of the clearest identifiable differences between these literacy curricula.

F.R. Adams has compared the process of developing national curriculum guidance across the UK:

The 5–14 Programme applies only in Scotland while the National Curriculum is the statutory guidance on the curriculum in England, Wales and N. Ireland. There have been marked similarities in the process of production of the national curriculum guidance in Scotland and England. In both cases subject based working groups were set up. In Scotland each Review and Development Group (RDG) produced its 'ideal' curriculum, the sum of which is a vastly complex map of the primary curriculum, while in England syllabus overload resulted from curriculum decisions made by isolated working groups using the strategy of include everything and cross-reference among curricular areas. Other similarities include the confidentiality of the working groups (lack of public access to minutes and working papers), tight time scales, tokenistic consultation and rapid introduction to schools.

Despite these similarities, there has been a fundamental difference in the overt political influence that has been exerted on the development in England arising from Conservative policies and the active involvement in curriculum policy of various political figures from Sir Keith Joseph through to Kenneth Baker. However, the lack of clear and consistent approaches to the content and assessment of the National Curriculum between 1988 and 1993 led to the review carried out by Sir Ron Dearing and the School Curriculum and Assessment Authority (SCAA) which resulted in the so-called 'slimmed down' National Curriculum which was to be implemented from August 1995.

Adams goes on to identify key differences in the English and Scottish national curricula:

The 1995 English National Curriculum differs principally from the Scottish 5–14 Curriculum and Assessment Programme in its separation of the primary stages from the secondary through presentation of curriculum at Key Stages 1 and 2 (5–7 years and 7–11 years) for primary and Key Stages 3 and 4 (11–14 years and 14–16 years) for secondary. While 5–14 occupies the longest timespan in the Scottish curriculum made up of 5–14 years (PI–S2), which includes attainment targets grouped at five levels of progression A–E, followed by Standard Grade (S3/S4) and Higher Still (S4–S6), there is no overall perception of the Scottish curriculum as a seamless garment from PI to S4. Differences also exist in the curriculum coverage at each of the stages. The 5–14 Programme covers all of the areas of the curriculum and does not prescribe a core curriculum, while the English National Curriculum labels English, mathematics and science as core subjects with technology, history, geography, art, music and PE as foundation subjects at Key Stages 1 and 2 and, with the addition of a modern language, as foundation at Key Stage 3. There are similarities in terminology within both structures but differences in interpretation of the terms used.

(F.R. Adams 1999, pp. 353–4)

The similarities in terminology in particular can mask important conceptual differences between the two national curricula. For example, in the National Curriculum in England and Wales 'attainment target' means the standard of pupil performance that is expected, but in the 9–14 Programme in Scotland it refers to a specific learning goal. In England and Wales 'programmes of study' indicate what should be taught to pupils, but in Scotland they constitute advice offered about appropriate forms of learning and teaching.

The nature of the 'programmes of study' in the two educational systems is of particular interest. The English National Curriculum is prescriptive in what is to be taught at each Key Stage, while the Scottish 5–14 Programme expects schools to use the information and advice contained in the 5–14 guidelines to review existing school programmes and to develop appropriate responses. The different underpinning structures and emphases of these two national curricula have in turn influenced the subsequent development of recent literacy curricula policies, pedagogy and research programmes at a local level in these two regions.

In England the overall literacy strategy operates within the curriculum guidelines of the English National Curriculum. The prescriptive approach in the National Curriculum can be seen to have given rise to an equally prescriptive approach in the NLS. This can be seen as a method of ensuring uniformity of delivery and the consistent meeting of statutory requirements within a 'very sound framework for teachers to plan within'. Furthermore consistency and uniformity is reinforced by OFSTED inspection:

> The literacy framework ensures that the statutory requirements for reading and writing in the national curriculum for English are covered and also contributes substantially to the development of speaking and listening. It unites the important skills of reading and writing and also includes some elements for the development of speaking and listening. The framework for teaching sets out objectives for pupils from reception to year 6 to enable them to become fully literate. It also gives guidance on the literacy hour in which this teaching will take place. And on page 3 of the framework it indicates what fully literate people should be able to do ...
>
> ... It's always the focus of an OFSTED inspection that inspectors must report on how literacy is delivered in that school. Every OFSTED inspector has had to undertake additional training. Although it's not statutory if schools choose not to adopt the

strategy they have to demonstrate why they haven't done that and what approach they've taken as an alternative ...

Some entire literacy lessons must be observed and, when evaluating literacy, inspectors must look for a thorough knowledge of the national literacy strategy framework for teaching, secure understanding of the literacy skills to be taught, secure knowledge and understanding of the literacy skills pupils will need. A good understanding of how to teach phonics, good use of the national literacy objectives in planning and a balance between word, sentence and text-level work ...

... During any OFSTED inspection the inspectors must comment on the delivery of literacy in that school. And all OFSTED inspectors have been required to undertake additional training in the inspection of the literacy hour. But as you're aware, it's not statutory but if schools choose not to adopt statutory they have to demonstrate why they haven't.

(interview with an OFSTED Inspector for Open University E801 course materials, 2002)

The prescriptive approach of the NLS can also be seen to provide uniformity and consistency in training and support, as well as in teaching strategies for teachers endeavouring to address difficulties in literacy:

In my view, each element of the hour enables opportunities for both of those and there's been a whole range of training across the country which will help teachers to do both of those things during the literacy hour. There's also been additional training for teaching assistants, again to help them identify how they might best help teachers to support pupils with learning difficulties in the hour. The whole ethos of the strategy has been to promote opportunities for inclusion and there are certain elements of the hour which are very helpful for such students; for example, the structure and routine offer clear predictability in what is going to happen, provide opportunities for focus teaching, opportunities for practice, reinforcement, and in group and individual activities teachers could use specific programmes which are appropriate to individual needs. It's important that teachers are aware of the specific objects ... for pupils that have IEP's [individual educational plan] and that those are reflected in every element of the literacy hour.

One of the things that pupils with literacy difficulties have benefited from are the clear expectations and rules which were introduced when the literacy strategy was first introduced into schools. Basically it's about good teaching, varied teaching styles which reflect individual learning needs. It's also about good classroom management, which ensures that there are structured activities again to meet learning needs. It's about effective differentiation, appropriate resources and also ensuring that the ethos of the classroom is appropriate and that there are strong interpersonal relationships too.

(interview with an OFSTED Inspector for Open University E801 course materials, 2002)

While the approaches and evaluation of the NLS are prescribed, it is argued that there is room to tailor these guidelines to the needs of individual children who may experience difficulties in their literacy development:

[A]ll schools, every year, are allocated monies through what we call the standards fund. And in recent years there's been increased flexibility in the way in which schools use those monies. Although there are certain specific areas that they must demonstrate that they are usin g the monies for, there are a lot of opportunities for schools to be flexible and use that money for staff training and for resources to meet the individual needs of pupils in their school. Also, schools can use their own budget to purchase resources, training, equipment etc., which again would address the individual needs of pupils in their school.

(interview with an OFSTED Inspector for Open University E801 course materials, 2002)

Whereas the English National Curriculum and the NLS stress prescription and uniformity, the Scottish 5–14 Programme expects schools to use the information and advice contained in the 5–14 guidelines to review existing school programmes and to develop appropriate responses. This ability to develop appropriate responses has been carried over into the Scottish literacy curriculum and assessment procedures:

First of all, it's important to note that there is no national literacy strategy within Scotland. There are, however, curriculum guidelines in all the key curriculum areas. They date from around about 1991. Not only do they apply to the curriculum, there are individual documents on assessment, and on reporting, so the key curriculum area here is entitled English language, and there are national 5–14 guidelines; 5–14 are the ages of the children who are involved, starting in primary 1 at age 5 and going through to secondary 2 at age 14. There are four key strands in English language – listening, talking, reading and writing – and this was the first time in 1991 that key areas like listening and talking were opened up to Scottish teachers. The rationale behind the guidelines is that it's an approach to learning and teaching, and that it's unlikely to be a radical departure from a lot of good practice that currently exists or was existing at the time. Within each curriculum area there are then broad attainment outcomes, and attainment targets which apply to each level. There are now six levels in 5–14, starting at Level A, which we would anticipate for youngsters in primary 1, 2 and 3. So Level A should be attained by nearly all pupils in primaries 1 to 3. And this goes through to, for example, Level D [which] should be attained by some pupils in primary 5 or primary 6, or even earlier, but certainly by most in Primary 7. Now, interestingly, this kind of use of attainment targets is now judged, not in terms of national testing or with national figures, but is dependent on when the teacher decides that a youngster should be presented for the test; but we can use the national testing information to collate how successful a school is in attaining its own attainment targets and obviously can set targets for the school within that system.

(interview with a Head of Early and Special Education in a Scottish LEA for Open University E801 course materials, 2002)

The ability of teachers to develop appropriate responses within the 5–14 Programme has been given further impetus by the development of the EPSEN document (HM Inspectors of Schools 1994), which has emphasised the motivation of learners and has enabled LEA administrators to link the raising of attainments to social inclusion, which in turn can facilitate community links and early-years literacy development:

[A] document called the EPSEN document ... was effective provision for special educational needs, and that's now been confirmed in a Scottish-wide manual of good practice for special educational needs. So this process should be consistent in authorities across Scotland. ... We have to take the 5–14 guidelines in English language and interpret them as far as we can in terms of literacy. In this we've been helped by the government, who have established new initiatives on early intervention and on developing literacy within an early-intervention programme. ... Within our early-literacy strategy there is a vision statement that requires pupil achievement or attainment to improve from the levels previously reported. There's an emphasis on heightening the motivation of learners and on value-added mechanisms to monitor the progress of youngsters. So the rationale is that literacy, for us, includes attention to reading, writing, within a context of real-world situations. A lot of our literacy is based on research evidence which confirms that the concentration of attention in the early years has positive benefits as a child grows older, and with this quality early experience a difference can be made to all children. So we don't just see it in terms of raising attainment; we also see it in terms of social inclusion. We also think that an early-literacy strategy is required to avoid failure and to help each individual achieve their true potential.

(interview with a Head of Early and Special Education in a Scottish LEA for Open University E801 course materials, 2002)

Early intervention in literacy difficulties is also facilitated by funds made available through the excellence fund:

The Council has obviously always made funding available for the Education Department, and the Education Department has leeway within its budget to move money to certain key priority areas, so literacy is seen as a key priority area. However, the Scottish Executive Education Department have made an excellence fund available to schools. The excellence fund totals £100 million per annum across Scotland, and is dedicated to ... different programmes. These range from alternatives to exclusion, to the National Grid for Learning, but crucially one of the programmes is entitled early intervention.

The government makes £13 million available across Scotland for early-intervention programmes, and East Renfrewshire gets £255,000 per annum from the excellence fund for early intervention. Now we use this money to give every school within the authority additional help in terms of early literacy co-ordinators. The first stage of the programme looked at schools in our most deprived areas, the second phase of the programme gave additional help to schools who had specific problems of social inclusion, and the third phase gave a little bit extra to every school within the authority. We would anticipate that early literacy co-ordinators should be working with their colleagues in primary 1 and primary 2 on early literacy, early number, and in 'working with parents' activities.

(interview with a Head of Early and Special Education in a Scottish LEA for Open University E801 course materials, 2002)

The Scottish approach to the curriculum has led to a range of regional and individual literacy curriculum developments and programmes designed to address literacy difficulties that differ markedly from the nationally co-ordinated developments initiated under the NLS. In Scotland it has been possible for individual LEAs to devolve a large percentage of their budgets to schools, creating a situation where schools and teachers working with LEAs have the flexibility to respond to local needs and design crucial, strategic aims to suit particular populations and geographic areas. The lack of a tightly prescribed literacy curriculum enables different schools to undertake different programmes of study within different timetables which will reflect the 5–14 guidelines on English language. This flexibility has had an impact on assessment, evaluation and the involvement of teachers and other professionals at the local and classroom level in research:

I am no expert in the English Literacy Strategy, but it does appear to me that there's certainly more flexibility in Scotland. We provide guidelines; we don't provide a straitjacket. We also appear to have a system which is less based on assessment, or a different type of assessment. Our assessments are more informal and more observational, and more to do with a screening procedure as opposed to assessment procedure. We also appear to have put in more opportunities for interaction between pupils and parents, between pupils and teachers, between teachers and authorities, between teachers and parents. We also appear in Scotland to have a better reaction to local circumstances, local monitoring and local evaluation, and I think crucially also we seem to be basing a lot of what we're doing on research, on new research, and on small pieces of research in a different local authority that's informing a lot of what we do. For example, in East Renfrewshire recently we've undertaken research on gender, and research on raising expectations. So the essential difference I think, though, is still one of flexibility.

(interview with a Head of Early and Special Education in a Scottish LEA, for Open University E801 course materials, 2002)

The literacy curriculum in the Republic of Ireland

The Republic of Ireland has a 'three-pronged', 'broad-based' literacy strategy (interview with Shiel for Open University E801 course materials, 2002). This strategy was developed through consultation with teachers, representatives from the colleges of education and the universities in the late 1990s. The three aspects of this strategy consist of revised English language curriculum guidelines, a learning support service with revised learning support guidelines, and special education provision for students with specific learning difficulties, including dyslexia. As in Scotland, there is a lot of flexibility, particularly at the classroom level, in how teachers might meet the needs of children with learning difficulties, and provision is underpinned by a notion of developing individual programmes to meet children's needs.

Like the Scottish curriculum, the general curriculum in the Republic of Ireland allows a considerable amount of flexibility and choice in teaching method and assessment. As in Scotland, the funding and inspection system also allows flexibility. A research fellow specialising in the assessment of reading and literacy at the Educational Research Centre at St Patrick's College in Dublin explains the key characteristics of this flexibility in relation to the literacy curriculum thus:

> I think that in terms of presenting the general curriculum, schools have an awful lot of flexibility. The curriculum tends not to be very prescriptive, the guidelines are general and broad, and schools are expected to devise programmes that meet their individual needs. Part of this involves putting together a system to assess students who are experiencing reading difficulties. Again, it's up to the school to decide how specifically this might be done. Whether, for example, in the infant classes checklists will be used by the teachers to identify those students who are having difficulty with very basic skills from an early age. It might involve the administration of group tests, individual tests or the use of curriculum profiles, for example. There's a variety of directions that schools can go in terms of specifying what might be done. Schools also have flexibility at another level ... schools are allocated a learning support teacher in the first instance, it's on the basis of need. They've established that forty students have a need for learning support services, in either reading, mathematics or both. In general schools retain that learning support in the long term, even

if their actual level of need changes. So schools have some flexibility, in terms of how they allocate that teacher's time. ...

... What also happens in some schools is that the principal teacher may decide to increase the pupil–teacher ratio in individual classes, so that an extra teacher can be allocated to working with students with learning difficulties, and reading difficulties in particular. ...

... There's a little bit of flexibility in funding as well, particularly in the last two or three years, with the implementation of the revised curriculum. Schools have been given funding to organise in-career training days for teachers. These training days are an addition to the sort of general in-career development that's provided to all teachers by national co-ordinators. The schools are provided with funding, to bring in experts to the school, to work with the school, on developing school-level plans for dealing with reading difficulties. So there are different layers of funding.

(interview with a research fellow from the Republic of Ireland for
Open University E801 course materials, 2002)

The speaker notes that, while the curriculum guidelines do not specifically address issues associated with supporting students who have difficulties in literacy, the focus within these guidelines is on meeting the needs of the average student. However, there is provision for catering for students who have difficulties in literacy within the learning support guidelines. Shiel sees these guidelines as providing a structure that enables schools to have a large degree of autonomy in developing their literacy curricula, as they facilitate the development of individual school-level plans for the teaching of literacy and meeting the needs of students with reading difficulties.

[T]he learning support guidelines are very specific in terms of what teachers, schools indeed, can do to better meet the needs of students with reading difficulties. In the first instance it suggested that all students be assessed using group level tests of achievement and reading, and that as a result of this initial assessment ... students with very low scores are identified and considered for additional testing. The whole process is done very closely in consultation with the student's class teachers and the learning support teacher. In some instances the class teacher conducts a comprehensive diagnostic assessment, in order to identify the student's specific areas of strength and weakness. The learning support guidelines provide specific suggestions for what that diagnostic assessment might consist of, and mentions several areas – for example phonological awareness, word recognition skills, reading fluency, reading comprehension, and so forth. As a result of the assessment, a decision is made based on input from class teachers, the student's parents and the learning support teacher as to whether the student would benefit from learning support, and what form that might take.

There is now a move towards developing an individual learning programme for each student who is to be in receipt of learning support, so that all the partners, parents, class teachers and the learning support teacher, are very clear on what the student's learning programme consists of, and how they might be involved in presenting that programme. There's a general guideline that learning support services be provided to students with achievement scores in reading … at or below the 10 per cent level on the standardised test. Schools vary in terms of how this guideline is implemented.

In disadvantaged schools, one might have more than 10 per cent of the students experiencing learning difficulties. In other schools, the percentage might be considerably less, and the school may decide to provide learning support to students in reading, and also in mathematics. So we have variation from school to school in terms of what type of provision this made and how intensive that provision might be.

> (interview with a research fellow from the Republic of Ireland for
> Open University E801 course materials, 2002)

While, as we have seen, the inspection system in England requires evidence that the specifics of the NLS have been adhered to, inspectors in the Republic of Ireland tend to take a broader view. They examine a variety of classroom programmes and additional literacy programmes. They also examine the literacy programme within the overall functioning of the school:

> [T]echnically inspectors are duty-bound to look at the entire literacy programme, [also] to look at classroom programmes in literacy, and also to look at any additional programmes, such as remedial learning support and special education provision. At this point in time, school-level inspections occur every four to five years. These tend to be comprehensive, and look at every aspect of the school's functioning. The literacy programme obviously is a

very important aspect of that, but it's not the only aspect. Issues such as school organisation, which ... ultimately may have an impact on the effectiveness of literacy programmes, are also looked at. The school-level inspections tend to focus on the overall functioning of the school, rather than what individual teachers are doing in their classrooms. In general inspectors look very closely at the work of individual teachers, and those teachers are in the initial probationary period, when they're in the first year or two years of teaching. After that, the focus of inspections tends to be much broader from the individual teacher's point of view.

(interview with a research fellow from the Republic of Ireland for Open University E801 course materials, 2002)

Conclusion

This chapter has explored the concepts and models underpinning the NLS in England and Wales and the implications for addressing the difficulties pupils can experience in becoming literate. There is apparent contradiction and fragmentation in recent government initiatives in relation to pupils who experience difficulties in literacy development. In England, for example, the tensions between inclusion and exclusion in literacy education are increasingly being pressured by the drives for teachers and schools to achieve acceptable literacy standards and standardised programmes for literacy achievement. The contradiction between raising the range of 'normal' development and catering for more extreme individual differences is still being played out in recent English-based curriculum policies, for example that relating to inclusion and that relating to the English NLS. The contrast between these two policies illustrates the tensions between the desire to cater for individuality and difference and the desire for inclusion and equal access that are inherent in national education systems and mainstream schooling. There is an obvious contradiction between the rhetoric in the General Statement of Inclusion (GSI) (Qualifications and Curriculum Authority 2000), which incorporates a recognition of the need to be responsive to the diversity of individual learning needs, and the pedagogy of the NLS as reflected in the literacy hour. As we have noted, a prescriptive approach to teaching outlined in the formal *Framework for Teaching* of the literacy hour sets out the pedagogical principles which teachers are expected to follow in their classroom practice. The pedagogical element within the literacy hour emphasises whole-class teaching of skills, and reduces the potential for developing differentiated curricula aimed at meeting the diversity of pupils' learning needs and family and social situations through a flexible approach to pedagogies and learning environments of the sort advocated by Piotrowski and Reason (2000).

This chapter has also contrasted the NLS approach with approaches and literacy curriculum initiatives in Scotland and the Republic of Ireland. In examining these models and approaches it is clear that there are variations in the extent to which current curriculum-based literacy initiatives and approaches in the UK emphasise child-centredness versus conformity to literacy standards, prescribed compared to flexible guidelines, phonics and skills-based versus whole-language approaches. As well as these differences in underpinning concepts of literacy and models of reading, there are also variations in the way individualised versus whole-class and group approaches are used. These regional and national differences in literacy curricula are also linked to funding differences, the use and integration of different programmes, and the formation of differing structures, teaching methods and ways of organising facilities to cater for students who experience difficulties with literacy.

Chapter 8

Assessment of barriers to literacy development

Introduction

Identifying and evaluating the barriers faced by pupils who experience difficulties in literacy is the key to addressing such difficulties. However, the whole issue of assessment is complex. Methods of evaluation, like the literacy strategies and programmes discussed in previous chapters, are underpinned by particular views of literacy and particular views of the source of the difficulty experienced by the student.

As Wearmouth and Reid (2002) note, a number of developments in the area of assessment of 'special' learning needs, including the needs of those who experience difficulties in literacy development, have been apparent in recent years. For example, there has been a growing awareness that assessment is highly political and that any kind of assessment rests on particular assumptions about the nature of human beings, human learning and achievement. Different ways of assessing individual differences carry different implications at a personal, school and also societal level. Furthermore, in order to plan appropriate teaching approaches there has been a move away from the solely 'medical' model of difficulties in learning to one that recognises the interactive nature of difficulties in learning (interview with Wedell for Open University E831 course materials, 2000) and to a broader concept of what specially 'needs' to be done to address such difficulties. In this 'interactive model' the barriers to pupils' learning arise as a result of the interaction between the characteristics of the student and what is offered through the pedagogy and supporting resources. This changed emphasis leads to a broader conception of what needs to be assessed beyond the characteristics of the individual pupil. Cognitive assessment of individuals and the assessment of attributes such as metacognitive awareness are clearly very important, but so is the question of how to assess the learning environment in which pupils acquire literacy. In addition, as a result of legal and moral considerations (Gersch 2001) and the implications of current models of learning which emphasise the agency of the learner (Vygotsky 1987), the issue of pupil self-advocacy has assumed an increasing significance. Lastly, the right of parents and carers to be actively engaged in the decision-making processes with regard to their children's education has been given explicit recognition in many countries, for example in England in the *Parents' Charter* (Department for Education and Science 1991).

Assumptions underlying the assessment of 'special' learning needs and their consequences

Underlying particular forms of assessment of pupils' 'special' learning needs are assumptions which carry particular consequences. Some of these assumptions intrinsically contradict notions of inclusion. For example, available resources have often dictated the provision made for individual pupils (Cline 1992). To determine eligibility for additional services, special educational provision depends on norm-referenced assessment designed to enable a comparison of individual pupils' achievement with that of peers, and therefore to identify some students who are 'different'. Standardised tests reflect innate views of intelligence to allow for a statistical definition of need. The underlying assumption disallows a view of the brain as having the potential to achieve anything given the right learning opportunities. Norm-referenced tests of ability and attainment have the potential selectively to decide how issues should be discussed and solutions should be proposed (Broadfoot 1996). The influence of psychometric thinking leads to deterministic views of ability and achievement which limit teachers' expectations of certain students and restrict developments in assessment.

In addition, Tomlinson (1988) argues that, for some students – for example those from the poor or lower class – lowered expectations can lead to a reproduction in society of underprivileged groups. Special educational arrangements appear to be the result of rational and pragmatic assessment of pupils. This, however, is questionable. Tomlinson considers that the function that such schools serve in maintaining the power of the privileged and dominant groups in society is a powerful determining factor in explaining its existence:

> The ideas of critical theorists can suggest that the stupidity or dullness of some individuals or social groups is not necessarily self-evident or 'true'. Acquiring the label and being treated as 'less-able' is likely to be the result of complex social economic and political judgements and considerations.
>
> (Tomlinson 1988, p. 45)

Some commentators feel that schools can help to reproduce the pattern of control and subordination within society which is linked to the economic context (Bourdieu and Passeron, 1973). There is a contradiction between the rhetoric of education to promote equality and the reality that the system of education functions to continue to put the children of underprivileged groups into powerless positions in society. 'Success' and 'failure' are not objective 'givens', but social categories whose labels serve the vested interests of dominant, powerful groups in society. The reason why children fail in the education system is explicable as a function of the social, economic and political status quo, which requires some children to fail in the education system. This explains individual pupil failure as much as the supposition of a deficit in the child.

In a post-industrial age where achievements assessed through reading and writing are the prerequisites for obtaining a job with a salary above subsistence level, education is in crisis. The inability of illiterate citizens to find well-paid employment is legitimised if they have been labelled in advance through special education: 'Special education reproduces and controls lower-status groups, and legitimates their life-long treatment, but is, in itself, an acceptable, legitimating, humane development' (Tomlinson 1988, p. 49). Low scores on standardised tests of reading and spelling allow schools to 'blame' the child and also absolve themselves of responsibility for that child's progress in school: 'The way the black and working-class Johnnys with reading problems are dealt with will usually ensure that they are reproduced into the low-status sections of society' (*ibid.*, p. 55). In the case of dyslexia, however, some groups of parents, seen from this perspective, have found a way of removing the stigma of failure from their children and of normalising them: 'The dyslexia label says to parents, "Your child has a problem, but your child is normal," and, by its nature, it discriminates against other disability labels' (Booth and Goodey 1996, p. 5).

To some extent the views of Tomlinson, Bourdieu and Passeron outlined here – in relation to the marginalisation of particular groups of children in schools and later in society as adults – reflect some of the concerns of the discussion of equity issues in previous chapters. On the one hand identification and labelling may bring additional resources, but on the other they may serve to perpetuate the existing social order.

Assessing students' difficulties in literacy development

Whatever the ideological arguments, the fact remains that some pupils experience difficulties in literacy development. It is important to tease out factors contributing to this difficulty if those pupils are to acquire literacy, one of the fundamentals of a cultural toolkit (Bruner 1986). However, identification of what needs to be measured to assess literacy development in terms of the characteristics of the individual student is not simple (Beard 1990). Certain aspects of the process of literacy acquisition – for example awareness of sound–letter correspondence during the process of reading – can be broken down into measurable skills, quantified and assessed. It is much more problematic to conceptualise how to assess and quantify others – for example assessment of the enjoyment of reading or of the finer points of the appreciation of text. Crucial to what professionals are trying to achieve in relation to the individual student are the distinctions in kind and purpose of different types of assessment.

In a number of countries in the UK and the Republic of Ireland, individual education plans (IEPs) or Records or individual profiles have become major tools in planning programmes of study for individual students who experience difficulty in literacy acquisition. In drawing up these individual programmes the assessment of students is both formative and summative. The assessment process can therefore be regarded as both formative and summative. Formative assessment is an ongoing process that can be carried out both formally and informally to collect information and evidence about individual pupils' learning and then used to plan the next step in their learning. In contrast, summative assessment is intended to provide a global picture of the learner's progress to date, without the addition of too much detail. Harlen and James (1997) explore these issues in more depth, arguing that formative and summative assessments are different in kind as well as in purpose. For example, formative assessment:

- is concerned with information about ideas and skills that can be developed in certain activities, and so is important for everyday teaching;

- is carried out by teachers;
- combines criterion-referenced and pupil-referenced (ipsative) techniques;
- can be contradictory as pupils' performance can be inconsistent – such differences can be used diagnostically;
- places more significance on validity and usefulness than on reliability;
- should involve the student.

Summative assessment, on the other hand:

- is concerned with the bigger picture of progress, across several activities perhaps;
- takes place at certain intervals when achievement has to be recorded;
- may involve a combination of different types of assessment, for example the measurement of individual pupil progression in learning against public criteria;
- requires a high degree of reliability, and therefore involves some quality assurance procedures.

As we have noted above, if difficulties in literacy learning can be seen as a function of the interaction between within-child and environmental factors, then it follows that there must be an assessment of the student's characteristics and also of the learning environment. Identification of what needs to be measured in terms of literacy development at the level of the individual student is not simple (Beard 1990). Some aspects of the process of literacy acquisition – for example awareness of sound–letter correspondence during the process of reading – can be broken down into measurable objectives. However, other aspects – for example assessment of enjoyment of reading or of the finer points of the comprehension and appreciation of text – is much more problematic.

Formative assessment

A useful way of collecting formative assessment data to inform teaching is classroom observation. Observational assessment is contextualised and can be used flexibly to ensure that the data obtained is the type of information required. It is important, however, that the observer recognises the drawbacks of observational assessment, in that often it only provides a snapshot of the student unless it is implemented in different contexts over time. Nevertheless, this type of assessment can be particularly useful for students with difficulties in literacy development, since, as Dockrell and McShane (1993) note, some standardised tests may not provide the kind of diagnostic information which is needed to develop a teaching programme.

We have noted above other problematic issues associated with the way in which the use of normative testing procedures may result in the marginalisation and exclusion of students who experience difficulty in learning. If assessment systems are to be inclusive, then, as Dockrell and McShane note, they need to be criterion based, using task analysis, and result in such measures as developmental profiles and checklists to 'help identify whether or not an individual possesses some particular skill or competence ... allow for the analysis of error patterns ... provide a clear indication of what a child can do and [indicate] what skills should be taught next' (*ibid*, p. 35).

Dynamic assessment

Whilst standardised assessment can provide information on the student's level of attainments in comparison with peers, it is static, since it emphasises what the learner can do unaided but does not provide information about the learner's thinking processes. Dynamic assessment, which focuses on the process of learning, can identify the strategies being used by the learner and can also be a useful teaching tool through the development of concepts and ideas during teacher/student interaction. An example of this is reciprocal teaching, which consists of a dialogue between teacher and student 'for the purpose of jointly constructing the meaning of text' (Palincsar and Brown 1984, p. 19) and can therefore combine assessment and teaching.

Assessing understanding through retelling

Assessment instruments are often based on restrictive criteria, examining what the student may be expected to know, often at a textual level. However, they may ignore other rich sources of information which can inform the teacher about the student's thinking, both cognitive and affective, and provide suggestions for teaching. Ulmer and Timothy (2001) developed an alternative assessment framework based on retelling as an instructional and assessment tool. This indicated that informative assessment of a student's comprehension could take place by using criteria relating to how the student retells a story. Ulmer and Timothy suggested the following criteria: textual – what the student remembered; cognitive – how the student processed the information; and affective – how the student felt about the text. Their two-year study indicated that 100 per cent of the teachers in the study assessed for textual information, only 31 per cent looked for cognitive indicators, and 25 per cent for affective. Yet the teachers who did go beyond the textual found rich information. Some examples of information provided by the teachers indicated that assessing beyond the textual level in relation to the use of the retelling method could provide evidence of the student's 'creative side', and they discovered that students could go 'beyond the expectations when given the opportunity'. This is a good example of how looking for alternative means of assessing can link with the student's understandings of text, and promote and develop thinking.

Metacognitive assessment

It is argued that dyslexic students may have difficulty with the metacognitive aspects of learning (Tunmer and Chapman 1996); that is, being consciously aware of, and being able to control and monitor, their own thinking processes. This implies that they need to be shown how to learn and that the connections and relationships between different learning tasks need to be highlighted. The emphasis should not necessarily be on the content or the product of learning, but on the process – that is, how learning takes place. Metacognition has an important role in learning, and can help to develop thinking skills and enhance an awareness of the learning process and the utilisation of effective strategies when learning new material. The teacher then has an instrumental role to play in assessing metacognitive awareness and supporting its development (Peer and Reid 2001). This can be done by asking the student some fundamental questions, and also through observing the learning behaviour of students such as that indicated in the example below. When tackling a new task does the student demonstrate self-assessment by asking questions such as:

- Have I done this before?
- How did I tackle it?
- What did I find easy?
- What was difficult?

- Why did I find it easy or difficult?
- What did I learn?
- What do I have to do to accomplish this task?
- How should I tackle it?
- Should I tackle it the same way as before?

The use of metacognitive strategies can help to develop reading comprehension and expressive writing skills.

Wray (1994) provides a description of some of the skills shown by good readers which can provide a good example of metacognitive awareness in reading. Good readers, according to Wray, usually:

- generate questions while they read;
- monitor and resolve comprehension problems;
- utilise mental images as they read;
- re-read when necessary;
- self-correct if an error has been made when reading.

These factors can help to ensure that the reader has a clear picture of the purpose of reading and an understanding of the text about to be read. There is considerable evidence to suggest that pre-reading discussion can enhance reading fluency and understanding.

Learning can be seen as a cognitive process. One perspective on formative assessment is to focus on the information processing cycle involved in literacy learning and to consider potential metacognitive aspects and learning styles within the information-processing cycle. The stages of the information-processing cycle essentially relate to input, cognition and output. Students may experience difficulties at any or each stage. Some suggestions of practical strategies for dealing with each of these stages are as follows:

- At the input stage it may be important to present information in small units, test at frequent intervals to ensure that over-learning is used, and vary this, using a range of materials, and present key points at the initial stage of learning new material.
- At the cognition stage, encourage organisational strategies, organise new material to be learned into meaningful chunks or categories at each of the stages of the information-processing cycle, relate information to previous knowledge to ensure that concepts are clear and the information can be placed into a learning framework by the learner, use specific memory strategies

such as mind-mapping and mnemonics, and assess learning frequently.

- At the output stage, use headings and subheadings in written work to help provide a structure, encourage the use of summaries in order to identify the key points and assess learning at each point.

Assessment of learning styles

Closely related to the notion of formative assessment is that of the assessment of learning styles. Clearly it is crucial to have some idea of the way in which a student learns in order to plan most effectively for future teaching. In addition to metacognitive approaches, consideration of learning styles can be useful for both assessment and teaching of students who experience difficulties in literacy development, and it can provide them with an opportunity to focus on their own understandings of text and utilise their own strengths in learning to access text across the curriculum. Currently there are over one hundred instruments specially designed to identify individual learning styles. Some were developed to evaluate particular aspects of learning associated most commonly with a cognitive perspective on learning, such as preference for visual, auditory, tactile or kinaesthetic input (Grinder 1991). Many approaches attempt to identify how individuals process information in terms of its input, memory and expressive functions (Witkin and Goodenough 1981). Riding and Raynor (1998) conceptualise cognitive style as a constraint which includes basic aspects of an individual's psychology such as feeling (affect), doing (behaviour) and knowing (cognition). The individual's cognitive style relates to how these factors are structured and organised. A few theorists emphasise the body's role in learning and promote cross-lateral movement in the hope of integrating the left and right brain hemispheric activity (Dennison and Dennison 1989).

Others included broader factors assumed to influence learning, and primarily associated with personality issues such as intuition, active experimentation and reflection (Gregorc 1982; Kolb 1984; G. Lawrence 1993; McCarthy 1987). Kolb's Learning Style Inventory is a derivative of Jung's psychological types combined with Piaget's emphasis on assimilation and accommodation, Lewin's action research model and Dewey's purposeful, experiential learning. Kolb's twelve-item inventory yields four types of learners: divergers, assimilators, convergers and accommodators.

The Dunn and Dunn approach (Dunn *et al.* 1996), Learning Styles Inventory, contains 104 items that produce a profile of learning-style preferences in five domains (environmental, emotional, sociological, physiological and psychological) and twenty-one elements across those domains. These domains and elements include environmental (sound, light, temperature, design); emotional (motivation, persistence, responsibility, structure); sociological (learning by self, in pairs, with peers, in a team, with an adult); physiological (perceptual preference, food and drink intake, time of day, mobility); and psychological (global or analytic preferences, impulsive and reflective).

Given (1998) constructed a new model of learning styles derived from some key elements of other models. This model consists of emotional learning (the need to be motivated by one's own interests), social learning (the need to belong to a compatible group), cognitive learning (the need to know what age-mates know), physical learning (the need to do and be actively involved in learning) and reflective learning (the need to experiment and explore to find what circumstances work best for new learning).

The use of a framework for collecting observational data can yield considerable information and can complement the results from more formal assessment. Observational assessment can be diagnostic, because it is flexible, adaptable and can be used in natural settings with interactive activities. Reid and Given (1999) have developed such a framework – the Interactive Observational Style Identification (IOSI). A summary of this (quoted in Wearmouth and Reid 2002) is included in the Appendices.

Summative assessment

One of the key issues in relation to summative assessment is the selection of assessment strategies. Amongst the types of strategies often used to assess within-child factors related to poor achievement in literacy are normative, psychometric tests. Norm-referenced tests, for example standardised reading and spelling scores, imply measurement and the use of standardised instruments, and typically produce measures in terms of ranks. It might be important to gain some understanding of the way in which a learner's comprehension of text, or their ability to read individual words or to spell accurately, compares with that of peers. We have already seen some of the problems associated with normative assessment in relation both to notions of inclusion and to the model of learning that it assumes. Whilst this type of assessment has some uses, particularly for supporting requests for additional resourcing of individual students' learning needs, it must be treated with some caution as the results of such norm based-tests can be misinterpreted and misused. They cannot, for example, indicate appropriate intervention strategies, because 'the scores do not provide details of what the child knows or does not know, nor do they elucidate the processes that are involved in the child's difficulty' (Dockrell and McShane 1993, p. 34).

One of the controversial issues that face professionals dealing with students who experience difficulties in literacy is the question of what needs to be assessed if a student is to be described as 'dyslexic'. Reason (2002) notes that the 'working definition' of dyslexia requires that three factors should be assessed:

- the level of fluent and accurate word recognition and/or spelling;
- the extent to which appropriate learning opportunities have been provided for a student;
- the extent to which progress in literacy acquisition has been the result of additional instruction and the persistence of difficulties in literacy development.

This does not mean, however, that only these factors require assessment. Reason comments on the importance of a comprehensive view of the difficulties that a student may experience in literacy development and therefore the comprehensive nature of the assessment that needs to be undertaken. One of Reason's most important conclusions about the purpose of assessment is that it is useful only insofar as it points to action which will benefit the individual student with literacy difficulties.

Below is an extract from an educational psychologist's report which gives a summative assessment of the cognitive difficulties experienced by a learner considered to experience specific difficulties in learning (SPLD) of a dyslexic nature. The definition of SPLD used by the psychologist who carried out this particular assessment is included in the Appendices:

Referral and background information

X was referred in order to assess her intellectual potential, her academic functioning and her educational needs.

X is the youngest of four siblings. Mrs Y had a normal pregnancy and delivery and X was born at full term. Mrs Y informed me that X reached her developmental milestones within the expected parameters. She also informed me that X suffered from ear infections at the infant stage and showed early indicators of clumsiness.

X attended two schools in xxxxx for a very short period (one to three months). Her family then moved to xxxxx where X was enrolled at S School. At the Year 3 level, X transferred to xxxxx. She is currently in Year 5. X receives tutoring every week (arranged privately by her parents).

Current tests administered

The Wechsler Intelligence Scale for Children – Third Edition UK (WISC–III UK), the Wechsler Individual Achievement Tests (WIAT) of Basic Reading, Spelling and Numerical Operations, the Monroe Sherman Tests of Reading, Writing and Motor Speed, and the Aston Index Test of Laterality.

Test behaviour

X presented as a lively, well-motivated girl who appeared to enjoy the assessment situation. She informed me that she experienced difficulties with spelling and mathematics.

X was under-confident in the area of verbal expression and often gave what would be termed a 'one-point' response to many of the verbal items of the WISC–III UK. However, when she was encouraged to elaborate her answers, she was usually able to give a more mature reply.

Results

Cognitive

WISC–III UK

On the Wechsler Intelligence Scale for Children – Third Edition UK, X obtained a Verbal and Full Scale score in the *average* range of intelligence and a Performance score in the *low average* range.

Strengths

Relative to her performance on the verbally oriented subtests of the WISC–III UK, a significant strength for X (in the *high average* range of intelligence) was on a measure of her ability to interpret social situations and make practical judgements.

She scored in the *average* range (63rd %ile) on a measure of her general fund of information and in the *average* range (37th %ile) on measures of her ability to express ideas verbally, her concrete and abstract reasoning skills and numerical reasoning.

Weaknesses

Relative to her performance on the verbal tasks of the WISC–III UK, a significant weakness for X (in the *low average* range) was on a measure of her ability to recall auditory information in proper sequence and detail.

Performance scale (nonverbal)

Strengths

X had no significant strengths relative to her performance on the visual perceptual tasks of the WISC–III UK. She scored in the *average* range of intelligence (50th %ile) on measures of her nonverbal reasoning skills when dealing with social situations and visual alertness to environmental detail, and in the *average* range (37th %ile) on a measure of part–whole integration (analysis of the parts into the whole).

X scored in the low *average* range (16th %ile) on a measure of her ability to duplicate abstract designs ('timed' paper and pencil task).

Weaknesses

Relative to her performance on the visual perceptual tasks of the WISC–III UK, significant weaknesses for X (in the *low average* range – 9th %ile) were on 'timed' paper and pencil tasks measuring her speed of information processing and spatial planning and spatial visualisation and nonverbal concept formation – analysis of the whole into its component parts (low range).

Aston Index

Laterality: X has indicators of mixed laterality. Mixed laterality can cause difficulties in both the language arts area (in terms of orientation and visual tracking often resulting in reversals, loss of place and lack of fluency in reading) and in the math/science area (in terms of directionality, orientation, spatial awareness and visual discrimination). Difficulties may also occur in the area of hand, eye and body co-ordination.

Educational data
The Wechsler Individual Achievement Tests

Basic reading: 8 years 0 months. Percentile (relationship to chronological age): 10.
Basic spelling: 8 years 6 months. Percentile: 25.
Numerical operations: 8 years 9 months. Percentile: 25.

Monroe Sherman
Writing speed: below the 10th percentile.
Motor speed: below the 10th percentile.
Reading speed: below the 10th percentile.

Summary

The results of the WISC–III UK indicate that X is a girl of *average* cognitive ability who is presenting with Specific *Learning Difficulties*. Factor analysis indicates that her verbal comprehension skills are significantly stronger than her visual perceptual skills. A difference of this magnitude can result in information-processing difficulties. For example:

- the individual attempts to process all information in the stronger mode, which widens the skills gap even further;
- extreme frustration and dichotomy is caused by, in X's case, the *comparative* ease with which she processes verbal information in comparison to completing visual perceptual organisation tasks;
- blocking (learning and emotional) can result as a consequence of the above.

Her performance on the tasks which require short-term auditory memory processing was weak. These subtests measure the mental manipulation of information in short-term auditory memory and suggest a comparative weakness in this form of processing. When short-term memory tasks were presented visually, X's processing skills were stronger but remained an area of weakness relative to her cognitive potential.

X scored in the *high average* range of intelligence on the subtest of Comprehension. This item measures the ability to process and understand incoming verbal information. There was, however, a significant difference between her performance on this item and the subtests of Vocabulary and Similarities, which measure the ability to express ideas verbally and verbal reasoning. I would suggest that X's comparative weakness in this latter area, in conjunction with her weakness with the organisation and sequencing of information, is significant in terms of the way she finds it difficult to formulate her thought processes verbally, and consequently organise her written work effectively and systematically.

This difference between the ability to process incoming, in comparison to outgoing, information has been found to cause frustration difficulties within the individual as s/he is unable to justify the level of his/her understanding and knowledge through the medium of spoken and consequently written language. It must be noted, however, that X's under-confidence over her performance (see Test behaviour) will also adversely affect her spoken and written language in terms of maturity of thought, content and creativity.

It was noted that X experienced difficulties with visual motor integration tasks requiring fine motor, visual tracking, spatial analysis, visual discrimination and speed of information processing.

To sum up, X's performance within the learning situation will be affected by an interaction between the following factors:

- a significant difference between her verbal comprehension abiities and her visual perceptual organisation skills;
- a significant weakness in the area of short-term memory processing;
- a weakness with the sequencing and organisation of information;
- a significant difference in her ability to process incoming, in comparison to outgoing, information (weaker verbal expression);
- mixed laterality;
- difficulties with visual motor integration tasks requiring fine motor, visual tracking, spatial analysis, visual discrimination and speed of information processing abilities;
- under-confidence in her intellectual and academic abilities as a result of the above.

As the academic results indicate, in terms of the teaching/learning situation, this has resulted in X's *inability to reach an academic level which is commensurate with her intellectual potential.*

(Head teacher and educational psychologist of the Red Rose School, 2001)

It is noteworthy that this report highlights the cognitive aspects of the assessment, and the principal test used is one of the closed tests which can be used by educational psychologists. The cognitive aspects of the assessment would, of course, need to be considered alongside the contextual factors relating to the whole school literacy curriculum and the views of parents. However, one of the strengths of adopting a cognitive view is that it provides the assessment tools to pinpoint particular cognitive weaknesses. When the results of these tests are used critically and carefully they can lead to a clear identification of strategies and programmes designed to address the cognitive difficulties that have been identified.

Assessment for planning particular interventions

Assessment of students' difficulties in literacy is not necessarily generic. One cannot assume that assessment is transferable across reading programmes. Particular types of screening and assessment procedures are inextricably tied to the conceptual underpinnings of the particular reading programmes with which they are linked. Two examples of assessment for the purpose of planning particular interventions are those of the Observation Survey assessment for Reading Recovery and the early screening procedures for dyslexia that have been adopted as an integral part of the early literacy-intervention initiative in East Renfrewshire (Crombie, unpublished). Reading Recovery appears to be rooted broadly in a meaning-based approach to the process of reading. The Observation Survey is designed for use with young pupils who have experience of one year of formal schooling only and therefore might be considered as in the early stages of literacy acquisition. Elements of this survey therefore assess aspects of literacy acquisition such as concepts of print and the usefulness of strategies employed in reading, writing and spelling, as well as knowledge of letter sounds. An example of this can be seen in the following extract taken from an assessment carried out in 2001 using the Observation Survey with 'B', a pupil in an inner-city school:

Cues used or neglected in reading: Errors all showed use of meaning and structure but only one also included visual information.
Concepts about print: B understood that print contains message, 1–1 matching and directionality. He couldn't identify changes in letter, word or line order. He understood first and last relating to the story but not to a word. He couldn't identify a word.

Useful strategies on text: B can use meaning and structure. He understands that print contains message. He knows where to start reading, which way to go and the return sweep. He can match 1–1 (CAPS).

Problem strategies on text: Errors showed him making very little use of visual information in his reading. He can lose 1–1 matching if the structure of the book alters.

Useful strategies with letters: B can name 24 letters giving an alphabet response. He also knows 12 sounds.

Problem strategies with letters: He could only link one letter to a sound in the dictation task. He showed confusions between letters of similar shape but different orientation. He mixes upper and lower case letters in the same word.

Useful strategies with words: B could read two words and write four words when tested. He showed some awareness of analogy.

Problem strategies with words: He could not identify a 'word' when asked (CAPS). His invented spelling showed consistency: AK/is AK/his. When writing he often used one letter to represent a word.

Summary: B is reading at Dictated Text level. He can use meaning and structure when reading but generally ignores the visual information. He is not secure with matching 1–1. He can read and write a small number of words but doesn't have the strategies needed to spell unknown words. He can link less than a quarter of letters with their sound. He shows letter confusions both when reading letters: eg w/m n/u and writing words: wnw/mum. He is consistent with these errors.

(Open University E801 course materials; adapted from Clay 1993)

Crombie's screening procedure has a different focus from that for Reading Recovery. This difference rests on the conceptual underpinning of the models of reading. Crombie's assessment is designed to identify indicators of a broad range of difficulties associated with the whole dyslexia syndrome, for example gross motor control. The assessments are also designed to be used at different stages. Crombie's nursery screening procedure is intended for use during the pre-school year. The purpose of this procedure is clear:

> While the profiles will give useful information on individual children's progress in all areas, it is intended that they should also flag up any children who show signs of specific problems. While they may give an indication of children who may be at risk of later problems in learning, they may merely indicate that a child is slightly

slower to develop certain specific skills or is less mature than the rest of the group. It is important not to write too much into this information at this stage. When considering children's profiles, account needs to be taken of children who may be up to a year younger than the rest of the pre-school year group. Some seeming problems may only be due to immaturity. What is important is that *targeted intervention is put in place for these children and the children are then monitored to ensure progress is made and maintained.*

(Crombie, unpublished)

The profile of attributes falls into five main areas and the profile sheets are set out under the five main areas of learning:

- emotional, personal and social development;
- communication and language;
- knowledge and understanding of the world;
- expressive and aesthetic development;
- physical development and movement.

Emotional, personal and social development

It is important to consider the strengths of the child, for it is the strengths that will guide future planning, and will provide channels to motivate and encourage children to develop areas which may be immature for their age or slow to develop.

Home background and culture – that is, social, background and cultural factors – are liable to have a strong influence on emotional, personal and social development as are the role models that have influenced the child during the early years.

Communication and language

The pre-school year is generally a period of rapid growth in language, with increasing awareness of sounds and words, and how they can be used to produce certain effects. Poor phonological skills at this stage, and a lack of awareness of rhyme and rhythm may indicate possible later difficulties in learning to read and write. However, it may be that these skills have not been encouraged at home, perhaps because of cultural or social factors, or in the case of a bilingual child it may be that the skills have been developed in the home language but not in English.

Most children enjoy stories. For those who have difficulty in listening at this stage, there may be indications of later attention problems. Children who are abnormally restless or inattentive may perhaps have an intolerance to certain foods or soft drinks. This is, however, a good stage to discuss possible food allergies with parents, and ask them to observe if there is a pattern to these types of problem following eating or drinking specific foods or drinks. Some children may simply be very active and need to move about a lot.

Memory is important to many language and communication skills. Children who are unable to remember more than two items of information, for instance, may appear as disobedient when in fact they are unable to remember what it is they were told to do. They may be unable to remember the sequence of events in a story or may be unable to repeat the syllables that make up a polysyllabic word.

A child's ability to put the message across can be assessed during any language activity, when the child is reporting on what they wish to do later etc. The child can be encouraged to retell a familiar story to observe awareness of sequence. Speech too can be informally observed to ensure that the child has sufficient control of the tongue and lips to reproduce sounds in the desired way. This can be assessed when the child is telling or retelling a story. Polysyllabic words and nonsense words can be repeated as part of a game. The teacher should note any problems with pronunciation.

Children who enjoy books, and have good awareness of print and phonology will have a distinct advantage when they start more formal learning of reading and writing.

Knowledge and understanding of the world

Children who have a natural curiosity for the world around them will investigate and learn with a small amount of guidance. Others will require considerable assistance to know what to do. Early activities of categorisation and naming will provide basic skills which will be required in dealing with mathematics and other areas of the curriculum. Ordering and sequencing can be observed through activities using concrete materials. Visual perceptual skills can be built through manipulating shapes and seeing how they fit, or do not fit, together.

Young children learn best through the interaction of all their senses. Children who are naturally able to take advantage of multi-sensory learning will require only a little help, but some may need to be presented with material to be remembered by use of all their channels of learning – hearing, seeing, touching, saying, acting out, singing, and the sense of smell where this is appropriate.

The emphasis in the number sections should be of a practical nature using many sorting toys, beads, linking elephants, etc. More able children will be observed through their problem-solving abilities and their strategies for coping with unusual or different situations.

There are numerous opportunities for assessing children's language and understanding of the concepts.

Expressive and aesthetic development

It is interesting to note if the child is able to represent by painting, drawing or modelling the objects they tell you they are representing.

An awareness of rhythm will facilitate language learning and will help in music. Provide opportunities for children who are weak in tapping out a rhythm or keeping reasonable time to music to gain expertise in these areas. Activity singing games and simple dance sequences will identify those children whose short-term memory is likely to inhibit their learning. They will also identify those children who seem likely to be able to develop a high level of expertise in these areas.

Physical development and movement

Movement can be assessed by the teacher as part of the routine observations made within the classroom situation. It is important that children build skills of co-ordination at this early stage to aid fine motor skills such as writing. While giving exercises which will generally aid co-ordination, it is important that the children should also have exercises which involve the use of both sides of the body in co-ordination.

Balance has been found to be an important ability for learning. Children who are poor at balance tasks while doing something else are likely to encounter other learning problems. Ask children to balance on one foot while they say the names of their group, or recite a rhyme such as Jack and Jill.

Pay particular attention to children whose toes turn in as they walk, or whose arms flap when they start to run or skip.

Ask the child to hold up their right hand. Then throw a ball or beanbag so that the child has to catch it in the right hand.

> Try also to investigate if the child can catch with their right
> hand when they have to cross the mid-line, i.e. when you
> throw the beanbag or ball towards their left.
>   Observe children who are reluctant to take part in physical
> play activities, or who choose to be on their own more than
> would be expected.
>   The child's attentiveness should be assessed as part of the
> routine observations made within the nursery situation. Note if
> there is a difference in attentiveness between different activi-
> ties and areas, and note if the child has bad or good days.
>
> (Crombie, unpublished)

Both the Observation Survey (Clay 1993) and Crombie's Nursery
Screening assess characteristics associated with the individual learner.
If difficulties in literacy learning can be seen as a function of the interaction between within-child and environmental factors, then it follows
that there must be an assessment of the student's characteristics and
also of the learning environment.

Understanding the demands of the learning environment

For many teachers there seems to be an inherent conflict between
addressing the individual learning needs of the pupil and meeting the
demands of the school curriculum. The learning environment can
support, or militate against, the learning needs of pupils who experience
difficulties in literacy development, and teachers need to be aware of
ways to appraise the teaching and learning context. Wearmouth and
Reid (2002) note that there are a number of ways of conceptualising the
interactional relationship between the learning environment and the
learner. For example, from an ecosystemic perspective, Bronfenbrenner
(1979) identifies four levels that influence student outcomes:

- microsystem, the immediate context of the student – school, classrooms, home, neighbourhood;
- mesosystem, the links between two microsystems, e.g. home–school
  relationships;
- exosystem, outside demands/influences in adults' lives that affect
  students;
- macrosystem, cultural beliefs/patterns or institutional policies that
  affect individuals' behaviour.

In their review of the literature on learning environments Ysseldyke and Christenson (1987b) identified three categories of environmental factors influencing instructional outcomes:

- school district conditions;
- within-school conditions;
- general family characteristics.

Ysseldyke and Christenson argue that it can be a very useful exercise to focus on features of classroom practice because these can be changed to support more effective learning. They identify a number of instructional factors in the classroom that influence student outcomes:

- planning procedures;
- management procedures;
- teaching procedures;
- monitoring and evaluation procedures.

They used their analysis of these features in the learning environment to design 'The Instructional Environment Scale' (TIES) as a framework for the systematic collection of data to analyse contextual barriers to pupils' learning. Data are gathered through classroom observation and interview with both pupil and teacher on twelve components of teaching:

- Instructional presentation: Instruction is presented in a clear and effective manner; directions contain sufficient information for the student to understand what kinds of behaviours or skills are to be demonstrated; and the student's understanding is checked before independent practice.
- Classroom environment: The classroom is controlled efficiently and effectively; there is a positive, supportive classroom atmosphere; time is used productively.
- Teacher expectations: There are realistic yet high expectations for both the amount and accuracy of work to be completed, and these are communicated clearly to the student.
- Cognitive emphasis: Thinking skills needed to complete assignments are communicated explicitly to the student.
- Motivational strategies: The teacher has and uses effective strategies for heightening student interest and effort.
- Relevant practice: The student is given adequate opportunity to practise with appropriate materials. Classroom tasks are clearly important to achieving instructional goals.

- Academic engaged time: The student is actively engaged in responding to academic content; the teacher monitors the extent to which the student is actively engaged and redirects the student when the student is not engaged.
- Informed feedback: The student receives relatively immediate and specific information on his or her performance or behaviour; when the student makes mistakes, correction is provided.
- Adaptive instruction: The curriculum is modified to accommodate the student's specific instructional needs.
- Progress evaluation: There is direct, frequent measurement of the student's progress toward completion of instructional objectives; data on pupil performance and progress are used to plan future instruction.
- Instructional planning: The student's needs have been assessed accurately and instruction is matched appropriately to the results of the instructional diagnosis.
- Student understanding: The student demonstrates an accurate understanding of what is to be done in the classroom.

(Ysseldyke and Christenson 1987b, p. 21)

An important aspect of the learning environment comprises the texts in use with classes and particular pupils. Selection of published texts can be complex and problematic as well as costly. Piotrowski and Reason's list of questions provides teachers with a very useful framework against which to assess the potential use of expensive resources for students who experience difficulties in literacy development:

Piotrowski and Reason (2000) compared three kinds of commercially published materials with a strong emphasis on the teaching of phonics. First, those developed for all children as meeting the requirements of the NLS [National Literacy Strategy] at the word level; second, those intended for learners making slower progress in literacy; and, third, those targeted at learners regarded as having difficulties of a dyslexic nature. The materials were audited in terms of the following eight questions:

1   A *comprehensive model*: With their focus on phonics, do the materials reflect a comprehensive model of reading and/or spelling development, i.e. NLS searchlights that include comprehension of the text as a whole and the anticipation of words and letter sequences?

2 *Progression*: Do the materials show a clear progression of phono-logical targets, starting from phonological awareness and moving gradually to more advanced phonic structures?

3 *Speaking and listening*: Are children exploring and reinforcing the learning of phonological regularities through both speaking and listening?

4 *Reading and writing*: Are children exploring and reinforcing the learning of phonological regularities through both reading and writing?

5 *Assessing to teach*: Do the materials provide guidance on 'assessing to teach', i.e. on assessing what the children know in order to plan, in appropriately small steps, what should be learnt next?

6 *Mastery learning*: Are the materials based on 'mastery learning', i.e. on planned repetition and revision that ensures the retention of what has been learnt?

7 *Role of the learner*: In terms of motivational influences, is there explicit guidance on the involvement of the children themselves in setting their own targets and monitoring progress?

8 *Home–school links*: Is there clear guidance on how parents and carers can help their children at home?

(Reason 2002, p. 195)

Cultural context and assessment

Bilingualism and multiculturalism are important factors in students' cultural contexts. There are particular issues related to the assessment of literacy difficulties among bilingual students. For example, we need to be aware of whether a student is experiencing difficulty as a result of cultural factors or of cognitive factors. These issues are raised by Cline (2002), who suggests that children who are learning English as an additional language (EAL) will be likely to vary in their intellectual performance over time and across settings more than monolingual pupils. This highlights the shortcomings of using a single test for assessment purposes. Instead, it is important to draw upon multiple sources of evidence. Cline and Shamsi (2000) suggest that this might involve one or more of the following:

- sampling the child's performance and behaviour in different roles and in different situations;
- using multiple indicators to assess progress over time;
- sampling a child's reading across a range of texts and genres;

- comparing performance in settings where L1 is the main medium of communication with performance in the mainstream classroom;
- consulting any religious or community school that children attend.

Cline also suggests that an analysis of cumulative records makes it possible to identify changes in the rate of progress over time. When children start school at an early stage in learning EAL, it can be expected that their progress in literacy, particularly in reading comprehension, will speed up as their oral use of English improves and their vocabulary increases. Cline therefore proposes that it is a reasonable working hypothesis that if the pace of progress does not pick up in this way the original obstacle to reading progress is more likely to have arisen from learning difficulties relating to literacy and not simply from a lack of knowledge of English.

It is important to motivate children who are learning EAL to engage with a wide range of texts. The literacy curriculum, therefore, according to Cline, must be designed to empower them to acknowledge the benefits of such wide reading for further cultural and intellectual heritage. Cline suggests they will be deprived of these experiences if the educators working with them fail to identify specific learning difficulties that inhibit their progress.

Pupil perspectives

The notion of pupil self-advocacy is supported by international law, and by one piece of British legislation. In the United Nations Convention on the Rights of the Child, Article 12 states:

> Parties shall assure to the child who is capable of forming his or her own views the right to express those views freely in all matters affecting the child, the views of the child being given due weight in accordance with the age and maturity of the child.
>
> For this purpose the child shall in particular be provided the opportunity to be heard in any judicial or administrative proceedings affecting the child, either directly or through a representative or an appropriate body, in a manner consistent with the procedural rules of national law.
>
> (United Nations Convention on the Rights of the Child 1989, Article 12; available online, May 2000, at www.freethechildren.org/uncrcdoc.htm)

Article 13(1) states:

> The child shall have the right to freedom of expression; this right shall include the freedom to seek, receive and impart information and ideas of all kinds, regardless of all frontiers, either orally or in print, in the form of art or any other media of the child's choice.

(United Nations Convention on the Rights of the Child 1989, Article 13(1); available online, May 2000, at www.freethechildren.org/uncr-cdoc.htm)

There is conflict between these rights and practice in many schools, however, since:

- within schools teachers are regarded legally as in loco parentis and therefore participation by children is more in terms of an indulgence that may be granted;
- pupils have no right to see their files until they are 16;
- pupils cannot appeal directly against exclusions but must rely on parents or carers to do so;
- pupils have no automatic right to be present at appeals against exclusions.

Pupils are now encouraged to express their own views during the assessment process to ascertain their 'special educational needs'. This is highlighted by the British Psychological Society's (1999) advice to its members about the importance of taking pupils' perspectives into account. The rationale given for this in the original Code of Practice was as a disclosure of information from child to professional, in part as enlisting the support of the child for the programme that is devised, and in part as a matter of human rights. The benefits are:

- practical – children have important and relevant information. Their support is crucial to the effective implementation of any individual education programme
- principle – children have a right to be heard. They should be encouraged to participate in decision-making about provision to meet their special educational needs.

(Department for Education 1994, para. 2:35)

However, there are major challenges facing those with responsibilities for planning provision in schools for pupils who experience difficulties in literacy development. On the one hand, there is an expectation that pupils' views will be sought over provision made for them and that teachers as well as pupils will be willing and able to engage in this activity, however much their interests may be in conflict. On the other hand, traditional school structures and bureaucracy often present barriers to the expression of pupil opinion particularly. Institutionalised resistance to change is a well-known problem in schools (Hopkins 1991). Teachers are professionals in the education industry. It is their role to make informed decisions based on their knowledge and experience. In many school staff rooms, attempting to claim the high moral ground by appealing to colleagues to respect the rights of the individual child is insufficient to justify pupil participation in decision-making processes. It is important, therefore, that a greater degree of pupil participation can clearly be justified. Moreover, the assumption that 'teachers know best' can become a barrier to participation. Research (Wade and Moore 1993) suggests that teachers believe pupil consultation is time consuming and of little value; that decisions are made at a higher level and preclude consultation; that even if they were given the opportunity for participation pupils would not take the task seriously; and that the range of perspectives within a given group would not be coherent.

Problems associated with a number of philosophical and practical issues surrounding self-advocacy have been identified by Garner and Sandow (1995). These issues undermine any notion that supporting pupils' self-advocacy is straightforward in the manner that is implied in the 1994 code because they suggest a conflict of values both within and between individuals. For example:

- The model of pupil as participant and self-directed learner rather than passive receiver and empty vessel to be filled implies that the traditional role of the teacher as one who purveys wisdom and transmits knowledge must change to that of one who guides learners' participation (Freire and Macedo 1999). This development in the teacher's role may be uncomfortable and not always welcome.
- Some pupils may be seen as undeserving of the right to self-advocacy, for example those whose behaviour is seen as disruptive. Others may be perceived as incapable of contributing

rationally to decisions about their own lives, for example those identified as experiencing severe difficulties in learning:

> The dilemma for the teacher is thus to decide whether to extend to such children the same rights to self-representation as are afforded to others, or whether to act instead as a guardian, protecting the child from the world and the world from the child.
>
> (Garner and Sandow 1995, p. 20)

- It may be that not all children wish to be self-advocates and that choosing not to engage with the decision-making process may be a valid choice in itself. It may also be the case that forcing children to make their own choices where the learning goals do not seem relevant to the individual is counterproductive.
- Self-advocacy may be viewed as a threat to the existing order and may therefore be unpopular with some teachers. Pupils may openly verbally challenge teachers' authority, as well as the structure and organisation of the school. In addition, self-advocacy involves a transfer of power from teacher to pupil in the degree of legitimacy accorded to pupils' opinions.

It is questionable how often pupils identified as having special educational needs are asked their opinion about which sort of provision is most appropriate for them. Gersch notes that, although over the past twenty years there has been progress in involving children more actively in their education, 'such progress as has occurred has been patchy, unsystematic and slow' (2001, p. 228). In Gersch's opinion, lack of progress in promoting pupil self-advocacy is a matter of regret, because in listening to what students say about their education and their needs there remains a 'wealth of untapped resource for teachers, schools and other professionals'. Awaiting discovery there is a 'gold mine of ideas, views, feedback, information and motivational energy' (*ibid.*).

Wearmouth (2000) quotes Gersch (2001) in listing a number of dilemmas encountered during the development of research initiatives in schools designed to support the development of active pupil participation in decision-making processes in schools:

- how to deal with other colleagues who might feel that children should be seen and not heard;

- the question of whether some children are mature or capable enough to participate [in the author's experience even very young children and students with severe learning difficulties can make some choices about their educational programmes];
- how to deal with parent–child dislike;
- how much scope children need to negotiate, try things and change their minds;
- how adults can distinguish what a child needs from what he or she prefers or wants;
- what status should be given to the pupil's views if the professional responsible for organising the special or additional provision comes into conflict with their head teacher over ways of meeting a pupil's needs.

These dilemmas represent, essentially, conflict between the roles of the participants. Clearly there are no easy solutions. Gersch himself does not offer a single answer, but feels that if a positive way forward is to be found a mutually trusting, listening, open, non-judgemental relationship must be established between teacher and pupil. The learning support guidelines for the Republic of Ireland offer guidance on how this might be achieved:

The involvement of pupils in the development, implementation and review of their own learning programmes is an important principle underlying effective supplementary teaching. Pupils can become more independent as learners if they perceive themselves to be stakeholders in the learning process. Pupils who are in receipt of supplementary teaching should, as appropriate:

- become familiar with the medium and short-term learning targets that have been set for them, and they should be given the opportunity to contribute to the setting of such targets;
- contribute to the selection of texts and other learning materials that are relevant to the attainment of their learning targets;
- develop 'ownership' of skills and strategies that are taught during supplementary teaching and learn to apply these learning strategies and skills to improve their own learning;
- contribute to the evaluation of their progress by participating in appropriate assessment activities, including self-assessment.

(Ireland 2000, p. 51)

Engaging with parents'/carers' perspectives

In some countries of the UK there is overt acknowledgement of effective working relationships between home and school in supporting the
literacy learning of students who experience difficulties. For example,
in England the Department for Education, then the Department for
Education and Science (DES), produced a document in the Citizen's
Charter series, *Children with Special Needs: A Guide for Parents* (first
published in 1992), supporting the rights of parents to be involved in
decisions about their children's education.

Parent power

The power of parents to influence the organisation of a school, especially when supported by the force of law, is illustrated by the way in
which staff at 'Downland' were forced to restructure its overall
curriculum response to meeting the diversity of pupil learning needs:

> In Downland there were a number of pupils with statements of
> special educational needs, largely for specific learning difficulties.
> These statements had included reference to individual non-
> specialist support. This was at odds with the ethos of inclusion and
> non-withdrawal from the mainstream classroom. Initially, the
> response of the school had been to provide non-specialist support
> in the context of the classroom, but this had been challenged by
> the parents of the statemented pupils who demanded that the
> requirements of the statement were fulfilled. The response of the
> school was to set up an alternative system in which the state-
> mented pupils were to become the responsibility of a former
> member of the girls' school and to receive the 'entitlement' of
> their statement through her specialist teaching. ... The solution
> was in effect to 'hive off' a small sub-group of pupils in an effort to
> retain the liberal values of the school for the overwhelming
> majority by leaving the existing system intact.
>
> (Clark *et al.* 1997, p. 65)

Effective communication with parents

It is important to keep in mind what parents expect and professionals
aspire to in the parent–professional relationship. Mittler (2000)
suggests that schools need to rethink the basis of home–school links
for all children in order to promote children's learning as well as

social and school inclusion. He refers to a study of OFSTED reports by Blamires *et al.* (1997) which indicates that schools congratulated by the inspectorate for effective partnerships with parents are characterised by:

- a rapid response to parental requests;
- regular newsletters which include diaries of future events;
- responsibility for home–school liaison assigned to designated members of staff or working parties;
- clear presentation of information on children's progress and opportunities for further discussion;
- clear lines of communication between parents and the school through the use of diaries and logs;
- parental involvement in educating children through lending libraries of materials such as books and games.

Friend and Cook (1996) have made a number of suggestions about how schools might relate to parents and deal with their concerns. To some extent they parallel Mittler's views above:

- create an environment that is welcoming;
- schedule the meeting at the convenience of the parent;
- provide an advance summary of the topics to be covered and a list of questions the parent might want to ask;
- suggest they bring to school copies of work the child has done at home;
- let the parent be seated at the meeting table first;
- provide the parent with a file folder containing copies of the information the professionals have in their folders;
- use your communication skills to structure the meeting so the parent has opportunities to provide input throughout the meeting.

(Friend and Cook 1996, p. 232)

Friend and Cook go on to outline how parents might prepare for their meetings with school personnel:

- review records on past meetings;
- talk with other family members and friends about what questions to ask and what information to share;
- make a list of questions to ask;

- make a list of information to share;
- ask another person to go to the meeting with you;
- take all relevant records to the meeting;
- bring a pencil and paper;
- check the time and place of the conference.

(Open University 2000b, p. 96)

In 1997 Russell made a plea to schools to take seriously their power to affect the lives of children and their families and carers through the kind of assessment and provision that they make, and this was reiteration in 2000 by Mittler:

Please accept and value our children (and ourselves as families) as we are.

Please celebrate difference.

Please try and accept our children as children first. Don't attach labels to them unless you mean to do something.

Please recognise your power over our lives. We live with the consequences of your opinions and decisions.

Please understand the stress many families are under. The cancelled appointment, the waiting list no one gets to the top of, all the discussions about resources – it's our lives you're talking about.

Don't put fashionable fads and treatments on to us unless you are going to be around to see them through. And don't forget families have many members, many responsibilities. Sometimes, we can't please everyone.

Do recognise that sometimes we are right! Please believe us and listen to what we know that we and our children need.

Sometimes we are sad, tired and depressed. Please value us as caring and committed families and try to go on working with us.

(Russell 1997, p. 79)

Parents and dyslexia

Over the years in the area of dyslexia there have been many debates around the cause of the difficulty and appropriate forms of curriculum differentiation or intervention which have involved parents and carers. A number of researchers (Clark et al. 1997) have pointed out the significance of the alliance between parents and psychologists in the emergence of the category 'specific learning difficulties'.

[P]sychologists employed by, for example, the Dyslexia Institute, appear to play a key role in helping parents secure resources and provision for their 'dyslexic' children, often in the face of opposition from professional educators and educational administrators.

(Clark *et al.* 1997, p. 110)

Often the pupil him/herself is ashamed of his/her inability to learn to read properly. The pupil's family may feel guilty that they have not been able to help him/her more. Whatever the cause, it remains the case that attributing a pupil's problems to a sensory, neurological or psycholinguistic impairment is one way of absolving the pupil and his/her family from the blame for lack of progress.

Conclusion

Pupil achievement in the area of literacy is influenced by a multitude of factors, singly and in complex interaction. Some factors are intrinsic to the individual learner. Some relate to the learning environment and methods of teaching. Others are associated with the external environment outside the control of the teacher. Information on student achievement can be elicited from a number of sources: teachers, other professionals, parents or carers, and the students themselves. It can be gathered in a variety of ways, both formal and informal. Inside educational institutions, those responsible for supporting the literacy development of those learners who experience difficulties must be familiar with the whole range of techniques appropriate to assessing the factors over which they have some control. They should also be aware of the underlying assumptions of particular forms of assessment and the potential effects of their use. Assessment of students who experience difficulties in literacy needs to have a clearly stated rationale and be embedded in the whole school curriculum. It is crucial that responsibility for assessment should not rest with one individual but should be a whole–school responsibility.

Chapter 9

Framework for planning

Introduction

Planning for the literacy development of any learner or group who experiences difficulties should be based on a comprehensive assessment of factors related both to the individual and the learning environment in which she or he is educated. It needs to include an overall long-term programme based on a global view of the individual; an awareness of the immediate and broader context within which any individual education plan, individual profile or record must take effect; and an understanding of issues related to equal opportunities. It must also take account of what constitutes 'literacy' and the underpinning models of literacy acquisition assumed by different intervention programmes. From this long-term programme it is possible to draw up medium- and short-term plans, which should clearly be related to it.

Planning for literacy learning in the long, medium and short term

An initial assessment of the difficulties in literacy acquisition experienced by the learner might lead to long-, medium- and short-term planning within the context of the whole-school curriculum. Principles described in the work of Tod, Castle and Blamires (1998) and Wearmouth (2000) might lead to the conclusion that this initial assessment of the strengths and difficulties in literacy development experienced by the learner is based on the following:

- teachers' assessments;
- results of formal testing procedures;
- prior records/reports;
- assessment by outside agencies;

- the pupil's views;
- the parents'/carers' perspectives;
- consideration of the learning environment.

However, before any plans are formulated, account should be taken of:

- contextual factors related to the whole-school literacy curriculum, including national requirements, school priorities, approaches to diversity and equal opportunities, and issues of differentiation;
- contextual factors relating to the student's background;
- perspectives on literacy;
- models of reading.

A long-term plan for the learner's literacy development might then be drawn up which is based on:

- personal and parental aspirations;
- strengths and weaknesses in literacy development;
- provision for access to the whole curriculum.

Planning for the long term will depend on the age of the learner, the degree and type of need, and the length of time during which an individual plan, profile or record has been structured for the learner, and it might imply taking a view about the pupil's future over the next few years. Tod, Castle and Blamires (1998), in their work on Individual Education Plans (IEPs), suggest that 'long-term' might be as short as a year. This equates with the cycle of annual reviews. Individual learners' progress and personal development should be reviewed annually, as well as changes in the learning environment and the stage reached in the National Curriculum, and a considerable amount of revision and amendment to a pupil's programme might be needed in the light of this. However, the annual cycle does not detract from the need to consider potential directions for learners over a much longer period than this. It is important to have a longer-term vision of a range of possibilities for a learner that can be shared between the learner, the parent/carer and the professionals in order to give a sense of direction to the whole planning process. Individuals' needs change over time, however. Flexibility of thinking is very important here, so that the planning process facilitates rather than restricts literacy learning.

From the long-term plan might flow a medium-term plan for the learner's literacy development which must:

- reflect strategies appropriate to the school context and learning environment, and to the individualism of the learner;
- incorporate termly and yearly achievable targets designed to lead to the learner's long-term goal;
- reflect the Key Stage and associated programmes of study;
- offer regular assessment opportunities.

Flowing from the medium-term plan, short-term, day-to-day planning for literacy learning must:

- incorporate medium-term targets in literacy achievement;
- offer opportunities for daily, formative assessment of literacy development.

IEPs

Since the inception of the *Code of Practice for the Identification and Assessment of Special Educational Needs* (Department for Education 1994; Department for Education Northern Ireland 1998) the IEP has become a major tool for planning individual pupils' programmes of study in England, Wales and Northern Ireland. The term 'individual education plan' can be used to refer both to the process of planning the next steps in a pupil's learning programme on the basis of an analysis of pupil needs, and to the summative document (Tod *et al.* 1998). In the Republic of Ireland the Individual Profile and Learning Programme and in Scotland the Record of Needs serve the same purpose.

Statutory requirements of the IEP in England, Wales and Northern Ireland

Whether or not assessment leads to the issuing of a statement of special educational need, the IEP must have regard to the models of assessment outlined in the codes of practice that operate in the different countries of the UK. In general terms, the codes require that IEPs should contain details of the nature of the child's learning difficulties, the special educational provision to be made and strategies to be used, specific programmes, activities, materials, and/or equipment, targets to be achieved in a specified time, monitoring and assessment arrangements, and review arrangements and date. The details vary slightly in the different codes in England, Wales and Northern Ireland.

The Record of Needs in Scotland

'Good practice' in negotiating the Record of Needs in schools in Scotland has been defined by the inspectorate of the Scottish Executive:

EPSEN APPROACH TO ASSESSMENT AND RECORDING

At the primary stage the first three steps in identifying and assessing pupils' special educational needs [SEN] are outlined as:

STEP 1 Identification of difficulties in learning: Through the procedures normally used in the classroom, the class teacher assesses individuals' learning difficulties. Where relevant, reference is made to pre-school reports and to information given by parents. The teacher takes action to overcome the learning difficulties within a defined period, generally by adjusting the class programme. The teacher reassesses, making a record of the problems faced by individuals, and their learning strengths.

STEP 2 Referral to learning support co-ordinator: The class teacher consults with the learning support co-ordinator and together they plan, record and implement courses of action and necessary adjustments are made.

STEP 3 Referral to support services outwith the school: Where a pupil's special educational needs are not being met within the resources of the school, the learning support co-ordinator and class teacher consult with the headteacher. Where it is decided that further assistance is required, the headteacher may first seek advice from an adviser or learning support specialist from outwith the school. The next step is to seek parents' permission to refer the child to the psychological service. In good practice referral is in writing and specifies (a) the individual's strengths, and any needs which have been identified; (b) the parents' views; (c) actions taken by the school; and (d) indications of the assistance required.

(SEED 2001, p. 3)

Pupils' needs are considered by an educational psychologist at Step 4:

STEP 4 … The educational psychologist meets the parents and assesses the pupil in the school and in other contexts as required. A course of action is recommended in writing with, where appropriate, advice on the content of the curriculum and learning and teaching strategies. Other members of support services may also assess the pupil at this stage and make recommendations. Where action is some form of educational programme, arrangements are made for review and evaluation, in consultation with parents and school staff. No further steps are required for many pupils but the support services and school, in consultation with parents, continue the process of monitoring progress and adjusting provision in line with needs.

STEP 5 Consideration is given to opening a Record of Needs: The headteacher, parents and, normally, the educational psychologist consider whether a Record of Needs should be opened. If there is agreement, the directorate is informed and statutory procedures are initiated. School staff prepare a report on their view of the child's strengths and needs.

STEP 6 Medical examination and psychological assessment: The child is assessed. Parents have the right to be present at the medical examination and should be invited to discussions with the educational psychologist. The medical officer and the psychologist prepare reports. Staff in school, meantime, continue to give the pupil assistance.

STEP 7 Meeting to discuss opening of Record of Needs: The professionals, including representatives of school staff, meet with parents to discuss assessments. If the decision is that a Record of Needs should be opened, then the pupil's special educational needs are defined and the provision required to meet these needs is specified. Learning and teaching targets should be set and the date of the review agreed. The drafted terms are sent to the directorate for consideration and action. School staff prepare or update their individualised educational programme for the pupil.

STEP 8 Opening the Record of Needs: The Record is drafted and a copy is sent to parents for approval. Once approved it is 'opened' and copies are sent to parents, school and psychological service. Parents may appeal against the decisions to open or not to open a Record, against the terms of the Record and against proposed placement.

(SEED 2001, p. 4)

The Individual Profile and Learning Programme in the Republic of Ireland

The Learning Support Guidelines provide a detailed procedure for developing an Individual Profile and Learning Programme for each student who is to receive supplementary teaching (Swan 2002). This programme is intended to form the basis for short- and medium-term planning, and will contain a record of all relevant information. It should be drawn up by the learning support teacher, in consultation with the class teachers, the parents and the pupils themselves, through three stages:

1 Details of the pupil, the names of the class teacher and the learning support teacher are obtained and recorded.
2 Information from the screening and diagnostic assessment procedures used is recorded, both from standardised tests or other instruments, and from informal checklists. Relevant information from the pupils' parents, from the pupils themselves, and from other professionals who may have assessed or worked with the pupil – for example psychologists and therapists – may be added to this.
3 A profile of the pupil's attainments, strengths and needs in learning is drawn up, in order to develop specific learning targets appropriate to the individual. These targets might refer to the development of skills, or of pupil motivation, the time-scale allowed for their achievement and the date when a particular target has been achieved will, in due course, be noted.

The specific learning activities required in order to meet a given target will be planned by all the adults concerned, or communicated to them. The details of each person's responsibility for implementing the learning programme and the times, location and duration of the intervention will be recorded. A weekly Planning and Progress Record is recommended for each week of instruction throughout the school term, together with the specific activities planned for each contributing adult, with a record of observations of learning and lesson evaluation, including successes in learning or obstacles encountered (Swan 2002). The weekly Planning and Progress Records will build cumulatively into an invaluable record of progress to date, of the basis for future long-term planning and of the effectiveness of the programme itself.

Issues relating to planning for individual pupils

Planning for individual pupils within the context of the whole-school and the whole-class curriculum raises a number of issues which are not easy to resolve. Tod (2002) addresses concerns which she specifically relates to IEPs in England, Wales and Northern Ireland. Many of her comments are of generic interest as they are associated with planning for individuals within the curriculum for all students in any national curriculum context.

- There appears to be little evidence to support the view that written IEPs are systematically integrated into teacher planning, or translated into classroom practice (Lynch and Beare 1990; Sigafoos *et al.* 1993; OFSTED 1999).
- That although 'clear goals' (targets) have been identified as a component of effective pedagogy (Ireson, Mortimore and Hallam 1999) the emphasis on predetermined quantifiable targets in IEPs linked to predetermined teaching strategies and programmes is not supported by research (Deforges 2001). 'Research into literacy learning suggests that pupil involvement in learning, active experimentation with a range of strategies and the opportunity for learning to "occur" is crucial' (Grainger and Tod 2000). These aspects of students' literacy acquisition may have been sacrificed to the desire to write precise IEPs which can fulfil their accountability function.
- IEPs cannot be divorced from the context in which they have been developed: 'Targeted, focused, additional, phonological support offered via the IEP needs to be housed within a rich interactive effective and affective literary curriculum' (Tod 2002, p. 264).
- theoretical assumptions about literacy acquisition on which IEPs are based need to be evaluated against empirical evidence.

Tod (2002) goes on to identify a number of principles for schools to use to evaluate the development of IEPs for students who experience difficulties in literacy. These are:

- To be clear about the educational purpose of an IEP both for individual pupils and as part of whole-school planning and provision. Evaluation of IEPs should be undertaken in relation to the identified and agreed purpose. Clearly it is not enough to say that 'the purpose of an IEP is to show inspectors and parents that we have additional planning in place for SEN pupils'.
- To contextualise IEPs 'within the NLS and whole school planning for literacy in order to identify additional or different provision to that given for all pupils; IEP provision should not be compensatory or reduce entitlement to a rich, interactive literacy curriculum'.
- To ensure that IEPs 'impact upon curriculum development and delivery and upon pupil learning and progress'.

- To manage IEPs 'at whole school level with identified roles and responsibilities' in order to 'ensure that outcomes are monitored and responsive adjustments made'.
- To set targets that 'reflect high expectations, the need to develop social and academic aspects of learning, address skills and strategies, and build on pupil strengths'.
- To ensure that IEPs can support 'early identification of literacy difficulties and trigger proactive planning'.
- To ensure that IEPs 'support learning that is purposeful and motivating and reflect pupil involvement in the planning and assessment of their learning and progress'.
- To construct IEPs that are 'both enabling and empowering – possibly by linking literacy, PSHE [personal, social and health education] and Citizenship targets (Grainger and Tod 2000)'.
- To encourage staff 'to adopt a critical distance towards IEPs in terms of policy, practice and theory/research so that their impact on pupil's progress and whole school response to diversity can be evaluated and improved'.
- To 'harness and support efficient use of resources and reflect collaborative educational effort'.

(all quotations from Tod 2002, p. 266)

Three major issues continue to be raised by researchers, by teachers in schools and by OFSTED in relation to the compilation and use of IEPs. These issues are how to cope with the time demands on paperwork, how to embed IEPs into the curriculum and how to conceptualise targets relating to the whole-language/whole-book approach.

The pressure on schools to comply with the procedures relating to IEPs as outlined in the code, in particular the heavy demands on time, have been well documented (OFSTED 1997). It is therefore important for schools, with the support of the school staff, to develop ways of working which keep this pressure to a minimum whilst at the same time considering how to develop systems for ensuring that the learning programme is carried out, monitored and evaluated. Tod, Castle and Blamires (1998) note that attempts to reduce the bureaucratic demands of the IEP process in some schools include:

- allocating the meeting arrangements and collation and distribution of information to clerical staff;
- using in-service training to encourage class teachers and form teachers to prepare IEPs at stage 2 and to support all those

involved in the education of pupils with IEPs to monitor progress;

- delegating responsibility for IEPs to one person in each subject area to oversee the progress of all pupils experiencing difficulties in learning;
- training classroom assistants in aspects of the process;
- organising group learning plans which incorporate the monitoring of individual pupil progress;
- increasing the involvement of parents/carers, which can result in a higher degree of 'fit' for the individual pupil;
- using electronic means of communication (which has become increasingly common in schools) for generating reports for all pupils from, for example, data banks of pre-existing comments – many of the issues relating to the use of pre-specified comments for all pupils apply equally to the use of computerised files of comments for the specific purpose of generating IEP documents, in particular that of time efficiency versus individuality of approach.

(Open University 2000b, p. 101)

Target setting

In England OFSTED (1997) notes that the purpose of IEPs is to facilitate pupil learning by means of the effective planning of learning goals. However, in some schools there is confusion over the level of detail required for the targets that are set for pupils. Similar issues arise in relation to target setting for IEPs and individual profiles as in the notion of targets within the national context. The strength of targets may be that they provide a focus for the combined efforts of all those concerned to support a learner's progress, and highlight the need to link planning and provision. However, a very important underlying assumption of targets is that they must be measurable and quantified. This is clearly questionable if this assumption is applied to targets operating in every aspect of the curriculum.

The school curriculum can be seen as a ladder of progression up which it is expected that a student will climb, and from rung to rung of which it is feasible to set learning goals which can be clearly specified, quantified and assessed. However, not all children learn the same way. For this reason, setting targets which follow the same sequence for all pupils is not necessarily appropriate. Dockrell and McShane elaborate on the problems of this approach:

One of the major criticisms of task analysis and learning objectives is the conceptualization of the learning process. There may be a number of routes by which a child can acquire mastery, rather than a single instructional hierarchy that is common to all children. When a task analysis is being performed, it is assumed that each child will learn the task components in the same order, because the task is analysed and not the learning processes or the learning context. An over-reliance on task components can lead to a rigid application of prescriptive teaching, which takes no account of the knowledge a child brings to any given task or the specific strategies that a child utilizes.

(Dockrell and McShane 1993, p. 51)

In addition, some areas lend themselves to this approach more easily than others. Literacy is an obvious area of the curriculum where it is problematic to conceptualise measurable targets in every aspect of its acquisition. The series of activities designed by Lewis (1995) to encourage children's early reading makes clear the reason why it is problematic to assume that every area of the curriculum can lend itself easily to quantifiable objectives. This list is intended neither as a linear sequence of teaching activities, nor as a set of tasks that can be broken down easily into teaching objectives which together would add up to the goal of reading:

- watching another child, or an adult, looking at a book;
- sharing a book with an adult;
- sharing a book with another child;
- sharing a book to look at from a classroom book area;
- hearing print in a familiar context, e.g. from a known story;
- hearing print in an unfamiliar context, e.g. from a birthday card;
- activities linking the written symbols with meaningful messages, e.g. counting from a written list of names the number of children having school dinner;
- collecting a variety of printed media (e.g. music scores, birthday cards, bottle labels) that convey information;
- 'reading' a book in role play (later recognizing rules concerning the direction of print);
- letter/word games, e.g. finding the first letter of the child's name in other contexts (e.g. on road signs, in a teacher's name), at first with adult help then independently;

- decoding some basic sight vocabulary words from the daily environment (e.g. classroom, street, home);
- 'playing' with rhyming words;
- games involving recognizing individual letter sounds in different contexts;
- games involving identifying individual letter sounds in different contexts;
- games involving recognizing individual letter symbols in different contexts;
- games involving identifying individual letter symbols in different contexts;
- games involving matching individual letter sounds with their written symbols (and vice versa);
- retelling to an adult, with some prompting, incidents from (and later the main story-line) of a story, film or event;
- retelling, without any adult prompting, a sequence of events;
- inventing [their] own stories stimulated by a variety of media (pictures, events, objects, dramatic play, etc.);
- making [their] own story and reading books using words/sentences written by an adult but dictated by the child (building up from single word to simple sentences, and beyond).

(Open University 2000, p. 103)

It is important that curriculum planning for individual learners should be embedded within whole-school procedures and policies (OFSTED 1996). The implication of this is that targets for IEPs need to be embedded in the regular cycle of classroom activity and the whole learning experience offered to the child through the curriculum (Cowne 2000). Teachers and classroom assistants need to be aware of which pupils have individual plans, profiles or records and be conversant with their content so that they can take adequate account of individual pupils' needs in lesson planning. Cowne advises that teachers must have a very clear grasp of eight issues when planning lessons that take plans, profiles or records for individual pupils into account:

1   how the principal curriculum objectives and key concepts for the lesson relate to the overall schemes for the school;
2   the way in which the principal objectives and key concepts are to be assessed, the criteria which indicate a satisfactory level of skills and understanding of key concepts, ways in which the assessment

process might be differentiated and the means by which the outcome of the assessment is to be recorded as part of the IEP for individual pupils;

3   the prerequisite skills for the principal objectives, and the prior level of knowledge required to understand key concepts;

4   the extent to which all pupils in the classroom, including those identified as having special learning needs, have the prerequisite skills and prior knowledge in order that any 'pre-teaching', or a different resource to assist access to information, might be arranged;

5   relevant skills and knowledge that might be cross-referenced from another curriculum area;

6   ways in which various kinds of group work, with or without additional assistance from adults, might assist learning in a particular lesson;

7   the extent to which those pupils with the greatest needs might be expected to fulfil the principal objectives and grasp all key concepts;

8   whether an alternative set of objectives will be needed for any children.

The implications of Cowne's views are a flexible approach and a thorough grasp of, and familiarity with, the National Curriculum structure and its underlying principles, in particular the structure and requirements of the National Literacy Strategy, together with knowledge and understanding of the strengths and needs of individual pupils. Tod (2002) notes the guidance that has been offered in the national literacy guidance on ways to plan differentiated teaching approaches for pupils who experience difficulties in literacy during the literacy hour. Teachers can:

- reduce 'whole-class' time to give more group time;
- use objectives from earlier terms where appropriate;
- group together pupils who may share IEP objectives;
- institute setting across a number of classes;
- take pupils out of the hour to work in parallel, e.g. to give access to talking books – however, pupils should return to class for the final part of the hour;
- adopt a differentiated delivery style to secure access for pupils with SEN, for example by adapting questions or giving additional visual/tactile cues;
- increase group time whilst keeping class time the same;

- allow more time for teaching some objectives;
- plan time within the group and independent work to allow some time during the week for intensive work with individual pupils;
- use additional resources, for example more than one copy of the 'big book' so that learning support assistants can support individual pupils; make use of information and communications technology through speaking books, tape recorders, spelling games;
- employ additional adult support within the literacy hour;
- make use of parents and other volunteers, including older pupils, to provide support for additional reading practice;
- make explicit links in literacy with other curriculum subjects to offer extra opportunities for pupils to extend and practise their literacy skills.

Conclusion

Planning for the learning of individual students who experience difficulties in literacy can only be as effective as the rigour of the thinking within which the IEP, Record or Individual Profile was designed. If a pupil is experiencing difficulty it is essential to tease out whether the problem lies at the level of conceptual understanding or is the result of some aspect of the learning environment – for example the mode of communication, especially that which is reliant on text. Lessons may be planned to facilitate the understanding of content, develop concepts or skills, practise problem-solving, or encourage pupils' personal interests. However, barriers may be created to children's learning simply by the way in which material based on the same underlying concept is presented in particular ways.

Chapter 10

School responses to difficulties in literacy

In the context of a national education system, plans for supporting the literacy acquisition of students who experience difficulties focus crucially on the institution of the school. Plans for individuals cannot be considered in isolation from what occurs generally in policy and practice in the school literacy curriculum. Policy is enacted most crucially in the classroom where pedagogy, including student grouping arrangements and the organisation of support for students' literacy learning, can serve to include and motivate, or exclude and alienate, those who experience difficulties. Peer support and collaborative learning can, for example, be harnessed to facilitate many aspects of literacy acquisition, including reading comprehension, and the development of writing skills. Some literacy intervention programmes are designed to be used with individual students. The same arguments about employing literacy programmes to meet clearly identified learning needs whilst acknowledging the underlying theoretical assumptions apply whether an intervention is targeted at an individual or at a group.

School literacy policies

School literacy policies must acknowledge the needs of students with difficulties in a way that enables teachers to resolve some of the major debates and issues discussed in this book through classroom practice and practice in home–school partnerships to support literacy development. It is important to take account of the assumptions of underlying models of the reading process and top-down, bottom-up and/or interactive approaches within a view of the student as active agent in his/her own learning; issues related to gender, ethnicity and literacy acquisition; and the tension between catering for the literacy needs of all children versus individual approaches and differentiation for those with special difficulties.

Policies for reading

Medwell (1995) goes some way towards encompassing the literacy needs of all students in her discussion of school policies for reading:

- We recognise that there is no one method of teaching and that different children may need different approaches.
- Literacy involves creating the right environment in class both in terms of organisation of resources and of time.
- Reading with a supportive adult is at the centre of our reading instruction.
- Assessment for formative and diagnostic purposes as well as statutory assessment is the basis of our teaching and must be continuous and systematic.
- All children need to learn to use reading strategies like skimming and scanning as well as information skills.

(Medwell 1995, pp. 70–1)

D. Smith notes that it is especially important to link reading schemes to school policy on literacy acquisition and provides some points to consider when selecting a reading scheme for a school:

- Who is the scheme for?
- Why has it been written?
- How does it fit in with other reading material used within the school?
- Is there a handbook providing its rationale and giving helpful information?
- Can parents work through the scheme?
- Is there information about the reading books inside the children's books for parents?
- How are the books sequenced or grouped?
- Is there a range of styles or genres?
- Is the language close to speech patterns or is it stilted and unnatural?
- Is the language too simple or does it appear to be complex?
- Is the scheme a sight word scheme, using repetitive words and phrases?

- Does the scheme use a language approach where high interest words can be guessed through contextual cues?
- Is the scheme phonic using a sequence of phonic features or letter strings?
- Is the scheme a mix of all reading strategies?
- Does the scheme have back up materials and activities?
- Are the books well illustrated, colourful, attractive and well printed?
- Is the size of print suitable for the intended age levels?
- Which age group will enjoy the scheme?
- Have gender and racial issues been considered?
- Are there any special features which might make them particularly interesting?
- Are the books durable?
- Do the books give value for money?

(D. Smith 1999, pp. 25–6)

Spelling policies

Marking and spelling policies as they relate to the learning needs of individual pupils can also stimulate a fair amount of controversy. Bentley (2002) feels that it is possible to identify the stages of development in students' spelling errors as reflective of learners at the pre-communicative stage, where a child clearly knows what writing is for but cannot spell words in any decipherable way; the semi-phonetic stage, where the child's attempts to spell words show some letter–sound correspondence; the phonetic stage, where all surface sound features are represented; the transitional stage, where the child relies more on the visual appearance of words rather than sound; and the correct stage. From this standpoint, students should be encouraged to make the transition from one stage of spelling development to another when they have mastered the previous stage. She feels that, for the most part, class or group spelling tests are a waste of time since learners will be at different stages in spelling acquisition. Spelling tests may be a required part of a school's approach to supporting pupils' literacy development. Teachers may feel that set spelling tests are very important to assess the development in spelling of a whole class or group. On the other hand, they may feel that whether spelling tests are a waste of time may closely reflect the way in which spellings are chosen for pupils to learn and how far they are tailored to the needs of the individual child.

In order to identify the stage of development a student has reached in his/her spelling it is very important to take the time to scrutinise samples of writing very carefully. Bentley's comment that students' spelling errors often span the developmental stages indicates that there is much overlap between one stage and the next. A student who is tired and/or in a hurry may well make more mistakes than s/he would do otherwise. There is probably no one rule about how long a student might remain at one stage of spelling development. Perhaps the most important issue is to ensure that, overall, a student is making progress towards greater competence in spelling, and, if s/he is 'stuck' at one stage, to work out ways of supporting him/her to move on to the next.

Bentley argues that, in addition, schools should have very clear marking policies. On the one hand, it can be argued that, for some students, repeatedly getting back scripts covered with marks indicating errors is very demoralising. On the other, there has to be a rational, structured approach to ensuring that students make progress in recognising mistakes and learning how to correct them. Some teachers may feel it is appropriate to encourage students to proof read their own, or peers', work before handing it in and/or, perhaps, to correct only words or sentence structure with which they feel students should already be familiar. Whichever strategy schools choose, it should be supported by reasoned argument. Whatever decisions are made have both advantages and disadvantages, which need to be recognised.

Classroom practices

In recognising that different children need different approaches and that children may benefit from individual support, these researchers imply the need for differentiated approaches to meet the individual literacy needs and learning styles of pupils.

Differentiation

In the *Special Educational Needs Code of Practice* in England, differentiation is claimed to support the learning of all students, including those who experience difficulties in literacy: 'Differentiation of learning activities within the … curriculum framework will help schools to meet the learning needs of all children' (Department of Education and Skills 2001, 5:18; 6:18). In Northern Ireland *The Code of Practice for the Identification and Assessment of Special Educational Needs* (Department for Education Northern Ireland 1998) claims that 'differentiation of classwork within a common curriculum framework will help the school to meet the learning needs of all pupils'. This statement, however, begs a number of questions. Among these are the following:

- What constitutes 'differentiation'?
- How is it possible to make special provision for some whilst maintaining overall curriculum coherence?
- How can special provision be made without risking marginalising and stigmatising some pupils?

Visser and Phillips (1993) define differentiation as a process through which teachers select appropriate teaching methods to match an individual child's learning strategies within a group situation in order to support the child's progress through the curriculum. Phillips *et al.* offer the following definitions of differentiation:

> Differentiation is the process whereby teachers meet the need for progress through the curriculum by selecting appropriate teaching methods to match an individual child's learning strategies, within a group situation.
>
> (Visser 1993)

> Differentiation is a process whereby planning and delivering the curriculum takes account of individual differences and matches what is taught and how it is taught to individual learning styles and needs. It seeks to provide opportunities for ALL children to participate and make progress in the curriculum by:
>
> - building on past achievement
> - presenting challenges for further achievement
> - providing opportunities for success.
>
> (Phillips 1999, p. 33)

These writers also distinguish between different types of differentiation: input, task, outcome, output, response, resource and support.

There is a particular dilemma accompanying the choice of appropriate curricula. Young people sharing identical learning aims may be deprived of the opportunity to develop competencies appropriate to their needs, yet may be made to feel inferior if their curriculum is different. Whatever alterations teachers make to enable pupils who experience difficulties in the area of literacy to engage more fully in any aspect of the curriculum might solve some problems but create others (Norwich 1994). Solutions commonly adopted include:

- reducing the content coverage of the curriculum to release more time for literacy development;
- enabling some pupils to access the curriculum through alternative means, for example through the use of information and communications technology;
- providing different pedagogy, materials or specialist teaching for some pupils.

One example of differentiating for pupils at secondary level is planning to meet the learning needs of pupils who experience difficulties in the area of literacy. It must incorporate assessment of learning needs, a global view of the learner, together with future career possibilities, and also the overall curriculum structure that relates to all pupils in a school (OFSTED 1996). It is essential to consider the implications of curriculum differentiation for future life chances, as well as ways of embedding individual plans into the whole school curriculum.

At secondary level, few years of compulsory schooling remain. There is a very fine line between constricting curriculum choices so that they impact adversely on future life chances and not offering sufficient support to encourage the competence in literacy necessary for independent, successful life as an adult.

The issue of the readability of text is linked to that of differentiation, in that it is a major concern in thinking about the appropriateness of reading materials for all students. There are at least three major considerations for any of us who are thinking about how easily students can read text (Lunzer and Gardner 1979):

- the interest level of the text – and/or prior knowledge of the subject matter. If pupils are interested in, or already understand, what they are reading, they can cope with more difficult text;
- sentence length and complexity, word length and familiarity;
- conciseness of explanation of concepts – more pupils can understand higher-level concepts if ideas are expanded and explained step by step.

Formulae to work out the reading age of a text are mechanical, in the sense that they only take word/sentence length into account, and not meaning or interest level. However, at least they provide a more systematic means of working out the approximate level of a text than merely subjective judgement. The Flesch Formula is an example of such a test of readability.

Using the formula yourself necessitates having samples of text of more than 100 words.

This formula takes the form of a reading ease score (RE): RE = 206.835 − (0.846 × No.Syll) − (1.015 × WperS).

No.Syll is the average number of syllables per 100 words, and WperS is the average number of words per sentence.

To use this formula:

1   Select at random 3 continuous passages of 100 words each from the text. Count the number of syllables in each 100-word sample, add them together, and divide by 3. Substitute this answer for No.Syll in the formula.

2   Count up the number of words altogether in all 3 passages put together. Divide by the number of sentences in all 3 passages put together. If there are any part sentences, put them together and call them one sentence. Substitute this answer in WperS in the formula.

3   Now use the following table to convert the final score into a reading age level:

Flesch Formula score	Reading-age level
90–100	10–11 years
80–90	11–12 years
70–80	12–13 years
65–70	13–14 years
60–65	14–15 years
55–60	15–16 years
Lower than 55	Above 16 years

(Lunzer and Gardner 1979; quoted in Open University E801 course materials, 2002)

It was noted above that the Flesch Formula has its limitations because it cannot account for meaning or interest level. There are, however, ways of allowing for these factors. Lunzer and Gardner (1979), for example, offer some guidelines on modifying texts to reduce reading and/or conceptual difficulty of text:

1 Shorten sentences.
2 Use easier, shorter, more familiar words. Cut out technical vocabulary, unless it is absolutely essential.
3 Spread out the text so that there is less per page.
4 Simplify sentence structure.
5 Turn passive verbs ('He was bitten by the dog.') into active verbs ('The dog bit him.').
6 Give a step-by-step explanation of concepts.

Motivational strategies

One issue often associated with the consequences of difficulties in literacy is that of the demotivation of students in classrooms. A number of motivational theories within a cognitive psychology perspective have proposed that the beliefs students develop about their abilities influence their efforts. Most motivational theories propose that pupils tend to take an active approach to learning if they believe their effort will succeed. 'Locus of control' theorists (e.g. Crandall *et al.* 1965) propose that to achieve successful outcomes it is important to believe that academic successes and failures are the result of the individual's own efforts and skills – that is, to 'internal' factors, rather than to 'external' factors, such as luck or the fairness of the task. One very important factor for many students in supporting improvement in their literacy development is an increasing sense of control over their own level of achievement. A number of studies have shown that when children find a task difficult those who attribute their difficulties to controllable factors, such as insufficient effort, are more likely to persist than are children who attribute their difficulties to uncontrollable factors, such as insufficient ability (Butkowsky and Willows 1980; Diener and Dweck 1978; Dweck and Reppucci 1973; Licht *et al.* 1985). 'Attributional' theorists (e.g. Dweck and Licht 1980; Weiner 1979) propose that willingness to try hard is more likely where previous academic difficulties are attributed to factors within the learner's control, such as lack of effort, rather than to factors beyond the learner's control, such as lack of ability. 'Self-efficacy' theorists (e.g. Bandura 1982; Schunk 1989) stress that if a learner is to succeed it is important for her/him to believe that s/he has the ability to perform well.

Licht and Dweck (1984) examined the relationship between children's beliefs about achievement and how they coped with confusing textual material in the classroom. One group of children were given two pages of confusing material immediately followed by five pages of non-confusing material on a separate topic. A control group were given only non-confusing pages to read. Licht and Dweck (1984) found that those children who attributed their difficulties to lack of effort were not put off by having read the confusing material. Children who attributed their difficulties to factors that were beyond their control, for example their own poor ability, were strongly affected by having read the confusing material. However, the poorer achievement of these children was *not* due to a lesser ability to learn the material. When the same straightforward material was *not* preceded by confusing material they achieved as highly as their peers. Licht and Dweck's conclusion from this study is highly significant for those pupils who experience difficulties in literacy development. They concluded that when children confront challenging or confusing material, those who do not believe that their efforts will help them overcome their difficulties will fail to learn material they are capable of mastering.

The notion of 'attribution' – that is, where individuals locate causal factors – is important in motivational theory. A number of 'attribution retraining' studies (Andrews and Debus 1978; Dweck 1975; Fowler and Peterson 1981; Shelton *et al.* 1985) have concluded that teaching children to attribute their difficulties to insufficient effort tends to improve their persistence and achievement on difficult tasks. For example, the child might be given more problems than he or she could solve in the time allowed and the researcher might tell him/her that s/he did not complete them all because s/he was not trying hard enough. In some studies (Fowler and Peterson 1981; Shelton *et al.* 1985), children's successes were attributed to their level of effort and they were congratulated and praised for trying hard.

From the perspective of those attempting to support pupils who experience difficulties in literacy, there is an obvious criticism of these studies. Motivational interventions are likely to be effective only if they are integrated with good teaching programmes, and they are no substitute for them. Many pupils with difficulties in the literacy area, for example, cannot read, write or spell better simply through trying harder. These pupils therefore also need strategies to help them improve their literacy level (Palincsar and Brown 1984). Later studies in relation to such pupils have integrated 'attribution retraining' with training in strategies for improving literacy, for example strategy training in improving reading comprehension

(Borkowski *et al.* 1988). Borkowski *et al.* concluded that pupils who receive both attribution retraining and training in literacy strategies are more likely to use the literacy strategies than pupils who receive the strategy training alone.

One important factor that contributes to the development of poor self-efficacy is the visibility of information relating to how a child performs relative to his or her peers. There are many adults who can recall being humiliated by public demonstrations of their lack of achievement in literacy in comparison with peers (audio interview for Open University E801 course materials, 2002). However unintentional this may have been on the part of those professionals concerned, the fact remains that many have had similarly upsetting experiences which they still remember vividly. Research conducted in mainstream classrooms suggests that children who experience difficulty in learning are more likely to evaluate their abilities as poor when information of this sort is highly visible (Ames and Archer 1988), for example when assessments of pupils' work are displayed publicly.

To ensure that pupils continue to believe that increasing their efforts will help them to succeed, they must experience some success. However, tasks set must not be so easy that they do not require much effort (Dweck 1975; Schunk 1989). They must be set at a level of difficulty where the learner can achieve if s/he tries hard.

Other researchers have tested out interventions designed to teach children who experience difficulties that they can succeed. For example, encouraging pupils to set specific, 'proximal' goals by indicating the number of problems they would aim to complete in one lesson tends to raise self-efficacy and achievement more than setting 'distal' goals, by indicating how many sessions it takes to complete an entire learning programme (Bandura and Schunk 1981). There are recorded instances of individuals with difficulties in literacy who can recall having set themselves goals for personal success in examinations and teaching themselves to increase their chances of achievement by focusing clearly on what was required in published syllabuses for external examinations, for example.

Verbalising strategies aloud can also increase pupils' level of performance on tasks and their self-efficacy (Schunk and Cox 1986). It is likely that verbalising aloud attains higher achievement levels because it forces additional rehearsal of the relevant strategies (Licht 1993). Seeing peers perform the skills and strategies being taught can also increase children's self-efficacy through the process of modelling

(Bandura 1986). In addition, watching a peer successfully complete a task can communicate to children that they too have the ability to achieve it (Licht 1993), particularly when children perceive the model as similar to themselves (Schunk et al. 1987). Modelling can have powerful effects, although where the peer possesses skills that the learner does not possess this may be a discouragement rather than a motivator (Licht 1993). A burning determination to achieve more highly than peers who have criticised obvious poor literacy levels can be a strong determining factor in later academic success.

The comments teachers make have also been shown to affect pupil motivation. For example, giving specific information about what the learner did well and what could be done differently and how this could be achieved, as well as comments about how the pupil's current level of achievement compares with past achievement, have been shown to enhance pupils' self-perceptions of success, and to lead to improved levels of achievement when compared to grades or comments that compare pupils with peers (Krampen 1987).

Support for learning: in-class and withdrawal

The issue of the particular forms of support offered in mainstream classrooms can be an important factor in maintaining, or undermining, motivation. There is no single clear-cut way of ensuring the inclusion of pupils who experience literacy difficulties in a way that encourages motivation. Lewis (1995) notes that the withdrawal group work focused on the teaching of specific skills for pupils who experienced difficulties in certain areas that was common practice in the 1970s and early 1980s has now largely fallen into disfavour, because:

- apparent gains made in the small group situation could not be sustained and/or generalised in the context of the classroom;
- students lose the continuity of classroom activity and instruction;
- the teaching methods used in the withdrawal groups may conflict with those in the main classroom;
- class teachers had less incentive to take an interest in examining how teaching for all pupils, including those with difficulties in literacy, might be improved.

Using support staff is common practice in many classrooms, but there seems to be little consensus among teachers, parents and pupils about what exactly the role ought to be. A recent University of Manchester research report on learning support assistants (LSAs; Farrell 1999) confirms the key role that many LSAs play in acting as the main source of support for children with exceptional needs in mainstream schools. Although teachers were often responsible for planning schemes of work that were then implemented by LSAs, in many cases, especially when LSAs were working in non-resourced schools or employed by LEAs [local education authorities], 'they took the lead in adapting programmes of work and in planning new programmes' (Farrell 1999, p. 17).

Farrell's (1999) report reflects a strong consensus among teachers and LSAs on how effective in-class support should be organised:

Report summary:

- LSAs must be fully informed about the aims and objectives of a lesson and about the learning needs of pupils who need assistance.
- LSAs need to be familiar with additional materials and equipment.
- Teachers and LSAs must get on well together, trust each others' judgement and have enough time to plan together.
- Pupils, teachers and LSAs were in agreement that they wanted support to be given from a distance – that is they preferred LSAs to 'float around a class' but to be immediately available when needed.

The report concludes with a review agenda for evaluating practice. This consists of a series of questions and issues grouped under three major headings of role, management and training (Farrell 1999):

Role

- LSAs work co-operatively with teachers to support the learning and participation of pupils.
- LSAs work with teachers to prepare lesson plans and materials.
- LSAs contribute to the evaluation of the outcome of lessons.
- LSAs make relevant contributions to wider school activities.

Management

- Teachers' management strategies provide clear guidance as to how LSAs should work in their classrooms.
- Schools have policies outlining roles and responsibilities of LSAs.
- LEA policies ensure that LSAs' conditions of employment foster effective practice.

Training

- Teachers and LSAs learn together to improve the quality of their work.
- School staff development programmes foster the competence of LSAs and teachers to carry out their respective tasks.
- LEAs provide relevant additional training and support for LSAs.
- Use is made of (institution based) external courses, or courses run by voluntary organisations to extend the expertise of LSAs.

(Farrell, reported in Mittler 2000, pp. 126–7)

The practice of support in class varies enormously from one school to another. In-class support is often something imposed on the class teacher from without to accompany the 'integration' of pupils 'with difficulties'. Potential clashes inhere in a situation where, conventionally, one professional is in control and another professional appears in the same place. Support teachers may lack status in the eyes of staff and pupils, and lack authority and subject-specific knowledge (Lovey 1995). Often, support teachers find themselves propping up the system by helping pupils through inappropriate lessons, thus unwittingly contributing to pupils' problems in the long run (Allan 1995). In this context, even the best qualified, most experienced support teacher can be humiliated by a lack of definition of role, being treated like one of the pupils, and not being able to act in the familiar capacity of authoritative adult (Best 1991; Thomas 1992).

Some schools have adopted a much more flexible and creative use of support teaching (Clark et al. 1997). For example, individual teachers or subject departments might be asked to put in a bid for in-class support to develop differentiated strategies and schemes of work for all pupils. Partnerships might be drawn up requiring class and support teachers to plan lessons together. Support teachers might be regarded as full members of a subject department.

Collaborative learning: peer support among children

In-class support may be offered by others apart from classroom assistants. Successful inclusion and participation in lessons and in the life of the school depends to a large extent on other children. In Western countries the practice of peer tutoring is increasingly used (Mittler 2000). A recent issue of *Support for Learning* was devoted to the theme of peer support (Charlton 1998). The articles emphasise the mutual benefits to be derived from such support and show that gains for the tutee go well beyond skill acquisition or mastery.

Peer tutoring has been shown to be particularly effective in the teaching of reading, provided the tutor is properly prepared and supported, and the pupil is willing to accept such help. Westwood summarises four essentials of peer tutoring as:

- clear directions as to what they are to do and how they are to do it;
- a specific teaching task to undertake and appropriate instructional materials;
- a demonstration of effective tutoring behaviours; and
- an opportunity to role play or practise tutoring, with feedback and correction.

(Westwood, cited in Mittler 2000, p. 124)

Children also support one another informally and without teacher planning. Research reviews on inclusion of children with severe learning difficulties report that other children in the schools are generally supportive and accepting (Farrell 1997; Sebba with Sachdev 1997), although warm friendships are not frequently reported.

Linking the social and the individual is an important concept in addressing barriers to students' literacy acquisition. Programmes to address difficulties are often underpinned by particular psychological models. For example, the social-constructivist approach is applicable to the social context of the classroom because it explains the dynamic of student learning in this context. It makes the links between the individual and the social, and emphasises the role of the more competent and experienced 'other', who initially offers guided instruction for the learner through a process of 'scaffolding' (Bruner 1986; Palincsar 1986; Stone 1989). The tutor then reduces the explicit instruction as the learner gains greater expertise as a result of internalising the instructions and self-directed verbalisations. Co-operative learning through peer discussion and group reading offer learners opportunities to model, discuss and evaluate their learning as they plan work together, revise, edit each others' work, and discuss the content of texts and the process of reading.

Reading comprehension

Reading comprehension is a particular area of difficulty for some students. Using a social-constructivist framework, Palincsar *et al.* (1993) report a research study into the successful use of 'reciprocal teaching' to enhance reading comprehension with pupils who experience difficulties in literacy development. Reciprocal teaching emphasises collaboration between teachers and learners to apply given concrete strategies to the task of reading comprehension. Teachers and pupils take turns to lead discussion about the meaning of a section of text that they are jointly trying to understand and memorise. This technique focuses on four strategies to assist understanding of the text and joint construction of its meaning: generating questions from the text, summarising its content, clarifying areas of difficulty, and predicting the content of subsequent sections of text based on the content and structure of the current portion. Learners are taught the terminology of reciprocal teaching through direct instruction in each of the four strategies prior to the start of the procedure. This technique emphasises the role of the teacher in modelling expert performance and the role of the learner as active participant in his/her learning, in addition to the function of social interactions in learning. Assessment of learners' progress is ongoing and judged through their developing contributions to discussion of the texts.

Oakhill and Yuill note 'three main ways' in which students' comprehension of text might be improved (1995, p. 177). First, additions such as pictures, subheadings and summaries might be made to the text. Second, teachers might encourage students to take notes, underline key passages or write summaries. Third, students can be taught consciously to think about the text as they read: whether it fits in with what they know already, whether they have understood it adequately, what they might infer about the meaning of a whole sentence or story from individual words, what questions they might ask themselves about the meaning of the text as they read it through. Students can also be taught to generate mental images of the events described or discussed in a text. This latter technique is, according to Oakhill and Yuill, more suitable for students over the age of 8 or so.

As Oakhill and Yuill note, research findings have repeatedly indicated that individuals who are less skilled in understanding text tend to experience difficulties in making inferences not only about the written, but also the spoken, word. In addition, they tend to be much less clear about the structure of text, either how to structure their own text or its significance for overall meaning. Oakhill and Yuill have proposed particular group activities for developing skills for the self-monitoring of text comprehension and also for using imagery to support comprehension. The extent to which teachers might find either or both of these group activities of value will depend on individual working contexts, and also on individual perspectives on the difficulties in literacy experienced by particular students.

Whilst many researchers link peer tutoring to a social-constructivist approach, it is possible to devise peer-tutored programmes based on other psychological models – for example behaviourist, which emphasises the links between stimulus and response and the reinforcement of desired behaviour rather than the internalised learning process evident in the social-constructivist model.

Developing thinking skills through Paired Thinking

Topping (2002) suggests that thinking skills should be embedded into the teaching of reading because reading is a vehicle which can achieve deep processing. He proposes that there is an unclear borderline between thinking skills and 'higher order reading skills'. Paired Thinking therefore aims to combine thinking skills and higher-order reading skills.

The method called Paired Thinking is essentially a framework for pairs working together. Some difference in reading ability is needed in each pair. The pairs can be peers of the same or different ages, parents working with children at home, teaching assistants working with children in school, or volunteer adults (such as senior citizens) working with children in school. Paired Thinking is very active, interactive, socially inclusive and flexible. It integrates thinking skills with reading skills, particularly upon the specific structured method of Paired Reading, and promotes paired reading in higher-order reading skills and beyond. This approach is essentially a behaviourist approach, because it looks upon reading and thinking as 'behaviours' which can be accommodated by the participant. It does not break these tasks into teaching components or demand that the learner has mastered the subskills of the task, but treats the activity as a complete task, a behaviour – that is, either reading or thinking. Topping suggests that these two activities can be combined into one behavioural activity and that, for example, thinking skills can have a spin-off effect for reading skills, and particularly higher-order reading skills.

Supporting the writing process

Writing is a complex task. In a further elaboration of the paired approach to literacy development, Topping has piloted a Paired Writing technique, using the same principles of 'training' parents/tutors in its use. For example, he advocates using the technique as frequently as possible after the initial training session in order to reinforce and promote fluency in its use. He recommends drawing up an informal contract to agree minimum frequency of usage and suggests Paired Writing for three sessions of twenty minutes per week for six weeks. Paired Writing works within clear behaviourist principles of constant inbuilt feedback and cross-checking, both to ensure that what is written makes sense to both partners, and to address the issue of the fear of failure and anxiety about spelling or punctuation. Again, Topping lays out a clear method:

> Paired Writing is a framework for a pair working together to generate ... a piece of writing – for any purpose they wish. ... Paired Writing usually operates with a more able writer (the Helper) and a less able one (the Writer), but can work with a pair of equal ability so long as they edit carefully and use a dictionary to check spellings. ...
>
> The structure of the system consists of six Steps, 10 Questions (for Ideas), five Stages (for Drafting) and four Levels (for Editing) .... Further details will be found in Topping (1995).
>
> Step 1 is Ideas Generation. The Helper stimulates ideas by using given Questions and inventing other relevant ones, making one-word notes on the Writer's responses.
>
> Step 2 is Drafting. The notes then form the basis for Drafting,

which ignores spelling and punctuation. Lined paper and double spaced writing is recommended. The Writer dictates the text and scribing occurs in whichever of the five Stages of Support has been chosen by the pair. If there is a hitch, the Helper gives more support.

In Step 3 the pair look at the text together while the Helper reads the Draft out loud with expression. The Writer then reads the text out loud, with the Helper correcting any reading errors.

Step 4 is Editing. First the Writer considers where s/he thinks improvements are necessary, marking this with a coloured pen, pencil or highlighter. The most important improvement is where the meaning is unclear. The second most important is to do with the organization of ideas or the order in which meanings are presented. The next consideration is whether spellings are correct and the last whether punctuation is helpful and correct. The Helper praises the Writer then marks points the Writer has 'missed'. The pair then discuss – and agree improvements.

In Step 5 the Writer (usually) copies out a 'neat' or 'best' version. Sometimes the Helper may write or type or word-process it, however. Making the final copy is the least important step.

Step 6 is Evaluate. The pair should self-assess their own best copy, but peer assessment by another pair is very useful. The criteria in the Edit levels provide a checklist for this.

(Topping 1996, p. 46)

Evaluation of Paired Writing has, to date, been descriptive only.

Using behaviourist techniques is not the only way to conceptualise support for pupils' writing. As we noted above, this approach tells us nothing about the learning process itself, or the processing of information which results in the production of writing. The cognitive approach is very useful in conceptualising the process of writing. One influential and explicit description of the cognitive processes involved in writing (Flower and Hayes 1980) suggests that:

- The writing process is driven by a series of goals which are hierarchically organised.
- Those engaged in the writing task achieve their goals through processes of planning, translating and revising what has been written. Planning involves generating information to be included in the script, selecting and organising what is relevant,

and deciding on criteria for judging successful completion of the script. Translation means converting the plan into the script. Revising includes editing for both grammatical errors and structural coherence.

- These goals overlap and are revisited many times before the whole task is completed.
- Competent writers can switch their attention between these processes as their perception of successful task completion requires.

(Scardamalia and Bereiter 1986)

Learning to write clearly and effectively has proven to be particularly problematic for pupils who experience difficulties in literacy development (Graham and Harris 1993). Writing problems may, in large part, be the result of three factors (Graham and Harris 1989):

- Lack of proficiency in text production skills, i.e. frequent errors in spelling, the use of upper and lower case, and punctuation. The amount of attention that has to be expended on lower-level skills is thought to interfere with higher-order skills of planning and the generation of content (MacArthur and Graham 1987).
- Lack of knowledge relating to the subject content of the script to be written, and/or of the conventions and characteristics of different writing genres.
- Ineffective strategies in planning or revising text.

Wray (2002) suggests that, of all the processes of literacy and language, writing is the most self-evidently metacognitive. He proposes that by expressing these thoughts in a visible way we can subsequently rethink, revise and redraft, and we are allowed, indeed forced, to reflect upon our own thinking. Wray suggests, therefore, that writing is metacognitive and that metacognitive knowledge consists of dimensions of personal, task and strategy knowledge. This implies that self-knowledge is important at both the pre-writing and the writing stage. The writer's ideas, sequences, starting and finishing points are reflected on, as well as the information to be covered and the ideas the writer wants to incorporate in the writing piece. Wray suggests that the actual task is important, and that the writer reflects on the different genre, and the structure and accessibility of the writing for the reader and how the reader may be guided through the writing piece.

Knowledge of the process is also important for metacognition and reflection. Wray suggests that pupils need to reflect on the processes they go through as they write, to reassure themselves that the processes they use are entirely normal and will, in the end, produce the right results. Being aware of how they as individuals learn, of the task and of the processes helps the writer to control the writing process, and allows them to check on their own progress, choose alternative strategies, change direction and make an evaluation of the emerging and completed product.

Wray therefore advocates that teachers ensure that children are given adequate opportunities to acquire the requisite knowledge about themselves as writers, about the writing process and about the demands of particular writing tasks, including textual structures. They also need to ensure that this knowledge develops beyond simply knowing that certain things can be done in writing to knowing *how* they can be done and *why* they *should* be done. Therefore the focus is on the process involved in the emerging and finished product, rather than on the product itself.

Some strategies to help integrate metacognitive skills in the writing process include thinking aloud while writing, and critically examining and revising writing decisions – for example asking why did you write this or why did you explain something in this manner? According to Wray, writers also need to anticipate potential difficulties, make judgements and reconciliations between competing ideas, as well as showing an alertness to the needs of their potential and actual readership.

Wray suggests that expert writers are more likely to have in mind several alternative ways of handling their writing task, and their writing consists not only of expressing what they wish to say, but of actually working this out as they write. This 'knowledge transforming' has been described by a variety of professional writers. On the other hand, pupils with learning difficulties tend to lack the metacognitive control that would enable them to implement and regulate a range of learning strategies. They are also less successful in regulating their textual understanding, and fail to monitor or correct potential confusions as they read others' texts and produce texts themselves for others to read. This lack of ability, according to Wray, means they cannot detect errors and prevents them from successfully rereading, monitoring and revising their texts. He therefore suggests that younger and less experienced writers are less able to operate metacognitively in their writing than expert writers, but, moreover, that the actual level of metacognitive awareness may be a major factor which differentiates between skilled and poor writers.

Graham and Harris (1993) note that one advantage of the cognitive approach for conceptualising ways of supporting the writing development of pupils who experience difficulties is that it emphasises the component processes of writing production, which can then be focused on individually. They go on to indicate that the area researched most thoroughly in relation to pupils with difficulties in literacy development is the use of strategies intended to highlight planning processes. Examples of this that have been highlighted by Wray (above) are self-directed techniques for generating words relevant to the content of the script (Harris and Graham 1985), the use of writing frames to generate and organise ideas (Englert and Raphael 1988; Graves et al. 1989), and the articulation of process goals for establishing the way in which the end product is to be achieved (Graham et al. 1989).

Individualised programmes

Reading instruction

There are a number of programmes with individualised instruction that are designed to address reading difficulties in schools. The Reading Recovery programme is a well-known example of an initiative that operates at the level of the individual child and teacher but relies for its continued existence on resourcing, in part through LEAs or from central government itself and in part through individual school budgets. Reading Recovery is an intervention programme that attempts to prevent failure in learning to read by providing an intensive, highly structured programme of instruction to children who experience difficulty in learning to read after one year of formal schooling. This programme was developed by Marie Clay for New Zealand schools in 1976.

Clay describes Reading Recovery as:

> A one-to-one tutoring programme which gives supplementary help to individual children after their first year at school if they are still low achievers in reading and writing relative to their agemates.
>
> (Clay 1993, p. 10)

It is 'a prevention strategy' with two distinct goals, both expressed in relation to norms of achievement in literacy:

- first, to accelerate the learning of the very weakest children to reach the average band of the class and to give them learning strategies so that they will be able to keep up;
- second, to identify those who fail to achieve the level of the average group at an early age as needing long-term support.

(Hobsbaum and Leon 1999, p. 1)

Reading Recovery focuses on the development of individual children's literacy acquisition through tuition by trained teachers working in a school. It has a highly organised, tightly structured training programme for teachers. An expert tutor leads regular teacher professional development sessions: teachers bring their own experiences of individual children's reading difficulties into the training sessions, and a one-way screen is used so that the trained tutor and the group of teachers can observe and comment on each others' teaching practices.

On the surface it might appear that in contexts where the school literacy curriculum is heavily constrained by the requirements of a centrally imposed national curriculum there is little room for an additional literacy programme focused on individual pupils' needs. However, there are schools which have deliberately embedded Reading Recovery into an integrated literacy curriculum which aims to meet national requirements for all students and also the individual learning needs of some.

Whilst it might appear that the apparent efficacy of any programme should be the most important factor in determining its successful uptake, there is considerable evidence to indicate that factors relating to the political context at the micro and macro levels are equally important. Openshaw et al. (2002) have argued that the development of Reading Recovery in New Zealand and England illustrates that it is not simply the efficacy of individual programmes, but a combination of that efficacy and the political context at the micro and macro levels that establishes, expands and eventually destabilises new reading initiatives. They comment that those who engage in reading debates should not only focus on which reading programme appears to match desirable goals in children's literacy development, but also strive for a more balanced appreciation of the complex socio-political context of debates within which reading failure and its various remedies remain contestable. They go on to add that, in turn, this will lead to a more critical and more academically sophisticated scrutiny of literacy and its diverse purposes.

The outcomes of Reading Recovery might well be higher levels of reading competence among the student cohort. As is noted in Chapters 2 and 3, there are many examples of individuals diagnosed as 'dyslexic' who have learned to read through predominantly top-down approaches. However, despite being able to read by using problem-solving, meaning-based approaches, many may still experience particular difficulties at the level of word accuracy and spelling. For these students it may be appropriate to introduce programmes with a more rigorous focused approach to the subskills of reading, bearing in mind the issue of maintaining student motivation and a sense of overall achievement.

Phonological awareness

As was noted in Chapters 2 and 3, phonological awareness is one of the areas which create barriers to some students' literacy acquisition. There are a number of programmes which have been designed to address this specific learning need through individualised instruction. Programmes which rely on individualised instruction are inherently costly. It is therefore important to assess their effectiveness in improving pupils' overall reading standards. The Qualifications and Curriculum Authority (QCA) commissioned a report (1998) comparing the outcomes of a phonological training programme with Reading Recovery that relies on individualised instruction but is not based on phonological awareness. This phonological awareness training programme (PAT) was developed from the work of Bradley and Bryant (1983) and is based on their research into the normal stages of children's development of phonological awareness. They argued that onset and rime, for example 'c' + 'at' is the most natural way to break words down into smaller units of sound, and their training programme emphasised sound categorisation, beginning with rhyme and initial sounds (Qualifications and Curriculum Authority 1998). They aimed to develop in the child an awareness of sound, moving from rhyme and alliteration towards a greater level of phonic distinctions. In the original study by Bryant and Bradley individual children received forty ten-minute sessions over the course of two years, whilst in the evaluation study this was spread over seven months.

The authors of the 1995 SCAA report comment that phonological awareness training was generally effective in encouraging the development of word accuracy and spelling. Reading Recovery had more general effects in relation to pupils' reading, and appeared to be particularly effective in situations where pupils had little access to books and texts prior to starting school. In the long term both interventions significantly improved the reading of children from homes 'with an impoverished literacy environment' (Qualifications and Assessment Authority 1998).

Phonics programmes

Some of the other popular programmes which can help to develop decoding skills and phonological processing include 'Toe by Toe', 'Sound Linkage' and the 'Hickey Programme'. These last two focus, in particular, on the subskills of reading. For example, in 'Sound Linkage' there are sections on syllable blending, phoneme blending, identification and discrimination of phonemes, and activities on phonological linkage, including multisyllabic words and establishing links between sounds and the written form of words.

Multisensory approaches

One way to reinforce the links between sounds and symbols in order to develop skills in phonics is to take a multi-sensory approach to teaching. Multi-sensory programmes should focus on all modalities – auditory, visual, kinaesthetic and tactile. Johnson (2002) describes in more detail what is meant by a 'multi-sensory approach':

> Multi sensory teaching is teaching done using all the learning pathways in the brain (visual, auditory and kinaesthetic–tactile) in order to enhance memory and learning. It is crucial that whatever pathways are being addressed in a particular exercise are directly focussed upon by both teacher and child. For example, they look at, feel, move and say the names of the wooden letters they are using to compose a word. When 'writing' a word in the air the left hand holds the right elbow and the eyes follow the pointing finger. A tray with salt or sand on it or the reverse side of a piece of hardboard can be used to 'write on' with a finger. The rough surface maximises the sensory input and in both cases the letters and the final word are said out loud.
>
> (Johnson 2002, p. 275)

Many reading programmes incorporate that principle and often teachers can develop supplementary materials to ensure that the activities are multi-sensory. This is particularly important when considering the learning needs of dyslexic students, for whom the acquisition of phonics skills is often problematic. One such individualised programme which incorporates this principle is the Multi-Sensory Teaching System for Reading (MTSR). This is how Johnson describes the programme:

> The MTSR is a cumulative, structured, multi-sensory programme designed to be delivered by a teacher (or assistant under a teacher's guidance) in a normal primary classroom. The programme is taught to groups of up to six children, and all the materials required are contained in the published package. Lessons normally take 10 to 20 minutes and should be delivered daily for four or five days each week. The lessons are fully scripted and a Handbook provides details about the teaching methods. Each course book also contains a copy of the essential instructions for teaching the lessons.
>
> (Johnson 2002, p. 377)

Johnson (2002) describes the way this programme is designed to tackle reading from a bottom-up perspective and to ensure that the child has a basic grasp of the subskills:

> The most frequently recurring graphemes (letters and letter clusters) together with their varying pronunciations are taught in MTSR. A fundamental principle is that about 85% of the English language follows predictable rules of pronunciation. Teaching about what is consistent and predictable will help pupils gain confidence in tackling the reading process. At the same time, they are not misled and do learn about 'irregular' words, particularly those which are used frequently.
>
> The concept of phoneme awareness is reinforced every time a letter is taught. A sound is first represented in the context of spoken words; the sound is analysed, then the letter that represents that sound is shown. Finally the pupil sees the letter in written form, reinforcing the idea that letters in written words represent sounds in spoken words. As soon as pupils have been taught 'i' and 't', they read the word 'it'. As new letters are taught they read more words that can be formed with those

letters. After nine letter sounds have been presented, they begin reading phrases and short sentences. Since some graphemes (letters or letter clusters) have more than one pronunciation, pupils are taught how to make the appropriate choice from possible multiple pronunciations of the same grapheme, such as how to tell if a vowel is short or long, or when 'c' is pronounced (k) or (s). In addition to teaching letter–sound correspondence and related concepts, there is a systematic study of basic syllable types, suffixes and prefixes. The goal is to teach pupils the science and structure of the written English language, together with processes for applying their knowledge, so that they will have lifelong skills for independent reading.

(Johnson 2002, pp. 275)

One criticism, however, is the extent to which the acquisition of these subskills can be assumed to be prerequisites of fluent reading. Whole-book approaches can also be effective in promoting fluent reading, but not at the level of individual word recognition. There is considerable evidence that the reading process operates through an interaction between both bottom-up and top-down skills. It can be argued, therefore, that there is a need for both approaches but that the emphasis for individual students may be a matter for the professional judgement of the teacher.

Spelling programmes

As was noted above, Bentley (2002) has identified five stages of spelling acquisition: the pre-communicative stage, the semi-phonetic stage, the phonetic stage, the transitional stage and the correct stage. She comments on the work of other researchers in outlining ways in which students might be encouraged to learn new spellings, and suggests that, for example, Bradley's (1981) suggestions might apply to students at the semi-phonetic stage of development:

The method consists of a series of steps in the following order:

1 The student proposes the word he [sic] wants to learn.
2 The word is written correctly for him (or made with plastic script letters).
3 The student names the word.
4 He then writes the word himself, saying out loud the alphabetic name of each letter of the word as it is written.
5 He names the word again. He checks to see that the word has

been written correctly; this is important, as less able readers are often inaccurate when they copy …. Repeat steps 2 to 5 twice more, covering or disregarding the stimulus word as soon as the student feels he can manage without it.

6   The student practises the word in this way for six consecutive days. The procedure is the same whether or not the student can read or write, and whether or not he is familiar with all the sound/symbol relationships, but it must not deteriorate into rote spelling, which is an entirely different thing.

7   The student learns to generalise from this word to similar words using the plastic script letters.

(Bradley 1981; quoted in Bentley 2002, p. 3)

Bentley also refers to the work of Peters (1967), who perceived 'good spellers' as having a good visual perception of word forms, the ability to see words within words and recognise letter sequences and patterns, and sensitivity to the coding system of the orthography of a language. Peters outlined a slightly different strategy for developing competence in spelling:

- LOOK at the word carefully and in such a way that you will remember what you have seen.
- COVER the word so that you cannot see it.
- WRITE the word from memory, saying it to yourself as you are writing.
- CHECK the word. If it is not correct then go back and repeat the steps.

(Peters 1967; cited in Bentley 2002, p. 4)

Students should never simply copy words but should always be encouraged to memorise them and then write them down. Bentley comments that this strategy appears to be suited to those students who are moving from the phonetic to the transitional stage of development in spelling.

Both Peters' strategy of look, cover, write and check and the method piloted by Bradley (1981) in her controlled training study include sight, hearing and the fine hand movements needed for handwriting. However, Bradley's method involves more repetition of the same sounds and movements, and considerable over-learning of the kind often advocated as useful in supporting the learning of students with significant difficulties in reading and spelling.

Bentley makes the point that parents (and carers) should not be expected to know how to help their children with spelling acquisition but should be given guidelines to help their children in order to reduce their own anxiety levels. There is also another issue, however. Many parents may genuinely not know how most appropriately to help their child to learn new spellings. Guidelines that include a description of Bradley's method or Peters' strategy may well be very welcome to some parents or carers.

Reason and Boote (1994) offer a similar but slightly different outline of four developmental stages of spelling acquisition. At stage one students can recognise rhyme, blend spoken sounds into words and make some attempt to represent phonic structures at the beginning of words in letter form. At stage two they can write single-letter sounds, simple, regular single-syllable words and the more common single-syllable irregular words. At stage three they can write words with consonant blends (for example 'tr-', '-nd') and digraphs (for example 'sh'), vowel digraphs (for example 'ea', 'ow') and the 'magic' 'e'; and at stage four they can spell most common words correctly (Reason and Boote 1994, p. 133). In order to avoid difficulties in spelling later on, children need to be familiar with vowels and syllables at an early stage, and to be taught techniques for learning the spelling of words they want or need to use in writing. They also advocate the look, cover, write, check routine. In addition, for students who find particular difficulty with spelling they describe a multisensory approach, which, whilst lengthy at first, can, in their view, be slimmed down as students gain confidence and competence in spelling:

- Look at the word, read it, and pronounce it in syllables or other small bits (re-mem-ber; sh-out).
- Try to listen to yourself doing this.
- Still looking at it, spell it out in letter-names.
- Continue to look, and trace out the letters on the table with your finger as you spell it out again.
- Look at the word for any 'tricky bits'; for example, gh in right. (Different pupils find different parts of a word 'tricky'.)
- Try to get a picture of the word in your mind: take a photograph of it in your head!
- Copy the word, peeping at the end of each syllable or letter-string.
- Highlight the tricky bits in colour (or by some other means).

- Visualise the word again.
- Now cover it up and try to write it, spelling it out in letter-names.
- Does it look right?
- Check with the original.
- Are there some tricky bits you didn't spot (i.e. the parts that went wrong)?
- Repeat as much of the procedure as necessary to learn the words thoroughly.

(Reason and Boote 1994, p. 138)

Conclusion

For many students school is fundamentally important in determining the extent to which difficulties in literacy development impact on future life chances. The school literacy curriculum, including policies, classroom practices and the kind of home–school relationship that the school is seen to promote, can serve to include or exclude individual students, and to address and ameliorate, or exacerbate, the literacy difficulties that are experienced. Even in situations where teachers are heavily constrained by highly prescriptive literacy curricula there is likely to be some room for manoeuvre to support literacy learning in ways that respect diversity and can make a difference to individual life chances.

Chapter 11

Supporting students' literacy acquisition at the level of the family

Introduction

When students experience difficulties in literacy acquisition it is clear that teachers and schools alone are unlikely to be able to address every individual learning need. In considering what it would take to mobilise more people and resources to support students' learning, it is important to recognise the potential for involving others as partners in the educational process, most notably parents and carers. Furthermore, as noted in previous chapters, one of the most significant issues raised by an awareness of cultural aspects of literacy is the importance of acknowledging the relationship between family and literacy in teaching practices and in the school context. It is crucial that educators have a clear view of how families and schools can work together to establish home–school links to support the learning of students who experience difficulties in literacy development in ways which take account of a diversity of family and cultural backgrounds.

Models of parent/carer/school partnerships

The partnership arrangements that currently exist between parents/carers and schools have the potential to constrain or facilitate the literacy development of those pupils who experience difficulties. The degree of schools' responsiveness to family culture can serve to include or alienate students, in particular those with difficulties in literacy acquisition. The indicators for 'parents as partners' published in *Early Learning Goals* outline clearly the potential role for parents as children's first educators in the area of literacy acquisition and the respect that should be accorded to this role by schools:

Parents are children's first and most enduring educators. When parents and practitioners work together in early years settings, the results have a positive impact on the child's development and learning. Therefore, each setting should seek to develop an effective partnership with parents.

A successful partnership needs a two way flow of information, knowledge and expertise. There are many ways of achieving partnership with parents but the following are common features of effective practice:

- Practitioners show respect and understanding for the role of parents in their child's education.
- The past and future part played by parents in the education of their children is recognised and explicitly encouraged.
- Arrangements for settling in are flexible enough to give time for children to become secure and for practitioners and parents to discuss each child's circumstances, interests, competencies and needs.
- All parents are made to feel welcome, valued and necessary, through a range of different opportunities for collaboration between children, parent and practitioners.
- The knowledge and expertise of parents and other family adults are used to support the learning opportunities provided by the setting.
- Practitioners use a variety of ways to keep parents fully informed about the curriculum, such as brochures, displays and videos which are available in the home languages of the parents and through informal discussion
- Parents and practitioners talk about and record information about the child's progress and achievements, for example through meetings or making a book about the child.
- Relevant learning activities and play activities, such as sharing and reading books, are continued at home.
- Similarly, experiences at home are used to develop learning in the setting, for example, visits and celebrations.

(Qualifications and Curriculum Authority and Department for Education and Employment 1999; quoted in Mittler 2000, pp. 155–6)

There are, however, many instances of home–school relationships which reflect views of parents as educators which are different from those implied in these indicators. Dale (1996) has identified five common partnership arrangements between schools and parents/carers:

- The Expert Model represents the traditional way of working. It is like the doctor–patient relationship. The professional uses his or her expertise to make judgements and take control of what needs to be done. The involvement of the parent is not of primary importance and is limited to providing information.

- In the Transplant Model, parents are seen as an untapped resource for helping in the teaching of the child. The role of professionals is to share their expertise – in other words, to transplant their skills to the parents to help the parents to become teachers, like the Portage program. The professional still has the ultimate responsibility for decision making.

- The Consumer Model involves more of a partnership between parents and professionals. In this model, there is a shift of power from the professional to the parent. This model uses ideas from the marketplace. The parent and the child with a disability are seen as consumers of services. They are acknowledged as having expertise about the child's needs. As consumers they have control over decision making because they draw upon their expertise in deciding what services they need and want for their child. Many recent educational reforms in industrialized western countries have incorporated this model of parent–professional partnership. A clear example of it is in countries where legislation gives parents the right to choose the school their child attends.

- A more recent model of parent professional partnership is the Empowerment Model. Here the right of the parent to choose as a consumer is combined with a professional recognition of the family as a social system. As a social system, the family is made up of interdependent relationships which have an important effect upon how a family is able to cope and the type of support they will need. Research suggests that parents rely as much or more on informal networks of support – neighbours, other family members, friends, their church – than on the formal network that exists between the professional and the parent ....
Under the Empowerment Model the job of the professional is to help empower the family to meet its own needs rather than to make judgements and decisions about those needs.

- The final model is the Negotiating Model. The idea of this model is that both the parent and the professional have separate and valuable contributions to offer and that negotiating about these differences in perspective is the key to developing partnerships that lead to the best decisions for children. This model proposes how parents and professionals might negotiate to reach a decision.

(Open University E801 course materials, 2002,
summarising Dale 1996, ch. 1)

Wragg et al.'s (1998) summary of the manner in which parents were involved in the reading development of their children in the schools surveyed during the Leverhulme Primary Improvement Project reflects many of the same issues of power and assumptions of expert knowledge identified by Dale:

> No school expressed disregard for parents ... Most children in the 5 to 7 age group read to someone at home ... home/school diaries are countersigned by many parents; spellings are checked; the general attitude of teachers towards parents is, in the main, extremely positive. On the surface, therefore, all appears to be well.
>
> (Wragg et al. 1998, p. 269)

However, as Wragg noted, beneath the surface the processes were not quite as unproblematic:

> The difficulties sometimes arose when parents tried to act in a manner regarded as professional, rather than amateur. In several schools ... when parents expressed reservations about what was happening, teachers saw it as their duty to explain what the school was trying to achieve, to persuade them about the rightness of existing practice, rather than change it: 'Some of these parents really don't understand what we're trying to do and how we go about it', as one teacher put it.
>
> (Wragg et al. 1990, p. 269)

Commonly there was a clash of ideology over how to hear children read:

> for some parents the only method of teaching reading they remembered from their own school days. Another was about the different interpretations of what constituted 'reading', since some parents

found it difficult to accept that looking at a picture book could constitute 'reading'. ...

Many parents interviewed expressed ignorance about the methods used to teach reading, even in schools that had held parents' evenings. ... Yet successful evenings involving parents were very much appreciated, explaining, for example, how children might recognise, at quite an early stage, longer and more complex-looking words, such as 'elephant'. ...

Some parents seemed eager to play a more professional role, rather than the well-intentioned amateur role that teachers expected. Teachers tended to stress that reading at home was for 'fun' and 'enjoyment', avoiding any suggestion of drudgery, coercion, or indeed systematic teaching. Parents too were anxious to prevent reading at home becoming a chore, but several did want to be able to work more positively with their children, sounding out words, actually 'teaching' reading, rather than just hearing it. In a number of families there was tension and frustration when parents tried to push children on, expecting performance beyond what the child was achieving, or employed methods and approaches that were in contrast to what the child did at school. ...

Parent helpers in the classroom also performed a modest role. Few were given any instruction on what to do.... As a result, ... parents usually operated in an informal, unstructured and ad hoc manner. ...

The generally positive reaction of schools to the involvement of parents is a strong foundation stone on which to build, but there should be no doubt about the gaps, misunderstandings and lack of knowledge that exist, even in schools as effective generally as the ones studied in this research. ... Unwittingly perhaps, some schools may patronise their children's parents by glossing over their concerns, assuming that they are capable of very little beyond the most rudimentary, or, in the case of ethnic minorities, assuming too readily that they may not be equipped to help.

(Wragg et al. 1998, pp. 269–70)

Until comparatively recently there has been an assumption that the homes of poor working-class and ethnic-minority families are less good literacy-learning environments than those of dominant-culture, middle-class families. A number of studies carried out in the 1970s and 1980s suggested that achievement on standardised tests of reading is strongly related to social class. For example, the National Child

Development Study (Davie *et al.* 1972) followed all the children born in one week in 1958 through from birth. Tests of reading attainment were carried out when they were 7 years old. These tests showed relatively poor achievement among 30 per cent of the children. A number of home factors were found to correlate with poor achievement, amongst which was social class. Children whose fathers were semi-skilled manual workers were more than twice as likely to be poor readers as those children whose fathers held professional or technical posts. Hannon and McNally's (1986) study found a 27-point difference in mean reading test scores between middle-class and working-class 7-year-olds. Research by Wells (1985), M.J. Adams (1994) and McCormick and Mason (1986), among others, suggests a number of factors that might predispose children to this apparent difference in reading achievement: the number of books to which children had access at home, the number of stories read to children by parents, and the overall number of reading interactions between parent and child.

The assumptions that we make about family life are very important in conceptualising ways in which those families might support the literacy development of their children. For example, the work on 'family literacy' in recent years has represented an interesting diversity of views on the ability of some families to support their children's literacy development, where those families have little tradition of literacy. Hannon (1999) distinguishes the kind of family literacy programmes which combine basic education for parents with early literacy education for pupils – that is, with a focus on two generations in a family simultaneously – from other kinds of programmes which address the family dimension in students' literacy learning. He terms the former 'restricted', and points out that 'restricted' family literacy programmes are premised on the notion that some families are 'literacy deficient'. Programmes that ignore pre-existing literacy in families are prescriptive and interventionist and may not recognise possibilities for drawing on existing patterns of family literacy to inform children's learning. A further inherent difficulty in the deficit perspective on some pupils' families for those conceptualising appropriate ways in which to support the improvement of children's literacy is that the school is absolved from responsibility for addressing the literacy difficulties of those pupils from 'literacy-deficient' families. In addition, the assumption of a necessarily reciprocal relationship between low levels of parental literacy and the poor literacy development of their offspring is not fully supported by research findings. One of the problematic areas in the evaluation of restricted literacy programmes is that there is insufficient evidence that programmes which involve both parents/carers and children in literacy development achieve greater and longer-lasting effects than 'standalone' programmes. Hannon argues that, rather than targeting a few families for restricted literacy programmes, it may be more profitable to provide universal literacy-rich early childhood education. This should seek to identify children's difficulties and develop appropriate interventions at an early stage, involve parents in their children's literacy development and offer opportunities for parents and carers to enhance their own literacy if they wish to.

Hannon identified a number of issues crucial to the discussion of parental willingness to participate in literacy programmes which all those intending to implement such initiatives might do well to address:

- the manner in which families are invited to participate;
- the substance of what they are expected to do;
- the extent to which the programme is responsive to the circumstances of the family – for example, programmes based in the home have achieved higher mean take-up and retention rates than programmes based in learning centres.

Despite these rather negative views on the ability of families with little history of literacy to support their children's literacy development, Blackledge (2000) cites a number of studies which refute the deficiency model of poor working-class and ethnic-minority-culture families. For example, Delgado-Gaitan (1992) found regular use of texts in Spanish and English in poor Mexican-American families. Auerbach (1989) and Ada (1988) found that poor minority-culture immigrant families often value and support their children's literacy development as one key to social mobility.

Supporting the literacy acquisition of Travellers' children

In the UK, a number of researchers have raised particular issues in relation to the literacy acquisition of students from the families of Travellers. Jordan (2002) notes that, since the inception of state education for all, Travellers have experienced difficulties in accessing, and maintaining coherent access to, formal education. She goes on to comment that amongst these families there are high levels of illiteracy and lack of formal qualifications, which indicate that state education has failed to overcome the barriers associated with mobility in lifestyle, racism and institutional discrimination. Currently Travellers continue to experience discrimination. A lack of formal qualifications adds to their exclusion from the waged job markets. Great value is attached to oral skills, since there is commonly oral transmission down the generations of skills, knowledge and cultural codes. Jordan reflects on the fact that many prefer to undertake their own traditional education within the family and community, and cites Liegeois (1998) in commenting that, within the Traveller community, education to be a Traveller is as important as education for employability. She adds that this is significant in maintaining ethnic role boundaries.

Reading programmes for families

In the past studies have shown that parents from every social class are often very keen to help their children with reading at home (Newson and Newson 1977). In the UK, as Wragg *et al.* (1998) note:

> The Plowden Report (1967) on primary education devoted a whole chapter to the role that could be played by parents. Young and McGeeney (1968) experimented in London schools by involving parents in attending school functions, hearing their children read, and various other forms of participation. They found some improvements in reading performance compared with control schools where there was no such participation. Many studies of parents simply record the implementation of specific projects, while others report the teachers' and parents' attitudes to such studies. A few studies have been conducted on parents coming into school to help, but the majority are on parents helping at home.
>
> (Wragg *et al.* 1998, p. 33)

Hewison and Tizard's (1980) study of the reading attainment of 7-year-old working-class children in Dagenham showed that many working-class children do become competent readers. None of the parents had been encouraged by the school to hear their children read, but half regularly did this. Following this study a number of research studies were set up to investigate the hypothesis that parental support at home for school-related literacy had a significant effect on improvement in children's reading, for example the Haringey Project (Tizard *et al.* 1982). This is an example of an initiative which combines a whole-book approach with an assumption that parents are the first educators of their children and, as such, should be in control of any parent–child home-based reading project. In this project two top infant classes were chosen at random from two schools also chosen at random from six multiracial inner-city schools in London. Every child in the two classes was heard reading from books sent home by the class teachers over a period of two years. At the end of this period the children's reading scores were compared with parallel classes at the same schools and with classes chosen at random at two schools where extra tuition in reading was given to pupils. The results indicated a highly significant improvement in reading by pupils who were heard reading at home in comparison with other pupils, and no comparable improvement by those pupils who received the extra tuition in school. Reflecting on what she felt was the crucial factor in the success of the Haringey Project, Hewison (1988) speculates that it may have been the motivational context of the home itself in which the opportunity for extra reading practice occurred.

Building on the apparent success of the Haringey Project, a number of replications were carried out. Among these, the Belfield Project (Hannon 1987) was conducted over five years in a school in a largely white, working-class Social Priority Area in the north of England. In terms of gains in standardised reading tests, the results indicated only a slight positive impact on performance in reading. Almost all parents, however, reported that they welcomed the chance of involvement in their children's reading development. One explanation for the relative success of the Haringey Project in comparison with Belfield was that a home-reading programme has a greater impact on minority language families, who can be excluded by schools.

In recent years, support for family-based literacy programmes for children in the early stages of literacy acquisition has come, in some areas, from the LEA. East Renfrewshire in Scotland is one LEA with a very clear policy for early intervention in the area of literacy, which operates in part through family literacy co-ordinators. In a recent interview (for Open University E801 course materials, 2002) one of the family literacy co-ordinators outlines some elements of the early literacy strategy:

> One of the reasons that we started using 'Story Sacks' was ... to set in motion some strategies that could get resources into houses, into homes, that perhaps didn't have books in the house ... we liaised with our health visitors, and we joined a nationwide scheme with 'Book Start', and 'Books for Babies'. A bag is issued through our health visitors, and they give this out at the eight months check up,

where they discuss the contents of the bag with the parents. There are two books inside it … the health visitor at that point, can take time to discuss with the parent, you know do they enjoy reading, do they do a bedtime story. It allows them to give them something which is non-threatening, and it's an easy way in. At that particular time, you can be made aware of maybe a mum or a dad, shying away from a situation about reading, other than is necessary, and they might come forward and say things like, 'I'm not very good at that. I'm not really confident', or 'I was never, I never stayed on at school, I can't read too well.' Then they [health visitors] can say, 'Well, do you know that within this authority there are people and places you can go to, there can be help for that. If you want to know, if you feel that you merit getting some more help.' You liaise with the health visitor, she can discuss things, and we as an authority can put our own information in about our nurseries, about play groups, about child care services within the area. … The other thing that we do, is we do a Reading Reward Scheme which is operational in our nurseries, and in our libraries. It's designed for children in and around three to five. This is for children to encourage them, to take a book home, sit down with mum, dad, granny, their big brother, sister, and just read side by side. It works in the nurseries. They have a little book bag, they come in [to the library] once a week, they choose a book, they then take this home, it's read at home, and the parent and child fill in a little smiley sheet. … They come back in, and they hand the book back in, and they get a card, a sticker on a card. Once they've collected ten stickers, they go up with their mum to a local bookshop, where they get a two pound book token, and then they can choose a book to the value of that. It seems to be working very well, because lots of the children are encouraging their mums and dads to sit down with them and, 'Tell me the story, teach me the story.' We had a couple of instances whereby children who were diagnosed as being dyslexic have had other younger children, their brothers or siblings, going in and getting the books on reward schemes. One in particular, he spoke to the librarian and asked if he could join, and although he was that little bit older, he was allowed to join in with the reading reward with his younger brother, because it was encouraging him, as a dyslexic child, to read a lot of the books, and it, and then he was getting a reward for this, and being able to take his reward forward and get a book of his own and he was able to choose books that he enjoyed … his progress in reading has come on.

One of the other things that's happened in here is we've been able to have very good liaison with library staff. I have a particularly good relationship with them in that, we now have a programme where the libraries visit some of our primary schools, even in the upper school, and they visit libraries, and are shown round libraries, introduced to the Dewey system and they're shown round their local community library. We've also through the family literacy increased the stock particularly down at the early years, by bringing in a lot more board books, and a lot more suitable reading material for younger readers, and the encouragement of, getting mums and dads to bring their babies into a library. ... We also got the money together and we put sofas into a library providing a comfortable seat for people to sit and read, with their younger children, giving them a focal point, and believe it or not, children do sit on this, and enjoy sitting, and sit reasonably quietly. It also ... links back to the home, because, inside the home they've normally got a sofa, and they sit there and the newspaper will be read, magazines will be read, they'll curl up and read a story, and read books together. So again you're providing a link all the way round. Most of our nurseries have those as well, and use it a lot, for focusing on the home corner, and story time.

... part and parcel of the literacy tool bag that goes out, when the children enrol in primary school, ... we very much have taken on board what teachers would also like to see in that ... and we have a pencil in it, with a little grip, which is used by the children to learn to write, a jotter and a book and tape, and that's very much come from the teacher's input into this, into the tool bag. There are leaflets contained in this, which have been made up by the professionals in East Renfrewshire, and these are about reading, and it gives step by step hints about choosing a book they like, involving them, sitting in a quiet place, talking about the cover. ... It's called our 'First Steps' leaflet, and there's four of them, and, the reading one goes through all the different sort of stages that you would go through, trying to settle down, talking about the cover of the book, the content of the book, who's done the pictures etc. We do a writing one, a maths one, and playing, learning and playing ... these have been made up by the professionals, and these are a link between the school and home.

I think the best advice I would offer to them [early literacy co-ordinators] is they've got to make good links with the community. They've got to build up relationships, and sometimes you can't do that on your own. You've got to be able to work and liaise with other agencies. Keep reaching out into the community. Try different things, try alternatives, try bringing in story tellers, professional people. Try making up the story sacks. They have been very successful. We're now moving on, we're doing rhyme bags, on parent's suggestions. Take on board what they want, make them feel comfortable, but constantly, constantly, reach out into the community. Be enthusiastic yourself, and check out what other people have done. You're not trying to reinvent the wheel. If somebody's been out there and done it, you can pick up on their good practices, and then you can put it into practice for yourself, and also, you've always got to be aware of your own community, what the needs are within your area.

(interview for Open University E801 course materials, 2002)

Current programmes

There are a number of literacy programmes or techniques currently in common use in different countries which enable parents and carers to support the literacy development of students who experience difficulties at home. Different approaches make different underlying assumptions about the reading process and also the degree to which parental collaboration with schools in supporting the literacy development of their students is legitimate.

Pause Prompt Praise

From the outset, Glynn and McNaughton's (1985) Pause, Prompt, Praise (PPP) technique was designed to be used with parents of pupils experiencing difficulties in literacy acquisition. The initial research work for PPP was carried out in 1977 in South Auckland, New Zealand, in home settings with a group of pupils and their parents. Subsequent research was carried out in the UK with the procedure's research monograph being published in the UK under the title *Pause, Prompt and Praise* (McNaughton *et al.* 1987). The PPP strategies are derived from the theoretical perspective on reading developed by Clay (1979, 1991). As Glynn notes, it is cognitive-developmental; that is, it assumes the emergence of literacy as the child develops in a literacy-rich environment. This perspective views proficiency in reading as resulting from the ability to use every relevant piece of information around and within a text to understand it. It is therefore based on the whole-book approach to the teaching of reading. Differences between proficient and poor readers are seen to lie in the flexibility with which they combine knowledge and letter–sound combinations with contextual information. PPP is designed for use with individual pupils in order to facilitate opportunities to self-correct errors and practise strategies for problem-solving. Tutors are taught to implement a simple but specific set of tutoring strategies: pausing to allow for self-correction, prompting to offer word meaning or for sound–symbol identification, and praising to reinforce the use of independent skills. McNaughton, Glynn and Robinson (1987) found that pausing before correction leads to a greater degree of self-correction by the learner and an increase in reading accuracy. Careful consideration of the type of errors made enables prompting to focus on either semantic considerations – that is, to prompt for meaning – or the graphical features of a word. The type of praise allows for reinforcement of the desired reading behaviour, especially where positive comment is specifically related to the learner's actions. Following Clay, the authors of PPP emphasise the importance of supplying reading material at a level appropriate to the learner so that the learner meets some unfamiliar words but can read enough of the text to make semantically good productions, even if these are miscues. In most respects the project was very successful in supporting children's reading development. However, in one respect – generalisation to school reading – it was less successful.

Recent developments of PPP in New Zealand (Glynn et al. 2000) have built on the view that tutoring skills should be given away to parents and carers. These developments have enabled respect for cultural diversity and sensitivity to cultural differences to be taken into account as enormously important factors in supporting children's literacy acquisition. As was noted by Wearmouth and Soler (2002b), there has been a greater awareness of the importance of cultural contexts for children's learning through the introduction of PPP. For example, the Rotorua Home and School Project (Glynn et al. 2000) was concerned with effective collaboration between schools and the communities they serve, with the shared aim of supporting the improvement of children's literacy achievement. This project was premised on respecting the family and community as primary learning environments for children in addition to that of the school:

> While it is clear that home and school exercise joint influences on children's literacy, facilitating learning across the two contexts depends on home and school knowing and understanding what

literacy values and reading and writing practices are operating in the other.

(Glynn *et al.* 2000, p. 9)

It was also premised on the importance of recognising that different patterns of literacy in different communities 'meet particular purposes in particular contexts of use' (*ibid.*, p. 12) and thus carry particular cultural meanings for all community members. The corollary of this respect and recognition is that collaboration between home and school entails the sharing of understandings and actions that are reciprocal, not unidirectional from school to home:

> [T]he report signals that participation involves schools learning from families, as well as families learning from schools. Shared understandings of ways of teaching and learning, as well as sharing of goals and forms of literacy instruction are pivotal in successful family literacy programmes.
>
> (Glynn *et al.* 2000, p. 8)

Furthermore, recent research into the use of PPP in a variety of settings, for example the Rotorua Home and School Literacy Project, recognises the importance of achieving reciprocal understandings between home and school in order to pay due regard to the cultural context of children's literacy development. In a recent interview Mere Berryman, from the Special Education Services in New Zealand, explained how she first became acquainted with PPP and the relationship as she sees it between the programme and the local community:

> I think the important thing that I found working with Pause Prompt Praise, and working with Maori communities, is actually enabling people from the Maori community to work with students who are Maori. So having that cultural togetherness, having the tutor and the child of the same culture, has, we have found, helped enormously. The other thing that is important for our tutors is they have a really good understanding of the types of stories that might interest Maori children. That's not to say that they know the stories alone that will interest Maori children but, they're able to pick up on stories with a cultural theme, that children will enjoy reading, and that children can, Maori children specifically, can relate to. The other thing that's really important about it is there is reciprocity in the learning, and by that I mean

that the tutor is able to learn about the child that they're working with, and the child benefits by being able to learn about the reading process. ... So from that point of view also I think it's important for Maori. It's, it's not directive, it's collaborative.

... I think it's important in any community, that the community can feel, in fact understand, that they are part of the decision-making processes, and I guess that that also comes through in the Pause Prompt Praise process. It's not the tutor telling the child how to do it and what to do, and where to read and how to read, it's the tutor providing some time for the child to think, the child to initiate some directions that they want to go in, and when it doesn't happen then they can give some prompts. So for me it's about the child being able to initiate some of the learning themselves, and having a supportive tutor who is providing them with the time and the space to do that.

... I think, one of the important things [in setting up a Pause Prompt Praise initiative in a school] is get to know your community, and get to know the resource. There are two things. You need to be competent in the use of the procedures yourself, and that's something, that I think is really important. It's more than being able to just tell people about how to use it, it's actually having credibility in the process yourself. The other thing that I think is really important is that, you have credibility within the community in which you work. Because if you don't have that credibility, then you are less likely to be able to draw people from the community into your school. ... I guess it comes down to knowing the culture in the communities in which you are working. It's being able to do a good deal of listening if you don't know what that culture is like, because only by listening, and being prepared to learn, can you actually become part of that culture. I guess for me, one of the huge things that I've learned is it's not about telling the community how they will do it, it's about being invited by the community to participate with them. So I think that is hugely important. Being able to listen to what the community want, and being able to support them in the initiative, rather than coming in and being really heavy handed, and saying, well this is how it's going to be. It's about sitting beside them and collaborating.

... Interest in the training has brought new people in, success in the tutoring, has enabled people to go out and get jobs, and again brought new people in ... what we should be doing is thinking how wonderful that is because it's building skills within the community.

(interview with Mere Berryman for Open University E801 course materials, 2002)

PPP has developed to incorporate rather different assumptions of control and ownership in relation to the way in which families can give support to their children's literacy development. Mere Berryman is working within the context of the Maori community. However, the issues that face this community have generic relevance to some other ethnic-minority communities internationally. They are:

- the separation between the culture of home and school;
- lower achievement in the area of literacy;
- the need for reciprocal understanding between home and school.

Comparison between Pause Prompt Praise and Reading Recovery

It might be argued that there are important similarities between PPP and Reading Recovery, which is reviewed earlier in the chapter. However, there are also important differences which schools interested in initiating either of these programmes should be aware of. Both programmes can be seen as based on similar top-down approaches to reading; that is, both Reading Recovery and PPP appear to be premised on the whole-book/whole-language, psycholinguistic view of reading development. The design of techniques within both Reading Recovery and PPP appear to relate psycholinguistic theory to practice. This does not mean that either of them ignores the phonological aspect of reading. It is simply that phonics is not taught with the same degree of emphasis as in a bottom-up approach. Both were developed in the New Zealand context. However, the initial focus of one inside the school and the other outside in the community, together with factors related essentially to evaluation of like with like, has meant that one, PPP, has been more easily adapted to accommodate to cultural diversity. Reading Recovery continues to be organised and 'quality controlled' centrally, with formal, structured central support for the training of teachers and the evaluation of pupil progress.

Some differences between the programmes are obvious. For example, for Clay the reading process is 'complex', teachers are often 'unable to think how to overcome the difficulties' and, as a consequence, tutor and teacher training must be long and rigorous (radio interview on the *Open Mind* programme, Dublin, 1995). However, for McNaughton and Glynn poor readers are less efficient than good readers in their use of appropriate cues in their reading. 'Simple' cuing procedures which 'ordinary' people can use can be taught systematically to children (McNaughton *et al.* 1979). The consequence of this is variation in the professional status, length and rigour of the training programmes for tutors, and in the cost of the infrastructure needed to maintain Reading Recovery and PPP. Different views of ownership and control have influenced the degree to which these programmes have been adapted to respond to the contextual factors in which they operate. Reading Recovery remains largely the same as its original version. However, recent literacy initiatives using the PPP procedures have been able to respond to significant contextual features, particularly the cultural background of the learner and local community.

The question of available resources is highly significant in determining uptake of a programme, but is by no means the sole issue. Where accountability is increasingly required to be transparent and institutions are subject to external inspection, in some countries on given criteria, it may be that a programme with structured central support mechanisms is more attractive to a school even if the cost implications are greater. This may be the case particularly where that programme has been named in a literacy taskforce report (as is the case with Reading Recovery; Department for Education and Employment 1997) as appropriate in meeting some pupils' literacy needs. On the other hand, where a school is setting out to involve its parents and/or carers in children's learning, or where the targeted student group is older, or where serious consideration is being given to the cultural diversity of students' family backgrounds, PPP might be seen as an appropriate programme.

PPP is an initiative that typically relies on collaboration between education experts, schools and, often, the whole community. In addition, there are examples of individual parent-led initiatives. A number of writers have described particular techniques and practices that they, as parents of children described as 'dyslexic', have found useful both in obtaining the additional or alternative educational provision that they have felt necessary to meet their children's learning needs and also in supporting their children in day-to-day living. Heaton (1996), for example, notes that, for her and many other parents like her, one of the most important factors is a sense that she has the ability and power to offer appropriate support and help to her own child and will be listened to when she discusses the barriers to literacy learning faced by her child as she sees them. From a questionnaire completed by parents and carers of students identified as dyslexic she offers various pieces of advice to families, amongst which are:

- be prepared to have to organise a management system for, and spend time on, all the paperwork involved in making the case for recognition and assessment of the student's difficulties in literacy acquisition;
- be proactive in finding out about difficulties in literacy, appropriate teaching methods and common terminology;
- maintain close liaison with the school and every year ensure that the student's teachers are aware of the difficulties s/he experiences;
- consider colour coding the child's school books;
- work out practical strategies for personal organisation;
- teach strategies for dealing with potential difficulties with the concepts of time, space and direction;
- make time to listen to the child, encourage strengths and be prepared for outbursts of frustration;
- do not waste time by becoming obsessive about the child's difficulties.

One major reason why Heaton's advice on steps that parents or carers might take to raise awareness of issues associated with literacy difficulties in schools or other institutions might be seen as uncomfortable relates to a feeling that parents might usurp some of the power and control more usually owned by professionals inside educational institutions. Heaton's practical advice stems from her own personal experiences. How much of this relates to the context in which educators work will depend on a number of factors, among which are the ages and stages of the students for whom they have some responsibility.

There are many examples of initiatives involving parents in the reading development of their children where the emphasis is much more on the teacher as expert and the parent as needing control from external experts (see discussion of Dale's 1996 work above). Among the techniques of this sort that have been piloted for use with parents are Topping's Paired Reading and Cued Spelling programmes. These are expert-led initiatives initiated at the school level. Topping (1992, 1996) has set out a number of steps for the generic 'training' of parents in programmes to support children's literacy development: Verbal instruction ® modelling ® prompted practice ® feedback and reinforcement ® independent practice ® reinforcement and monitoring (Topping and Wolfendale 1985, p. 25).

He feels that guidelines on techniques for parents to use should be straightforward and sensible, so that parents can accommodate them to their existing frameworks. He urges them to be careful with certain things:

- reading sessions too late in the evening;
- inappropriate setting;
- parents exerting too much pressure;
- not enough praise;
- anxiety or loss of temper;
- inappropriate reading material;
- incorrect/inadequate cues;
- imprudent use of friends/siblings.

Paired Reading

As can be seen below, Topping's (1992) Paired Reading technique is an example of an approach with strong directives from teachers to parents about how the technique should operate. Topping warns against assuming that 'any old thing that two people do with a book' constitutes Paired Reading. Topping describes the 'rules' of his Paired Reading method as follows:

> Paired Reading is characterized by the child choosing high interest reading material irrespective of its readability level (provided it is within that of the helper) from any source.
>
> Families commit themselves to an initial trial period in which they agree to do at least five minutes Paired Reading on five days each week for about eight weeks. Grandparents, siblings, friends and neighbours can be encouraged to help, but must all use the same technique – the target child is deliberately asked to quality control the tutoring they receive.
>
> In Paired Reading the child is likely to want to talk about a book they have chosen, and talk is also more necessary given the (probably) greater difficulty of the text, as a check on comprehension.
>
> A very simple and ubiquitously applicable correction procedure is prescribed. After pausing for 4 to 5 seconds to allow self-correction,

the tutor just models the correct way to read the word, the child repeats it correctly and the pair carry on.

Much verbal praise and non-verbal approval for specific reading behaviours is incorporated. Undesirable behaviours are engineered out of the system by engineering in incompatible positive behaviours.

Tutors support children through difficult text by Reading Together – both members of the pair read all the words out loud together, the tutor modulating speed to match that of the child, while giving a good model of competent reading.

On an easier section of text, the child may wish to read a little without support. The child signals for the tutor to stop Reading Together, by a knock or a touch. The tutor goes quiet, while continuing to monitor any errors, praise and pause for discussion. Sooner or later while Reading Alone the child will make an error which they cannot self-correct within 4 or 5 seconds. Then the tutor applies the usual correction procedure and joins back in Reading Together.

The pair go on like this, switching from Reading Together to Reading Alone to give the child just as much help as is needed at any moment, according to the difficulty of the text, how tired the tutee is, and so on. Children should never 'grow out of' Reading Together; they should always be ready to use it as they move on to harder and harder books.

(Topping 1996, p. 46)

Topping describes Paired Reading as suitable for pupils 'of all reading abilities' in order to 'avoid stigmatization' (1996, p. 48). He is fairly prescriptive about the choice of family for a pilot project in a school: 'A small group of fairly well motivated families is a good choice for a first effort' where children 'have easy and frequent access to a wide range of books'. Important is a consideration of how to promote a 'sense of group solidarity' among the families concerned. He lays down rigorous rules for organising Paired Reading:

- Parents, all other tutors and the learners are invited to a launch or training meeting.
- Reading Together and Reading Alone are demonstrated separately to start then in alternation.
- The 4 to 5 second pause and praise are highlighted,

- The pairs practise the technique with a book above the child's current independent readability level that has been chosen prior to the meeting,
- Professionals check on the technique, offer advice, and coach as appropriate.
- The pairs keep a diary noting the date, name of text read, length of reading time, name of tutor and any comments on how well the child did.
- The diary is checked in school each week by the teacher, who comments on progress and signs it.
- Pairs are given a handout, translated into another language if necessary, to remind them of the technique and to show to other family members.
- If students or tutors experience difficulties in the ensuing weeks it may be necessary to hold individual meetings to check the technique and difficulty level of texts in use.
- A further meeting should be held for feedback. Students' reading can be tested before and after the project so that overall, not individual, results can be fed back to the group.
- Each pair should decide how to continue from there.

(Topping 1996, p. 48)

In their review of research on the effectiveness of Paired Reading, Topping and Lindsay (1992) note that much of the evaluation has been in terms of gains on norm-referenced tests of reading before and after the initial intensive period of involvement. These tests are divorced from day-to-day classroom activities. Topping and Lindsay report that in the published studies, involving a total of 1,012 children, for each month of time that passed the average Paired Reader gained 4.2 months in reading age for accuracy and 5.4 months for comprehension. Of the published studies, nineteen included control or comparison groups. Although the control groups often also made gains above the expected level, the Paired Reading groups on aggregate did far better.

Follow-up studies appeared to indicate that, while the rate of initial improvement does not continue indefinitely, the gains do not 'wash out' subsequently (Topping 1992). Topping also notes other significant issues related to Paired Reading projects:

The data ... suggested that well-organized projects yielded better test results, that participant children from lower socio-economic classes tended to show higher gains, that home visiting by teachers increased test scores and that boys tended to accelerate more than girls. Also, second language Paired Readers accelerated more than first language Paired Readers in accuracy but less in comprehension (while of course accelerating a great deal more than non-Paired Readers of either type).

(Topping 1996, p. 49)

However, once Paired Reading is applied in a more complex family situation with control from the school, statistical evaluation becomes very difficult, since there are problems in establishing who is doing what and with which and to whom. Paired Reading has also been used in an adult literacy context, with spouses, friends, neighbours and workmates acting as tutors. Scoble (1988) reported the evaluation of a six-week project of this type, noting average gains of 10.4 months in reading age for accuracy and 13 months for comprehension for those students who could register on the scale at pre-test. On miscue analysis, most tutees showed a striking increase in self-correction.

Pragmatically, it may be very important to be able to indicate gains in norm-referenced tests of reading as a result of a particular intervention. Topping and Wolfendale argue that the main factors in the effectiveness of parental involvement are specifically related to the techniques themselves and can be interpreted along behaviourist lines (1985, p. 25). In comparison with teacher input, parental modelling is more powerful, practice is more regular and feedback is more immediate. Parental reinforcement is more valuable.

The advantages of being able to use more appropriate and more readily available reading material and receive tutoring on a little-and-often basis closely linked to everyday family life are also extremely important, especially for the majority of adults with literacy difficulties who cannot or will not attend a class. Teachers and researchers might therefore wish to use interview or observation techniques to identify differences in attitudes to reading, changes in relationships in the family and general attitudes to literacy, in the way learners feel about themselves, in the kind and number of books they read, in the match between learner and personal interest in particular books, and so on.

The description of Paired Reading suggests strongly that it is an example of a whole-book approach. Wragg comments on Hancock's (1991) observation that reading programmes for parents to use with their children usually fall into the category of whole-book approach:

It is interesting to note that, as Hancock (1991) points out, the involvement of parents in their children's learning sits more easily with meaning-based approaches to teaching reading than with those emphasising the acquisition of skills. It remains to be seen, therefore, whether the renewed stress on the importance of phonics and decoding skills will halt or alter the direction of the move to involve parents in the teaching of reading. When reading is seen as an enjoyable shared activity, the aim of which is understanding, then parents, relatives and siblings can all join in. If reading is seen as a series of skills to be mastered, however, then teaching it is more likely to be claimed as the prerogative of the professionals.

(Wragg *et al.* 1998, p. 34)

Other programmes for parents

However, from Topping's perspective it is also possible to develop programmes for parents to use which are designed to support the bottom-up skills of phonics and spelling. Topping has designed what he terms Cued Spelling, which relies on these principles of parent training and also on behaviourist principles of praise, modelling, swift error correction and support procedures 'in the hope of eliminating the fear of failure'. The issue of pupil motivation is addressed through the self-selection of target words and self-management. The steps are set out to represent progression through small incremental stages. When pupils are familiar with the technique, speed in spelling is emphasised in order to overcome the difficulty with generalisation over time and contexts. Topping has set out a clear statement of method:

The basic structure of the technique comprises 10 Steps, four Points to Remember and two Reviews ...

The 10 Steps and four Points apply to every individual target word worked upon by the pair, while the 'Speed Review' covers all target words for a particular session and the 'Mastery Review' covers all the target words for one week or a longer period if desired.

The child chooses high interest and utility target words irrespective of complexity (Step 1). The pair check the spelling of the word and put a master version in their Cued Spelling Diary (Step 2). The pair read the word out loud synchronously, then the child reads the word aloud alone (3).

The child (not the parent) then chooses Cues (prompts or reminders) to enable him or her to remember the written structure of the word (4). These Cues may be phonic sounds, letter names, syllables or other fragments or 'chunks' of words, or wholly idiosyncratic mnemonic devices.

The pair then say the Cues out loud simultaneously (5). The child then says the Cues out loud while the parent models writing the word down on scrap paper to this 'dictation' (6). Roles then reverse, the parent saying the Cues out loud while the child writes the word down (7). The child then says the Cues and writes the word simultaneously (8). At Step 9, the child is asked to write the word as fast as possible. Finally (10), the child again reads the word out loud.

The four Points cover aspects of the technique relevant to its practical application. At every attempt at writing a target word, the parent covers up previous attempts on the work paper, to avoid the possibility of direct copying (some children prefer to do this themselves). At every written attempt on a word, the child checks the attempt, the parent only intervening if the child cannot check his or her own attempt accurately. Tutors praise at various junctures which are specified.

(Topping 1996, pp. 50–1)

Each session ends with a 'speed review':

In the 'Speed Review' … the parent asks the child to write all the target words for that session as fast as possible from dictation in random order. The child then self-checks with the 'master version'. Target words which are incorrect at Speed Review have the 10 Steps applied again, perhaps with the choice of different Cues.

At the end of each week, a 'Mastery Review' is conducted – the child is asked to write all the target words for the whole week as fast as possible from dictation in random order. No specific error correction procedure is prescribed and it is left to the pair to decide what they wish to do about errors. Many pairs choose to include failed words in the next week's target words.

(Topping 1996, p. 52)

Research into Cued Spelling has followed many of the organisational guidelines for Paired Reading projects:

Each pair has a Cued Spelling [CS] Diary, each page including space to write the master version of up to 10 words on all days of the week, with boxes to record daily Speed Review and weekly Mastery Review scores and spaces for *comments* from tutor (daily) and teacher (weekly). The pair are asked to use the technique on about five words per day (implying a minimum time of 15 minutes) for three days per week for the next six weeks. The children are encouraged to choose words from their school spelling books, graded free writing, relevant project work or special Cued Spelling displays of common problem words, and collect these (in a CS 'collecting book'), so they always have a pool of suitable words from which to choose.

Children bring their CS Diaries into school once each week for the class teacher to view. The words chosen need to be monitored, since some children choose words they already know while others choose extremely difficult words of very doubtful utility – in this a formula of 'three for everyday use and two just for fun' is usual.

As Cued Spelling has been much used in a reciprocal peer tutoring format, its use in family literacy in situations where both members of the pair are of equal spelling ability is entirely possible, although it is then especially important that the master version of the word is looked up in the dictionary and copied correctly into the CS Diary. Thus a parent who is of limited spelling ability could work with their child of similar spelling ability or sibling tutoring could operate between children of similar or different ages. In reciprocal tutoring, the fact that everyone gets to be a tutor is good for the self-esteem of both members of the pair, who of course end up learning their partner's words as well as their own.

(Topping 1996, pp. 52–3)

One problem with advocating the use of Cued Spelling is that the initial evaluation reports on Cued Spelling tended to be descriptive only (Emerson 1988; Scoble 1988).

Conclusion

Potentially, parents and carers are an important resource in supporting the literacy learning of students who experience difficulties. The kind of partnership arrangements that exist between school and parents or carers and the way in which schools respond to family culture and background can serve to include or alienate students. Clearly, the attitude of any educational institution to the role of families as prime educators of children and to families' social and cultural backgrounds is of great significance. Different approaches and strategies have embedded within them different underlying assumptions not only about the reading process, but also about the ability and right of families and/or carers from a diversity of backgrounds and cultures to support the literacy development of their students. It is fundamentally important for schools to recognise these assumptions in order to plan programmes which will address difficulties in literacy development within the context of respect for students' family and cultural background.

Chapter 12

Towards inclusive schools: considering literacy difficulties

Introduction

Since the 1981 Education Act reaffirmed the principle of integration, the law has made provision for all pupils to be educated in mainstream schools. One of the problems associated with the continuation of an individualised notion of 'special educational need' is that provision is also targeted at the individual pupil. This provision therefore tends to remain on the periphery of the school curriculum rather than becoming an integral part of it. As Dyson (1997) has argued, an 'army' of special educators has 'colonised' rather than transformed mainstream schools. The full inclusion of pupils identified as experiencing particular difficulties in learning, for example in the area of literacy, therefore presents a number of challenges to mainstream schools:

> The challenge confronting the inclusive school is that of developing a child-centred pedagogy capable of successfully educating all children, including those who have serious disadvantages and disabilities. ... Special needs education incorporates the proven principles of sound pedagogy from which all children may benefit. It assumes that human differences are normal and that learning must accordingly be adapted to the needs of the child rather than the child fitted to preordained assumptions regarding the pace and nature of the learning process.
>
> (UNESCO 1994, p. 7)

Development and change in schools

Many researchers in the area of inclusion and special educational needs are agreed on the kind of changes that will have to occur in schools for pupils who experience difficulties in learning, for example difficulties in literacy acquisition, to be included. Mittler, for example, considers that the inclusion in schools of such pupils requires:

> a process of reform and restructuring of the school as a whole, with the aim of ensuring that all pupils can have access to the whole range of educational and social opportunities offered by the school. This includes the curriculum on offer, the assessment, recording and reporting of pupils' achievements, the decisions that are taken on the grouping of pupils within schools or classrooms, pedagogy and classroom practice.
>
> (Mittler 2000, p. 2)

Bringing about change in schools

Past experience of failure to effect educational-policy change in practice indicates that moves towards including all pupils in mainstream schools are unlikely to succeed unless sufficient account is taken of the teachers who are expected to put the change into operation (Fullan 1992). Initiatives designed to bring about change in pedagogy must take account of the teacher's purpose in his or her work (Fullan and Hargreaves 1996). Fullan (2001) has identified a number of features crucial to understanding the change process in schools, and exhorts those charged with responsibility for bringing about change to be very clear about the following:

- the scope of change;
- the extent to which there is common understanding and agreement about values and goals;
- how far the consequences are understood;
- the way in which change is to be implemented;
- the dynamics of change as a socio-political process;
- individual, classroom, school, local, regional, national factors.

Classroom practices: accounting for social/cultural and cognitive barriers

It is at the classroom level in relation to classroom practice that the most important interactions affecting pupils occur (Rouse and Florian 2000). Issues of power relations, the model of pupil as active participant in his or her own learning, models or reading development and views of what constitutes literacy should pervade thinking about practice in the classroom. While the theories of multi-literacies and new literacies address the wider learning environment and the micro-politics of the classroom, there is also a need to examine more closely the dynamics of the learning process at the individual level. It is in the classroom that most pupils will experience the degree to which a school might be considered 'inclusive' of all students and the difficulties some of them have in literacy development.

A useful model of literacy learning is that afforded by Vygotsky (1978). In his theory of social constructivism, language is seen as crucial for the development of cognitive skills. The cultural and social context within which learning takes place is crucial in mediating how a learner gains access to the signs and symbols in the environment. The meanings attached to the signs and symbols of a culture are all first acquired in interaction with more-experienced others (adults or peers) in a social context, and later internalised for personal use in the mental context. Vygotsky described a Zone of Proximal Development as the space between the level at which a child can solve problems and think independently and the level at which s/he can operate if assisted by more-informed others. The Zone of Proximal Development is the zone where learning can be 'scaffolded' by others (Wood *et al*. 1976), the area where independent cognitive activity will take place if this 'scaffolding' is gradually removed at appropriate moments. Vygotsky emphasises the child's active role in his/her own learning through meaningful interactions with others. Children first develop literacy within a social setting, in which cultural interpretations are communicated by more experienced members of society. They internalise literacy skills and knowledge, and also the culturally accepted way of valuing those skills and that knowledge.

In the classroom it is important to acknowledge the need to differentiate between the levels at which barriers to literacy can occur. In order to differentiate between cultural/social barriers and cognitive barriers to literacy acquisition, educators also need to consider the relationship between an individual's cognitive processes and the socio-cultural aspects of the learning environment. Green and Kostogriz (2002) draw upon the field of New Literacy Studies, critical literacy and the work of Vygotsky to explore the possibilities and outcomes associated with viewing students who experience difficulties in literacy from socio-cultural and cognitive psychological perspectives. They explore the possibility for managing classroom literacy programmes and teaching practices for students who experience difficulties in literacy from the perspective of socially orientated psychology. This viewpoint highlights a cultural-historical perspective rather than the more traditional scientific-cognitive and clinically based understandings of literacy 'difficulties' and 'disabilities'.

As we have seen in earlier chapters of this book, New Literacy Studies and socio-cultural perspectives lead us to see literacy learning as more than learning about print-based 'skills' which develop largely within the student and are unaffected by the surrounding contexts. From the New Literacy Studies perspective, we all learn and use literacy within particular sets of social and cultural contexts, which can vary, giving rise to the possibility of 'multiple literacies'. The skills associated with literacy are seen to be a product of social practices that have occurred in conjunction with the development of literacy-related technologies, such as the alphabet, the printing press and the computer. From this perspective, text and the related practices associated with learning to read are not seen as a unitary, neutral, disembodied activity. Reading, understanding and writing text are related to power and ideological relationships, which shape our interpretations of text on the page or the screen in front of us while also impacting upon the way we utilise and evaluate our production of text.

Green and Kostogriz (2002) point out that this perspective also implies that it is necessary for students to understand social interaction and associated political and social practices if they are to become literate in society. Literacy is not restricted to decoding the letters and words in text; it is also necessary to understand that words and text are used in particular ways related to social, cultural and political contexts. This perspective also draws our attention to the way in which people's identities are tied up with social constructions of literacy proficiency, correctness and normal development. It is these social constructions that mark out students as different or 'other', which in turn leads to the production of the label 'disabled'.

Green and Kostogriz note that if we view literacy as a set of individual, neutral or 'autonomous' skills 'it is easy to focus on brain disorders and the like to explain deviancy from the norm as a matter of individual defect. But, when we conceive of literacy as a matter of social practices and indeed, even more so, as *multiple literacies*, any notion of "mental deviation" becomes problematic' (Green and Kostogriz 2002, p. 104). They argue that the opposing perspectives of a socio-cultural and a biologically based view of literacy learning lead to two different models of literacy learning difficulties and disabilities.

The socio-cultural perspective takes into account the immediate and wider social surroundings and cultural contexts of the student in the learning situation. The scientific-cognitive model of autonomous literacy skills leads to an emphasis on a clinical model which entails a deficiency view, where literacy problems need to be understood in medical terms. They note that it is this latter model which has in turn influenced the clinical work on dyslexia, and the politics and testing surrounding the diagnosis of dyslexia, which we explored in Chapter 11. They describe the clinical model as a deficiency view of literacy, which has particular consequences for educators and students:

> In essence this model entails a deficiency view of literacy learning and literacy learners alike, and is based on what might be called scientised forms of normative judgement. There is, of course, a long heritage of clinical work in dyslexia and related to this literacy problems, understood 'medically' .... Importantly, there are links to be observed between clinical perspectives of this kind and 'autonomous' models of literacy, between logics of deficiency and neuro-psychological deviancy and the politics of testing and classification in literacy studies .... The over representation of minority and socially disadvantaged students in the category of 'disability' attests to the incapacity of clinical models to take into account the sociocultural complexity of learning difficulties.
>
> (Green and Kostogriz 2002, p. 107)

Green and Kostogriz argue that Vygotsky provides an alternative to this clinical model through his work with disabled children, which he utilised for his empirical data for conceptualising and articulating the principles of his cultural-historical theory of learning and psychological development. They argue that in Vygotsky's view the socio-cultural shapes the internal individual psychological processes. For Vygotsky, the human mind, and therefore learning and literacy development, is mediated by the tools and signs which humans use to transform the material world and their living conditions. These 'tools' or cultural-historical artefacts include the tools associated with language, such as written symbols and signs, graphs, maps, counting systems, mechanical and expressive drawings, etc. Through participation in social activities the child internalises social languages, bodies of knowledge, the use of cultural-technical artefacts such as the alphabet, as well as learning socially acceptable ways to act and behave. This internalisation through cultural and social artefacts and practices leads to the development of psychological tools which shape the child's consciousness and thinking.

This perspective led Vygotsky to view disability and the disabled child in a way that is significantly different from the clinical model, as it stressed the need to enrich and increase participation in the social and cultural contexts rather than attempting to compensate for biological deficiencies:

> Before Vygotsky, the main focus of 'defectology' was on the organic or biological nature of a handicap: deafness, blindness, etc. He turned this approach on its head, arguing that the problem is not the handicap itself but rather its effect on the sociocultural development of the child. While an organic or 'primary' disability has in many cases a biological origin, the main problem for education becomes how to compensate it *culturally*. Focusing only on biological compensation, such as by training sharpness of hearing or smell in a blind child, means for Vygotsky a training *in* disability. He calls this the production of a 'secondary' disability, one that increasingly separates a handicapped child from social life and its cultural resources, leading to her distorted psychological development and social deprivation …. In order to overcome the production of 'secondary' disability in children and their 'discontogenesis' in disabling practices of special education, Vygotsky proposes a culturally inclusive model of pedagogy … this was based on the idea that the cultural line of development transforms the natural-biological one. In the process of interaction between these two lines, individuals' consciousness and behaviour can no longer be explained in solely biological terms. Rather, active participation of the handicapped children in social practices is the key to the cultural compensation of disability.
>
> (Green and Kostogriz 2002, p. 108)

Green and Kostogriz argue that there are important implications, challenges and potential for engaging with students who experience literacy difficulties that arise from Vygostky's work:

- The need to be aware of the way in which we can produce literacy difficulties through our own actions and attitudes. We need to be aware that the cultural contexts that work within and create can themselves produce disability as our notions of disability are linked to the practices and contexts of our particular background and society values. We need to be aware that the ways in which we talk, think and construct literacy and literacy education practices feed into the creation of disability.

- We can view socio-cultural difference as a resource rather than a liability and use it to obtain the goal of helping all students learn literacy. Socio-cultural theories of literacy learning imply that we can utilise the full gambit of the social, cultural and linguistic resources of all our students, and create a classroom community that celebrates and recognises a diversity of culture, social background and ability.
- In terms of understanding 'learning difficulties in literacy', there is a need to take account of disability in ways that fully acknowledge its status and significance as a socio-cultural category but nonetheless provide for classroom practice that is both inclusive and productive in learning terms. This implies recognising differences but not pathologising them. It implies generating 'tasks and environments that draw upon and celebrate difference and value a full range of educational outcomes, and acknowledging the importance of becoming involved in active and critical citizenship.
- Finally, there is a need to view literacy practice as more than 'meaning making' and 'skills development'. They argue that notions of literacy need to include a richer understanding of literacy as linked to the complexity of social life – including events, practices, social networks and mediators, resources and repertoires.

Incorporating these suggestions for classroom practice is, however, dependent on the leeway given by current literacy curriculum policies. At present, in parts of the UK the National Curriculum is supported by statute and also by nationally organised inspection procedures. This has had a huge impact on classroom practices. Some pupils who experience difficulties in literacy in schools face barriers in relation to the delivery of the National Literacy Strategy. One of the reasons may be that this strategy is, in some ways, in opposition to research findings from projects into what effective primary schoolteachers of literacy know, understand and do. For example, Wragg *et al.* (1998) concluded that teachers' personal philosophy, awareness and understanding of literacy are the factors which guide pedagogy and predispose to effective teaching. In an important research project into the effective teaching of literacy at primary level, Wragg *et al.* identified ten factors that, from observations of classroom practices, appeared to characterise the teaching approach of many successful teachers of literacy:

It is tempting to try to find a number of universal truths from observations of these 'above-average' practitioners. As other investigators ... have discovered, this is not as simple as it may sound. For example, several teachers observed gave prominence to the display of children's work and the celebration of it, as well as to the use of environmental print and the labelling of classroom features. Two teachers whose classes achieved amongst the highest gains in reading proficiency on standardised tests given early and late in the school year, however, showed little interest in display, and their classroom walls were relatively bare. It is not safe to assume that certain elements must be universally present in effective lessons.

We did, nonetheless, attempt to pick out some similarities amongst these arguably successful teachers, though it is noteworthy that these were often expressed in individual form. An illustration of this is that most teachers managed to secure a very high degree of pupil attentiveness to the task in hand, so that was common. What was different was the manifold means through which they achieved this goal, sometimes by fast-paced enthusiastic interactions prior to reading or written work, in other cases though a more quietly supportive, even private, approach to individuals. Some teachers made a show of publicly alerting the class to what was expected, or implemented clear rules of conduct, such as no talking or movement being permitted during sessions when reading was the highest priority.

The ten broad common factors we managed to isolate ... were as follows:

- A high level of personal enthusiasm for literature, some even supplementing the school's reading resources with their own personal collection of books.
- Good professional knowledge of children's authors and teaching strategies.
- Literacy being made very important, within a rich literacy environment.
- Celebrating progress publicly and increasing children's confidence.
- Being able to individualise and match teaching to pupils, particularly in terms of their reading interests.
- Systematic monitoring and assessment, though the form of it varied.

- Regular and varied reading activities.
- Pupils being encouraged to develop independence and autonomy, attacking unfamiliar words, taking their own reading forward, or backing their own judgement as authors.
- A notably high degree of classroom management skill and good-quality personal relationships with pupils ....
- High positive expectations, with children striving to reach a high standard, whatever their circumstances.

(Wragg *et al.* 1998, pp. 265–6)

A number of these conclusions clearly relate to discussion in previous chapters of this book about barriers to literacy at the socio/cultural and individual cognitive level, as well as different models of reading and notions of literacy. For example, 'a high level of personal enthusiasm for literature, some even supplementing the school's reading resources with their own personal collection of books' links both with cultural aspects of literacy, particularly in the emphasis of literature and of 'good' authors implied in this statement. Notions of cultural literacy contain a value judgement and assume it is possible to make a distinction between literature and other forms of popular text. The decision about this distinction is related to socio-economic background. Certain groups are privileged to make this judgement and have access to 'good' literature. It is assumed that pupils will learn to read through reading and a literacy-rich environment. One reason for supplementing schools' resources with personal collections of books may be that these teachers are prepared to give their pupils access to, and an understanding of, 'good' literature. The implications of Wragg's conclusions for teacher professional development is that effective teaching in the area of literacy is based on personal knowledge, reflection and analysis.

Conclusion

Establishing literacy policies and practices which cater for individual differences and diversity in schools that are more accustomed to catering for majority interests is not straightforward. School practices in relation to pupils who experience difficulties are heavily constrained by national and local-authority policies. Schools must be accountable to the general public for the quality of education they provide for the nation's children. For example, in England and Wales since the 1988 Education Act national education policies have attempted to promote the majority interest by setting normative targets to be achieved within the lifetime of one parliament and by establishing league tables of academic achievement. Much of the assessment on which these achievement tables rest is carried out through the medium of literacy. The problems created for many pupils with difficulties in literacy acquisition are therefore very hard to resolve. How far the effect of imposing additional pressure on schools to improve their overall literacy standards will result in squeezing some lower-achieving pupils out of the system remains to be seen.

For any school there is a challenge in thinking through the way in which the whole school literacy curriculum might be made more inclusive of the diversity of its students, and different or alternative provision for individuals who experience difficulties might be developed and implemented, whilst simultaneously making adequate provision for the whole student cohort. Change in literacy policy and practice which cuts across what teachers feel is in the best interests of those they teach or which appears impractical is likely to be resisted and/or resented. The complexity of the issues related to the whole range of perspectives on what constitute barriers to literacy learning must be teased out; policy-makers must understand the long-term nature of embedding change; the implications of the change for teacher development must be taken seriously; and necessary resources and technology must be made available.

Appendix 1

Summary of the Interactive Observational Style Identification (IOSI)

Motivation
- What topics, tasks and activities interest the student?
- What kind of prompting and cueing is necessary to increase motivation?
- What kind of incentives motivate the student – leadership opportunities, working with others, free time or physical activity.

Persistence
- Does the student stick to a task until completion without breaks?
- Are frequent breaks necessary when working on difficult tasks?

Responsibility
- To what extent does the student take responsibility for his/her own learning?
- Does the student attribute success or failure to self or others?

Structure
- Are the student's personal effects (desk, clothing, materials) well organised or cluttered?
- How does the student respond to someone imposing organisational structure on him/her?

Social interaction
- When is the student's best work accomplished – when working alone, with one another or in a small group?
- Does the student ask for approval or need to have work checked frequently?

Communication
- Does the student give the main events and gloss over the details?
- Does the student interrupt others when they are talking?

Modality preference
- What type of instructions does the student most easily understand – written, oral or visual?

- Does the student respond more quickly and easily to questions about stories heard or read?

Sequential or simultaneous learning
- Does the student begin with one step and proceed in an orderly fashion or have difficulty following sequential information?
- Is there a logical sequence to the student's explanations or do her/his thoughts bounce around from one idea to another?

Impulsive or reflective
- Are the student's responses rapid and spontaneous or delayed and reflective?
- Does the student seem to consider past events before taking action?

Physical mobility
- Does the student move around the class frequently or fidget when seated?
- Does the student like to stand or walk while learning something new?

Food intake
- Does the student snack or chew on a pencil when studying?

Time of day
- During which time of day is the student most alert?
- Is there a noticeable difference between morning work completed and afternoon work?

Sound
- Does the student seek out places that are particularly quiet?

Light
- Does the student like to work in dimly lit areas or say that the light is too bright?

Temperature
- Does the student leave his/her coat on when others seem warm?

Furniture design
- When given a choice, does the student sit on the floor, lie down or sit in a straight chair to read?

Metacognition
- Is the student aware of his/her learning-style strengths?
- Does the student demonstrate self-assessment?

Prediction
- Does the student make plans and work towards goals or let things happen?

Feedback
- How does the student respond to different types of feedback?
- How much external prompting is needed before the student can access previous knowledge?

- There are too many manifestations of style to observe all at once. One way to begin the observation process is to select one of the learning systems and progress from there. The insights usually become greater as observation progresses.

(Given and Reid 1999)

Appendix 2
Definitions of the term 'specific learning difficulties' (SpLD)

The terms 'specific learning difficulties' and 'dyslexia' are often used synonymously and many recent UK publications on the subject have chosen to include both terms in their titles.

Specific Learning Difficulties can be identified as distinctive patterns of difficulties, relating to the processing of information, within a continuum from very mild to extremely severe, which result in restrictions in literacy development and discrepancies in performances within the curriculum.

(Moray House Centre for Specific Learning Difficulties; quoted in Reid 1994, p. 3)

Persons identified as having a Specific Learning Difficulty or Difficulties all show different intellectual and emotional profiles, strengths and weaknesses, learning styles and life experiences. Within this context, Specific Learning Difficulties can be identified as distinctive patterns of difficulties, relating to the processing of information, within a continuum from very mild to severe, which result in restrictions in literacy, language, number, motor function and organisational skills.

(from the school policy document of the Red Rose School, Lancashire, Lancashire Centre for Specific Learning Difficulties, 1997)

Dyslexia is best described as a combination of abilities and difficulties which affect the learning process in one or more of reading, spelling, writing and sometimes numeracy/language. Accompanying weaknesses may be identified in areas of speed of processing, short-term memory, sequencing, auditory and/or visual perception, spoken language and motor skills.

(British Dyslexia Association; quoted in Peer 2001, pp. 2–3).

Bibliography

Ada, F. (1988) 'The Pajaro Valley Experience: Working with Spanish-speaking Parents to Develop Children's Reading and Writing Skills in the Home through the Use of Children's Literature', in T. Skutnabb-Kangas and J. Cummins (eds), *Minority Education: From Shame to Struggle*, Clevedon: Multilingual Matters.

Adams, F.R. (1999) '5–14: Origins, Development and Implementation', in T.G.K. Bryce and W.M. Humes (eds), *Scottish Education*, Edinburgh: Edinburgh University Press.

Adams, M.J. (1994) *Beginning to Read: Thinking and Learning about Print*, Cambridge, MA: MIT Press.

Ainscow, M. (1999) *Understanding the Development of Inclusive Schools*, London: Falmer Press.

Allan, J. (1995) 'How Are We Doing? Teachers' Views on the Effectiveness of Co-operative Teaching', *Support for Learning* 10(3), pp. 127–32.

Alloway, N.G. and Gilbert, P. (1997) 'Boys and Literacy: Lessons from Australia', *Gender & Education* 9(1), pp. 49–60.

Ames, G. and Archer, J. (1988) 'Achievement Goals in the Classroom: Students' Learning Strategies and Motivation Processes', *Journal of Educational Psychology* 80, pp. 260–7.

Andrews, G.R. and Debus, R.L. (1978) 'Persistence and the Causal Perception of Failure: Modifying Cognitive Attributions', *Journal of Educational Psychology* 70, pp. 154–66.

Audit Commission (1992) *Getting in on the Act: Provision for Special Educational Needs*, London: HMSO.

Auerbach, E.R. (1989) 'Towards a Socio-cultural Approach to Family Literacy', *Harvard Educational Review* 59, pp. 165–81.

Badian, N.A. (1997) 'Dyslexia and the Double Deficit Hypothesis', *Annals of Dyslexia* 47, IDA.

Baker, C. (1996) *Foundations of Bilingual Education and Bilingualism*, Clevedon: Multilingual Matters.

Bakker, D.J. (1979) 'Hemispheric Differences and Reading Strategies: Two Dyslexias?', *Bulletin of the Orton Society* 29, pp. 84–100.

——— (1986) 'Electrophysiological Validation of L- and P-type Dyslexia', *Journal of Clinical and Experimental Neuropsychology*, 8, p. 133.

——— (1990) *Neuropsychological Treatment of Dyslexia*, New York: Oxford University Press.

——— (in press) 'Teaching the Brain', in A.Y. Springer, E.L. Cooley and A.L. Christensen (eds), *Pathways to Prominence: Reflections of 20th Century Neuropsychologists*, Philadelphia, PN: Psychology Press.

Bakker, D.J. and Vinke, J. (1985) 'Effects of Hemisphere-specific Stimulation on Brain Activity and Reading in Dyslexics', *Journal of Clinical and Experimental Neuropsychology* 7, pp. 505–25.

Bakker, D.J., Bouma, A. and Gardien, C.J. (1990) 'Hemisphere-specific Treatment of Dyslexic Sub-types: A Field Experiment', *Journal of Learning Disabilities* 23, pp. 433–8.

Bakker, D.J., Moerland, R. and Goekoop-Hoefkens, M. (1981) 'Effects of Hemisphere-specific Stimulation on the Reading Performance of Dyslexic Boys: A Pilot Study', *Journal of Clinical Neuropsychology* 3, pp. 155–9.

Bandura, A. (1982) 'Self-efficacy Mechanism in Human Agency', *American Psychologist* 37, pp. 122–47.

——— (1986) *Social Foundations of Thought and Action*, Englewood Cliffs, NJ: Prentice-Hall.

Bandura, A. and Schunk, D.H. (1981) 'Cultivating Competence, Self-efficacy, and Intrinsic Interest through Proximal Self-motivation', *Journal of Personality and Social Psychology* 41, pp. 586–98.

Baynham, M. (1995) *Literacy Practices: Investigating Literacy in Social Contexts*, London: Longman.

Beard, R. (1990) *Developing Reading 3–13*, 2nd edn, London: Hodder & Stoughton.

——— (1999) 'Influences on the Literacy Hour', *Reading: A Journal about Literacy and Language in Education* 33(1), pp. 6–12.

Bedford-Feuell, C., Geiger, S., Moyse, S. and Turner, M. (1995) 'Use of Listening Comprehension in the Identification and Assessment of Specific Learning Difficulties', *Educational Psychology in Practice* 10(4), pp. 207–14.

Bentley, D. (2002) 'Teaching Spelling: Some Questions Answered', in J. Wearmouth, J. Soler and G. Reid (eds), *Addressing Difficulties in Literacy Development: Responses at Family, School, Pupil and Teacher Levels*, London: RoutledgeFalmer, pp. 340–53.

Best, R. (1991) 'Support Teaching in a Comprehensive School', *Support for Learning* 6(1), pp. 27–31.

Blackledge, A. (2000) *Literacy, Power and Social Justice*, Stoke on Trent: Trentham.

Blamires, M. (1997) *Parent–Teacher Partnership: Practical Approaches to Meet Special Educational Needs*, London: Fulton.

Blamires, M., Robertson, C. and Blamires, J. (1997) *Parent–Teacher Partnership: Practical Approaches to Meet Special Educational Needs*, London: David Fulton.

Booth, T. and Goodey, C. (1996) 'Playing for the Sympathy Vote', *Guardian*, 21 May, p. 5.

Booth, T., Ainscow, M., Black-Hawkins, C., Vaughan, M. and Shaw, L. (2000) *Index for Inclusion*, Bristol: CSIE.

Borkowski, J.G., Weyhing, R.S. and Carr, M. (1988) 'Effects of Attributional Retraining on Strategy-based Reading Comprehension in Learning-disabled Students', *Journal of Educational Psychology* 80, pp. 46–53.

Bourdieu, P. and Passeron, J.C. (1973) *Reproduction in Education, Society and Culture*, London: Sage.

Bradley, L. (1981) 'The Organisation of Motor Patterns for Spelling: An Effective Remedial Strategy for Backward Readers', *Developmental Medicine and Child Neurology* 23, pp. 83–91.

Bradley, L. and Bryant, P.E. (1983) 'Categorising Sounds and Learning to Read: A Causal Connection', *Nature* 301, pp. 419–21.

British Psychological Society (BPS) (1999) *Dyslexia, Literacy and Psychological Assessment*, Report by a working party of the Division of Educational and Child Psychology of the British Psychological Society, Leicester.

British Psychological Society Division of Educational and Child Psychology (BPS DECP) (1983) *Specific Learning Difficulties versus Dyslexia, Controversy Resolved* 7(3).

Broadfoot, P. (1996) *Education, Assessment and Society*, Buckingham: Open University Press.

Bronfenbrenner, U. (1979) *The Ecology of Human Development*, Cambridge, MA: Harvard University Press.

Bruner, J. (1986) *Actual Minds, Possible Worlds*, Cambridge: Harvard.

Burden, B. (2002) 'A Cognitive Approach to Dyslexia: Learning Styles and Thinking Skills', in G. Reid and J. Wearmouth (eds), *Dyslexia and Literacy: Research and Practice*, Chichester: Wiley.

Butkowsky, I.S. and Willows, D.M. (1980) 'Cognitive-motivational Characteristics of Children Varying in Reading Ability: Evidence for Learned Helplessness in Poor Readers', *Journal of Educational Psychology* 72, pp. 8–422.

Byers, R. (1999) 'The National Literacy Strategy and Pupils with Special Educational Needs', *British Journal of Special Education* 26(1), pp. 8–11.

Cann, P. (1996) 'Walking the Corridors of Power', *Dyslexia Contact* 15(1), Reading: BDA.

Carson, S.A. (2002) 'A Veteran Enters the Reading Wars: My Journey', in J. Soler, J. Wearmouth and G. Reid (eds), *Contextualising Difficulties in Literacy Development*, London: RoutledgeFalmer, pp. 117–32.

Castles, A. and Coltheart, M. (1993) 'Varieties of Developmental Dyslexia', *Cognition* 47, pp. 149–80.

Central Advisory Council for Education (England) (1967) *Children and their Primary Schools (England) Volume 1, The Report*, London: HMSO.

Chall, J. (1967) *Learning to Read: The Great Debate*, New York: McGraw-Hill.

Charlton, T. (1998) 'Enhancing School Effectiveness Through Using Peer Support Strategies with Pupils and Teachers', *Support for Learning* 13(2), May, pp. 50–3.

Chase, C.H. (1996) 'A Visual Deficit Model of Developmental Dyslexia', in C.H. Chase, G.D. Rosen and G.F. Sherman (eds), *Developmental Dyslexia: Neural, Cognitive and Genetic Mechanisms*, Baltimore, MD: York Press.

Christie, F. (1990) 'The Changing Face of Literacy', in F. Christie (ed.), *Literacy for a Changing World*, Hawthorn, Victoria: Australian Council for Educational Research.

Christie, F. and Misson, R. (2002) 'Framing the Issues in Literacy Education', in J. Soler, J. Wearmouth and G. Reid (eds), *Contextualising Difficulties in Literacy Development: Exploring Politics, Culture, Ethnicity and Ethics*, London: Routledge.

Clare, J. (1990) 'Tests Reveal Fall in Standard of Pupils' Reading', *Daily Telegraph*, 29 June, p. 1.

Clark, C., Dyson, A., Millward, A. and Skidmore, D. (1997) *New Directions in Special Needs*, London: Cassell.

Clay, M.M. (1979) *Reading: The Patterning of Complex Behaviour*, Auckland: Heinemann.

—— (1991) *Becoming Literate: The Construction of Inner Control*, Auckland: Heinemann.

—— (1993) *An Observation Survey of Early Literacy Achievement*, Auckland, New Zealand: Heinemann.

Cline, T. (ed.) (1992) *The Assessment of Special Educational Needs*, London: Routledge.

—— (2002) 'Issues in the Assessment of Children Learning English as an Additional Language', in G. Reid and J. Wearmouth (eds), *Dyslexia and Literacy: Research and Practice*, Chichester: Wiley.

Cline, T. and Frederickson, N. (1999) 'Identification and Assessment of Dyslexia in Bi/Multi-lingual Children', *International Journal of Bilingual Education and Bilingualism* 2(2), pp. 81–93.

Cline, T. and Shamsi, T. (2000) *Language Needs or Special Needs? The Assessment of Learning Difficulties in Literacy among Children Learning English as an Additional Language: A Literature Review*, London: DfEE. (The research brief and the full report can be accessed at http://www.dfee.gov.uk/research/re_paper/RR184.doc.)

Coltheart, M. (1978) 'Lexical Access in Simple Reading Tasks', in G. Underwood (ed.) *Strategies of Information Processing*, London: Academic Press.

Coopers and Lybrand/Society of Education Officers (1996) *The SEN Initiative*, London: Coopers and Lybrand/Society of Education Officers.

Cowne, E. (2000) 'Inclusive Education: Access for all – Rhetoric or Reality', Offprints Booklet, pp. 119–31, E831 *Professional Development for Special Educational Needs Co-ordinators*, Milton Keynes: Open University.

Cox, E. (1995) 'Men Must Change the System, Not Play the Victim', *The Australian*, 9 February, p. 13.

Crandall, V.G., Katkovsky, W. and Crandall, V.J. (1965) 'Children's Beliefs in their Own Control of Reinforcements in Intellectual–Academic Achievement Situations', *Child Development* 36, pp. 91–109.

Crombie, M. (2002) 'Dealing with Diversity in the Primary Classroom – A Challenge for the Class Teacher', in G. Reid and J. Wearmouth (eds), *Dyslexia and Literacy: Research and Practice*, Chichester: Wiley.

Crystal, D. (1995) *The Cambridge Encyclopedia of the English Language*, Cambridge: Cambridge University Press.

CSIE (1986) *Caught in the Act?*, Bristol: CSIE.

Cummins, J. (1984) *Bilingualism and Special Education: Issues in Assessment and Pedagogy*, Clevedon: Multilingual Matters.

Dale, N. (1996) *Working with Families of Children with Special Needs: Partnership and Practice*, London: Routledge.

Davie, C.E., Butler, N. and Goldstein, H. (1972) *From Birth to Seven: A Report of the National Child Development Study*, London: Longman/National Children's Bureau.

Davis, O.L. Jnr (2002) 'When Will the Phonics Police Come Knocking?', in J. Soler, J. Wearmouth and G. Reid (eds), *Contextualising Difficulties in Literacy Development*, London: RoutledgeFalmer, pp. 83–6.

Deforges, C. (2001) *Learning, Thinking and Classroom Work*, Paper presented at United Kingdom Reading Association (UKRA) conference, 6–8 July 2001, Canterbury Christ Church University College, Kent.

Delgado-Gaitan, C. (1990) *Literacy for Empowerment*, London: Falmer.

—— (1992) 'School Matters in the Mexican–American Home: Socializing Children in Education', *American Educational Research Journal* 29, pp. 495–516.

Dennison, P.E. and Dennison, G.E. (1989) *Brain Gym: Teacher's Edition, Revised*, Ventura, CA: Edu-Kinesthetics, Inc.

Department for Education (1994) *The Code of Practice for the Identification and Assessment of Special Educational Needs*, London: DfE.

Department for Education and Employment (1997) *Excellence for All Children*, London: Stationery Office.

—— (1998) *The National Literacy Strategy: Framework for Teaching*, London: DfEE.

—— (1999) *The National Literacy Strategy: Additional Literacy Support. Modules 1–4*, London: DfEE.

—— (2000a) *Making Links: Guidance for Summer Schools and Year 7 Catch-up Programmes*, London: DfEE.

—— (2000b) *The National Literacy Strategy: Supporting Pupils with Special Educational Needs in the Literacy Hour*, London: DfEE.

—— (2000c) *Supporting Pupils Working Significantly Below Age-related Expectations*, London: DfEE.

—— (2000d) 'Literacy & Numeracy Consultants play vital role', press release, 13 July; http//web.lexis-nexis.com.

—— (2001) *Making Links: Guidance for Summer Schools and Year 7 Support Programmes*, London: DfEE.

Department for Education and Science (DES) (1972) *Children with Specific Reading Difficulties. Report of the Advisory Committee on Handicapped Children* (Tizard Report), London: HMSO.

—— (1978) *Special Educational Needs: Report of the Committee of Enquiry into the Education of Handicapped Children and Young People* (Warnock Report), London: HMSO.

—— (1991) *The Parents' Charter: You and Your Child's Education*, London: DES.

—— (1992) *Children with Special Needs: A Guide for Parents*.

Department for Education Northern Ireland (DENI) (1998) *The Code of Practice for the Identification and Assessment of Special Educational Needs*, Bangor: DENI.

Department of Education and Skills (DfES) (2001) *Special Educational Needs Code of Practice*, London: DfES.

Dick, M., Glynn, T. and Flower, D. (1992) *Pause Prompt and Praise Reading Tutoring Procedures: Tutor Training Video*, Audiovisual Unit, Higher Education Development Centre, University of Otago, Dunedin, New Zealand.

Diener, C.I. and Dweck, C.S. (1978) 'An Analysis of Learned Helplessness: Continuous Changes in Performance, Strategy and Achievement Cognitions Following Failure', *Journal of Personality and Social Psychology* 36, pp. 451–62.

Dillon, J.T. (1994) *Using Discussion in Classrooms*, Milton Keynes: Open University Press.

Diorio, J. (2002) 'Justice, Literacy and Impediments to Learning Literacy', in J. Soler, J. Wearmouth and G. Reid (eds), *Contextualising Difficulties in Literacy Development: Exploring Politics, Culture, Ethnicity and Ethics*, London: Routledge.

Dockrell, J. and McShane, J. (1993) *Children's Learning Difficulties: A Cognitive Approach*, Oxford: Blackwell.

Dow, R.S. and Moruzzi, G. (1958) *The Physiology and Pathology of the Cerebellum*, Minneapolis, MN: University of Minnesota Press.

Duffield, J., Riddell, S. and Brown, S. (1995) *Policy, Practice and Provision for Children with Specific Learning Difficulties*, New York, Avebury Publishing.

Dunn, R., Dunn, K. and Price, G.E. (1996) *Learning Style Inventory*, Lawrence, KS: Price Systems (first published in 1975).

Duranti, A. and Ochs, E. (1996) 'Syncretic Literacy in a Samoan American Family', in L.B. Resnick *et al.* (eds), *Discourse, Tools and Reasoning*, Berlin: Springer.

Dweck, C.S. (1975) 'The Role of Expectations and Attributions in the Alleviation of Learned Helplessness', *Journal of Personality and Social Psychology* 31, pp. 674–85.

Dweck, C.S. and Licht, B.G. (1980) 'Learned Helplessness and Intellectual Achievement', in J. Garber and M.E.P. Seligman (eds), *Human Helplessness: Theory and Applications*, New York: Academic Press.

Dweck, C.S. and Reppucci, N.D. (1973) 'Learned Helplessness and Reinforcement Responsibility in Children', *Journal of Personality and Social Psychology* 25, pp. 109–16.

Dyson, A. (1997) 'Social and Educational Disadvantage: Reconnecting Special Needs Education', *British Journal of Special Education* 24(4), pp. 152–7.

East Renfrewshire Council (2000) 'Specific Learning Difficulties', policy document, East Renfrewshire Council, Scotland.

Eden, G.F., Van Meter, J.W., Rumsey, J.M. and Zeffiro, T.A. (1996a) 'The Visual Deficit Theory of Developmental Dyslexia', *Neuroimage* 4, S108–S117.

Eden, G.F., Van Meter, J.W., Rumsey, J.M., Maisog, J.M., Woods, R.P. and Zeffiro, T.A. (1996b) 'Abnormal Processing of Visual Motion in Dyslexia Revealed by Functional Brain Imaging', *Nature* 382, pp. 67–9.

Edwards, A.D. and Westgate, D.P.G. (1994) *Investigating Classroom Talk*, 2nd edn, London: Falmer Press.

Edwards, J. (1994) *The Scars of Dyslexia*, London: Cassell.

Ehri, L.C. (1991) 'Development of the Ability to Read Words', in R. Barr, M.L. Kamil, P.B. Mosenthal and P.D. Pearson (eds), *Handbook of Reading Research*, vol. 2, New York: Longman.

—— (1999) 'The Unobstrusive Role of Words in Reading Text', in A.J. Watson and L.R. Giorcelli (eds), *Accepting the Literacy Challenge*, Sydney: Scholastic Publications.

—— (2002) 'Reading Processes, Acquisition and Instructional Implications', in G. Reid and J. Wearmouth (eds), *Dyslexia and Literacy: Research and Practice*, Chichester: Wiley.

Elliot, C.D., Smith, P. and McCullock, K. (1996) *British Ability Scales*, 2nd edn (BAS II), London: NFER–Nelson.

Ellis, S. and Friel, G. (1999) 'English Language', in T.G.K. Bryce and W.M. Humes (eds), *Scottish Education*, Edinburgh: Edinburgh University Press.

Emerson, P. (1988) 'Parent Tutored Cued Spelling in a Primary School', *Paired Reading Bulletin* 4, pp. 91–2.

Englert, C. and Raphael, T. (1988) 'Constructing Well-formed Prose: Process, Structure and Metacognition in the Instruction of Expository Writing', *Exceptional Children* 54, pp. 513–20.

Everatt, J. (2002) 'Visual processes', in G. Reid and J. Wearmouth (eds), *Dyslexia and Literacy: Research and Practice*, Chichester: Wiley.

Fabbro, F., Pesenti, S., Facoetti, A., Bonanomi, M., Libera, L. and Lorusso, M.L. (2001) 'Callosal Transfer in Different Subtypes of Developmental Dyslexia', *Cortex* 37, pp. 65–73.

Farrell, P. (1997) *Teaching Pupils with Learning Difficulties*, London: Cassell.

—— (1999) *The Management, Role and Training of Learning Support Assistants*, Research Report RR 161, London: DfEE.

Fawcett, A.J. (2002) 'Dyslexia and Literacy: Key Issues for Research', in G. Reid and J. Wearmouth (eds), *Dyslexia and Literacy: Research and Practice*, Chichester: Wiley.

Fawcett, A.J. and Nicolson, R. (1994) 'Computer-based Diagnosis of Dyslexia', in C.H. Singleton (ed.), *Computers and Dyslexia. Educational Applications of New Technology*, Hull: Dyslexia Computer Resource Centre, University of Hull.

—— (1996) *The Dyslexia Screening Test*, London: Psychological Corporation.

—— (1999) 'Performance of Dyslexic Children on Cerebellar and Cognitive Tests', *Journal of Motor Behaviour* 31, pp. 68–79.

—— (2001) 'Dyslexia: The Role of the Cerebellum', in A. Fawcett (ed.), *Dyslexia: Theory and Good Practice*, London: Whurr.

Fawcett, A.J., Nicolson, R.I. and Dean, P. (1996) 'Impaired Performance of Children with Dyslexia on a Range of Cerebellar Tasks', *Annals of Dyslexia* 46, pp. 259–83.

Feuerstein, R., Rand, Y., Hoffman, M. and Miller, R. (1980) *Instrumental Enrichment: An Intervention Programme for Cognitive Modifiability*, Baltimore, MD: University Park Press.

Finch, A.J., Nicolson, R.I. and Fawcett, A.J. (2002) 'Evidence for an Anatomical Difference within the Cerebella of Dyslexic Brains', *Cortex*.

Flesch, R.F. (1955) *Why Johnny Can't Read – And What You Can Do About It*, 1st US edn, New York: Harper.

Flower, L. and Hayes, J. (1980) 'The Dynamics of Composing: Making Plans and Joggling Constraints', in L. Gregg and E. Steinberg (eds), *Cognitive Processes in Writing*, Hillsdale, NJ: Erlbaum.

Fowler, J.W. and Peterson, P.L. (1981) 'Increasing Reading Persistence and Altering Attributional Style of Learned Helpless Children', *Journal of Educational Psychology* 73, pp. 251–60.

Fredrickson, N., Frith, U. and Reason, R. (1997) *Phonological Assessment Battery*, London: NFER–Nelson.

Freire, P. (1996) *Letters to Cristina: Reflections on My Life and Work*, London: Routledge.

Freire, P. and Macedo, D.P. (1999) 'Pedagogy, Culture, Language and Race: A Dialogue', in J. Leach and B. Moon (eds), *Learners and Pedagogy*, London: Paul Chapman.

Friend, M. and Cook, L. (1996) *Interactions: Collaboration Skills for School Professionals*, White Plains, NY: Longman.

Frith, U. (1986) 'A Developmental Framework for Developmental Dyslexia', *Annals of Dyslexia* 36, pp. 69–81.

—— (1997) 'Brain, Mind and Behaviour in Dyslexia', in C. Hulme and M. Snowling (eds), *Dyslexia: Biology, Cognition and Intervention*, London: Whurr.

—— (2002a) 'The Causal Modelling Framework', in G. Reid and J. Wearmouth (eds), *Dyslexia and Literacy: Research and Practice*, Chichester: Wiley.

—— (2002b) 'Resolving the Paradoxes of Dyslexia', in G. Reid and J. Wearmouth (eds), *Dyslexia and Literacy: Research and Practice*, Chichester: Wiley.

Fullan, M.G. (1992) *The New Meaning of Educational Change*, London: Cassell.

—— (2001) *The New Meaning of Educational Change*, 3rd edn, London: Routledge.

Fullan, M. and Hargreaves, D. (1996) *What's Worth Fighting for in Your School?*, New York: Columbia Press.

Galaburda, A.M. (1989) 'Ordinary and Extraordinary Brain Development: Anatomical Variation in Developmental Dyslexia', *Annals of Dyslexia* 39, pp. 67–79.

Galaburda, A.M. and Rosen, G.D. (2001) 'Neural Plasticity in Dyslexia: A Window to Mechanisms of Learning Disabilities', in J.L. McClelland and R.S. Siegler (eds), *Mechanisms of Cognitive Development: Behavioral and Neural Perspectives*, Mahwah, NJ: Erlbaum.

Galaburda, A.M., Sherman, G.F., Rosen, G.D., Aboitiz, F. and Geschwind, N. (1985) 'Developmental Dyslexia: Four Consecutive Patients with Cortical Anomalies', *Annals of Neurology* 18, pp. 222–33.

Gallagher, A., Frith, U. and Snowling, M.J. (2000) 'Precursors of Literacy-delay among Children at Genetic Risk of Dyslexia', *Journal of Child Psychology and Psychiatry* 41, pp. 203–13.

Gallagher, J.J. (1976) 'The Sacred and Profane Uses of Labels', in *Exceptional Children* 45, pp. 3–7.

Galton, M., Hargreaves, L., Comber, C., Wall, D. and Pell, A. (1999) *Inside the Primary Classroom: 20 Years On*, London: Routledge.

Gambell, T. and Hunter, D. (2002) 'Surveying Gender Differences in Canadian School Literacy', in J. Soler, J. Wearmouth and G. Reid (eds), *Contextualising Difficulties in Literacy Development: Exploring Politics, Culture, Ethnicity and Ethics* London: RoutledgeFalmer.

Garner, P. and Sandow, S. (1995) *Advocacy, Self Advocacy and Special Needs*, London: Fulton.

Gee, J.P. (1990) *Social Linguistics and Literacies: Ideology in Discourses*, London: Falmer Press.

Gee, J.P., Hull, G. and Lankshear, C. (1996) *The New Work Order: Behind the Language of the New Capitalism*, Sydney and Boulder, CO: Allen & Unwin/Westview Press.

Gerber, M.M. (1996) 'Educational Ethics, Social Justice and Children with Disabilities', in J. Soler, J. Wearmouth and G. Reid (eds), *Contextualising Difficulties in Literacy Development: Exploring Politics, Culture, Ethnicity and Ethics* London: RoutledgeFalmer.

Gersch, I. (2001) 'Listening to Children: An Initiative to Increase the Active Involvement of Children in their Education by an Educational Psychology Service', in J. Wearmouth (ed.), *Special Educational provision in the Context of Inclusion*, London: Fulton.

Gilbert, P. (1989) 'Personally (and Passively) Yours: Girls, Literacy and Education', *Oxford Review of Education* 15(3), pp. 257–65.

Given, B.K. (1998) 'Psychological and Neurobiological Support for Learning-style Instruction: Why it Works', *National Forum of Applied Educational Research Journal* 11(1), pp. 10–15.

Given, B.K. and Reid. G. (1999) *Learning Styles – A Guide for Teachers and Parents*, St Anne's, Lancashire: Red Rose Publications.

—— (2001) 'Assessing Learning Styles', in I. Smythe (ed.), *The Dyslexia Handbook 2001*, Reading: British Dyslexia Association.

Glynn, T. and McNaughton, S. (1985) 'The Mangere Home and School Remedial Reading Procedures: Continuing Research on their Effectiveness', *New Zealand Journal of Psychology* (1985), pp. 66–77.

Glynn, T., Berryman, M. and Glynn, V. (2000) *Reading and Writing Gains for Maori Students in Mainstream Schools: Effective Partnerships in the Rotorua Home and School Literacy Project*, paper presented at the 18th World Congress on Reading, Auckland, New Zealand.

Glynn T., McNaughton, S., Robinson, V. and Quinn, M. (1979) *Remedial Reading at Home: Helping You to Help Your Child*, Wellington, New Zealand: New Zealand Council for Educational Research.

Goodman, K. (1967) 'Reading: A Psycholinguistic Guessing Game', *Journal of the Reading Specialist* 6(4), pp. 126–35.

—— (1976) 'Reading: A Psycholinguistic Guessing Game', in H. Singer and R.B. Ruddell (eds), *Theoretical Models and Processes of Reading*, Newark, DE: International Reading Association.

—— (1986) *What's Whole in Whole-language?*, 1st US edn, Portsmouth, NH: Heinemann.

—— (1996) *On Reading*, Portsmouth, NJ: Heinemann.

Graff, H. (1987) *The Labyrinths of Literacy: Reflections on Literacy Past and Present*, London: Falmer Press.

Graham, S. and Harris, K.R. (1989) 'Improved Learning Disabled Students' Skills at Composing Essays: Self Instructional Strategy Training', *Exceptional Children* 56, pp. 201–16.

—— (1993) 'Teaching Writing Strategies to Students with Learning Disabilities: Issues and Recommendations', in L.J. Meltzer (ed.), *Strategy Assessment and Instruction for Students with Learning Disabilities*, Austin, TX: Pro-Ed.

Graham, S., MacArthur, C., Schwartz, S. and Voth, T. (1989) *Improving LD Students' Compositions Using a Strategy Involving Product and Process Goalsetting*, paper presented at Annual Meeting of the American Educational Research Association, San Francisco.

Grainger, T. and Tod, J. (2000) *Inclusive Educational Practice: Literacy*, London: David Fulton.

Grampian Region Psychological Service (1988) *Reeling and Writhing: Children with Specific Learning Difficulties*, Grampian Education Authority, Aberdeen.

Graves, A., Montague, M. and Wong, Y. (1989) *The Effects of Procedural Facilitation on Story Composition of Learning Disabled Students*, paper presented at Annual Meeting of the American Educational Research Association, San Francisco.

Green, B. and Kostogriz, A. (2002) 'Learning Difficulties and the New Literacy Studies', in J. Soler, J. Wearmouth and G. Reid (eds), *Contextualising Difficulties in Literacy Development*, London: RoutledgeFalmer.

Gregorc, A.F. (1982) *An Adult's Guide to Style*, Columbia, CT: Gregorc Associates Inc.

Gregory, E. (1998) 'Siblings as Mediators of Literacy in Linguistic Minority Communities', *Language and Education: An International Journal* 11(1), pp. 33–55.

—— (2002) 'Childhood Memories of Reading in London's East End', in J. Soler, J. Wearmouth and G. Reid (eds), *Contextualising Difficulties in Literacy Development*, London: RoutledgeFalmer.

Grinder, M. (1991) *Righting the Educational Conveyor Belt*, 2nd edn, Portland, OR: Metamorphous Press.

Gross, J. (1996) 'The Weight of the Evidence', *Support for Learning* 11(1), pp. 3–8.

Hackett, G. (1999) 'Boys Close Reading Gap But Still Trail in Writing', *Times Educational Supplement*, 8 October, p. 2.

Hagtvet, B.E. (1997) 'Phonological and Linguistic-cognitive Precursors of Reading Disabilities', *Dyslexia* 3, pp. 163–177.

Hancock, R. (1991) 'Parental Involvement in Children's Reading: A Survey of Schools in Tower Hamlets', *Reading* 25(1), pp. 4–6.

Hannon, P. (1987) 'A Study of the Effects of Parental Involvement in the Teaching of Reading on Children's Reading Test Performance', *Cambridge Journal of Education* 16, pp. 28–37.

—— (1995) *Literacy, Home and School: Research and Practice in Teaching Literacy with Parents*, London: Falmer.

—— (1999) 'Rhetoric and Research in Family Literacy', *British Educational Research Journal* 26(1), pp. 121–38.

—— (2000) *Reflecting on Literacy in Education*, London/New York: Falmer Press.

Hannon, P. and McNally, J. (1986) 'Children's Understanding and Cultural Factors in Reading Test Performance', *Educational Review* 38(3), pp. 269–80.

Hardman, F. and Williamson, J. (1998) 'The discourse of post-16 English teaching', *Educational Review* 50(1), pp. 5–14.

Harlen, W. and James, M. (1997) 'Assessment and Learning: Differences and Relationships between Formative and Summative Assessment', *Assessment in Education* 4(3) pp. 365–79.

Harris, K.R. and Graham, S. (1985) 'Improved Learning-disabled Composition Skills: Self-control Strategy Training', *Learning Disability Quarterly* (8), pp. 27–36.

Harrison, C. (1994) *Literature Review: Methods of Teaching Reading*, Edinburgh: SOED.

Hatcher, J. (1994) *Sound Linkage*, London: Whurr.

—— (2000) *Sound Linkage*, 2nd edn, London: Whurr.

Hatcher, J. and Snowling, M.J. (2002) 'The Phonological Representations Hypothesis of Dyslexia: From Theory To Practice', in G. Reid and J. Wearmouth (eds), *Dyslexia and Literacy: Research and Practice*, Chichester: Wiley.

Hatcher, J., Hulme, C. and Ellis, A.W. (1994) 'Ameliorating Early Reading Failure by Integrating the Teaching of Reading and Phonological Skills: The Phonological Linkage Hypothesis', *Child Development* 65, pp. 41–57.

Heath, S.B. (1983) *Ways with Words: Language, Life and Work in Communities and Classrooms*, Cambridge: Cambridge University Press.

Heath, S.B. and Mangiola, L. (1991) *Children of Promise: Literate Activity in Linguistically and Culturally Diverse Classrooms*, Washington DC: National Education Association of the United States.

Heaton, P. (1996) *Dyslexia: Parents in Need*, London: Whurr.

Henry, J. (2001) 'Is It a Boy Thing?', *Times Educational Supplement*, 25 May, p. 3.

Hewison, J. (1988) 'The Long-term Effectiveness of Parental Involvement in Reading: A Follow-up to the Haringey Reading Project', *British Journal of Educational Psychology* 58, pp. 184–90.

Hewison, J. and Tizard, J. (1980) 'Parental Involvement and Reading Attainment', *British Journal of Educational Psychology* 50, pp. 209–15.

HM Inspectors of Schools (1994) *Effective Provision for Special Educational Needs (EPSEN)*, Edinburgh: SOED.

HMG (UK) (1981) *Education Act 1981*, London: HMSO.

—— (1993) *Education Act 1993*, London: HMSO.

Hogben, J.H. (1997) 'How Does a Visual Transient Deficit Affect Reading?', in C. Hulme and M. Snowling (eds), *Dyslexia: Biology, Cognition and Intervention*, London: Whurr.

Hopkins, D. (1991) 'School Improvement and the Problem of Educational Change', in C. McLaughlin and M. Rouse (eds), *Supporting Schools*, London: Fulton.

Hopkins, D. and Harris, A. (1997) 'Improving the Quality of Education for All', *Support for Learning* 12(4), pp. 162–5.

Hornby, G. (1999) 'Inclusion or Delusion: Can One Size Fit All?', *Support for Learning* 14(4), pp. 152–7.

Hulme, C. and Snowling, M. (1992) 'Deficits in Output Phonology: An Explanation of Reading Failure?', *Cognitive Neuropsychology* 9, pp. 47–72.

Ireland (2000) *Learning Support Guidelines*, Dublin: Department of Education and Science.

Ireson, J., Mortimore, P. and Hallum, S. (1999) 'The Common Strands of Pedagogy and their Implications', in P. Mortimore (ed.), *Understanding Pedagogy and its Impact on Learning*, London: Paul Chapman.

Irlen, H. (1991) *Reading by the Colours*, New York: Avery.

Johnson, M. (2002) 'Multisensory Teaching of Reading in Mainstream Settings', in J. Wearmouth, J. Soler and G. Reid (eds), *Addressing Difficulties in Literacy Development: Responses at Family, School, Pupil and Teacher Levels*, London: RoutledgeFalmer.

Johnson, M., Phillips, S. and Peer, L. (1999) *A Multisensory Teaching System for Reading (MTSR)*, Manchester: Manchester Metropolitan University.

Jordan, E. (2002) 'Partnership Approaches: New Futures for Travellers', in J. Wearmouth, J. Soler and G. Reid (eds), *Addressing Difficulties in Literacy Development: Responses at Family, School, Pupil and Teacher Levels*, London: RoutledgeFalmer.

Jordan, I. (2002) *Visual Dyslexia, Signs, Symptoms and Assessment*, North Lincolnshire: Desktop Publications.

Knight, D.F. and Hynd, G.W. (2002) 'The Neurobiology of Dyslexia', in G. Reid and J. Wearmouth (eds), *Dyslexia and Literacy: Research and Practice*, Chichester: Wiley.

Kolb, D. (1984) *Experiential Learning: Experience as the Source of Learning and Development*, Englewood Cliffs, NJ: Prentice-Hall.

Krampen, G. (1987) 'Differential Effects of Teacher Comments', *Journal of Educational Psychology* 79, pp. 137–46.

Landon, J. (1998) 'Say "No" to Extraction; Curriculum', *Times Educational Supplement*, 12 June, available at http://www.tes.co.uk/search/search_display.asp?section=Archive&sub_section=Friday&id=301425&Type=0.

Lankshear, C. (1994) 'Literacy and Empowerment: Discourse, Power, Critique', *New Zealand Journal of Educational Studies* 29(1), pp. 59–72.

Lankshear, C. and Knobel, M. (1997) 'Different Worlds: New Technologies in School, Home and Community', in C. Lankshear (ed.), *Changing Literacies*, Buckingham: Open University Press.

—— (1998) 'New Times! Old Ways?', in F. Christie and R. Misson (eds), *Literacy and Schooling*, London/New York: Routledge.

—— (2002) 'New Times! Old Ways?', in J. Soler, J. Wearmouth and G. Reid (eds), *Contextualising Difficulties in Literacy Development*, London: RoutledgeFalmer.

Lankshear, C. and Lawler, M. (1987) *Literacy Schooling and Revolution*, Lewes: Falmer Press.

Lankshear, C., Gee, J.P., Knobel, M. and Searle, C. (1997) *Changing Literacies*, Buckingham: Open University Press.

Lawrence, D. (1971) 'The Effects of Counselling on Retarded Readers', in *Educational research* 13(2), pp. 119–24.

Lawrence, G. (1993) *People Types and Tiger Stripes*, 3rd edn, Gainsville, FL: Center for Applications of Psychological Type, Inc. (first published in 1979).

Lawton, D. and Chitty, C. (1988) *The National Curriculum, Bedford Way Papers 33*, London: London University Institute of Education.

Lewis, A. (1995) *Special Needs Provision in Mainstream Primary Schools*, Stoke: Trentham.

Licht, B.G. (1983) 'Cognitive-motivational Factors that Contribute to the Achievement of Learning-disabled Children', *Journal of Learning Disabilities* 16, pp. 483–90.

—— (1993) 'Language, attention and motivation', in L.J. Meltzer, *Strategy Assessment and Instruction for Students with Learning Disabilities: From Theory to Practice*, Austin, TX: Pro-Ed.

Licht, B.G. and Dweck, C.S. (1984) 'Determinants of Academic Achievement: The Interaction of Children's Achievement Orientations with Skill Area', *Developmental Psychology* 20, pp. 628–36.

Licht, B.G., Kistner, J.A., Ozkaragoz, T., Shapiro, S. and Clausen, L. (1985) 'Causal Attributions of Learning Disabled Children: Individual Differences and their Implications for Persistence', *Journal of Educational Psychology* 77, pp. 208–16.

Licht, R. (1994) 'Differences in Word Recognition between P- and L-type Reading Disability', in R. Licht and G. Spyer (eds), *The Balance Model of Dyslexia: Theoretical and Clinical Progress*, Assen, Netherlands: Van Gorcum.

Liegeois, J.-P. (ed.) (1998) *School Provision for Ethnic Minorities: The Gypsy Paradigm*, Hatfield: University of Hertfordshire.

Literacy Task Force (1997) *A Reading Revolution: How We can Teach Every Child to Read Well*, Preliminary Report of the Literacy Taskforce, London: Institute of Education.

Little, A. (2001) 'Summer Schools Don't Bring Pupils Up to Standard; "Catch-up" Classes Fail', *Express*, 15 October, p.11.

Livingstone, M.S., Rosen, G.D., Drislane, F.W. and Galaburda, A.M. (1991) 'Physiological and Anatomical Evidence for a Magnocellular Defect in Developmental Dyslexia', *Proceedings of the National Academy of Science of the USA* 88, pp. 7,943–7.

Lovegrove, W.J. (1996) 'Dyslexia and a Transient/Magnocellular Pathway Deficit: The Current Situation and Future Directions', *Australian Journal of Psychology* 48, pp. 167–71.

Lovey, J. (1995) *Supporting Special Educational Needs in Secondary Classrooms*, London: Fulton.

Luke, A. (1993) 'The Social Construction of Literacy in the Primary School', in L. Unsworth (ed.), *Literacy, Learning and Teaching: Language as Social Practice in the Primary School*, Melbourne: Macmillan Education.

Lunzer, E. and Gardener K. (1979) *The Effective Use of Reading*, London: Heinemann.

Lynch, E.C. and Beare, P.L. (1990) 'The Quality of IEP Objectives and their Relevance to Instruction for Students with Mental Retardation and Behavioural Disorders', *Remedial and Special Education* 11, pp. 48–55.

McCarthy, B. (1987) *The 4mat System: Teaching to Learning Styles with Right/Left Mode Techniques*, Barrington, IL: EXCEL Inc. (first published in 1980).

McCormick, C.E. and Mason, J.M. (1986) 'Intervention Procedures for Increasing Preschool Children's Interest in and Knowledge about Reading', in W. Teale and E. Sulzby (eds), *Emergent Literacy: Writing and Reading*, Norwood, NJ: Ablex.

MacKay, G. and McLarty, M. (1999) 'Special Educational Needs of Scottish Children', in T.G.K. Bryce and W.M. Humes (eds), *Scottish Education*, Edinburgh: Edinburgh Press.

McLoughlin, D., Fitzgibbon, G. and Young, V. (1994) *Adult Dyslexia: Assessment, Counselling and Training*, London: Whurr.

McNaughton, S. (1987) *Being Skilled: The Socialisation of Learning to Read*, London: Methuen.

McNaughton, S., Glynn, T. and Robinson, V. (1987) *Pause, Prompt and Praise: Effective Remedial Reading Tutoring*, Birmingham: Positive Products.

Marsh, A. (1998) 'Resourcing Inclusive Education: The Real Economics', in P. Clough (ed.), *Managing Inclusive Education*, London: Paul Chapman.

Martin, D. (2002) 'Bilingualism and Literacies in Primary School', in J. Soler, J. Wearmouth and G. Reid (eds), Contextualising Difficulties in Literacy Development: Exploring Politics, Culture, Ethnicity and Ethics.

Mathieson, M. (1975) The Preachers of Culture: A Study of English and Its Teachers, London: Allen & Unwin.

Medwell, J. (1995) 'A School Policy for Reading', in C. Gairns and D. Wray (eds), Reading Issues and Direction, Tamworth: NASEN.

Mehan, N. (1979) Learning Lessons, Cambridge, MA: Harvard University Press.

Miles, T.R. (1983) Dyslexia: The Pattern of Difficulties, London, Collins Educational.

—— (1996) 'Do Dyslexic children have I.Q.'s?', Dyslexia 2(3), pp. 175–8.

Mittler, P. (2000) Working towards Inclusive Education: Social Contexts, London: Fulton.

Morton, J. and Frith, U. (1995) 'Causal Modelling: A Structural Approach to Developmental Psychopathology', in: D. Cohen (eds), Manual of Developmental Psychopathology, NY Psychological Assessment of Dyslexia: Wiley.

Moser, C. (2000) Better Basic Skills – Improving Adult Literacy and Numeracy, London: Department for Education and Employment.

Moss, G. (2002) 'Texts in Context: Mapping out the Gender Differentiation of the Reading Curriculum', in J. Soler, J. Wearmouth and G. Reid (eds), Contextualising Difficulties in Literacy Development, London: RoutledgeFalmer.

Mroz, M., Smith, F. and Hardman, F. (2000) 'The Discourse of the Literacy Hour', Cambridge Journal of Education 30(3), pp. 379–90.

Muter, V., Hulme, C. and Snowling, M.J. (1997) The Phonological Abilities Test, London: Psychological Corporation.

NCET (1995) Access Technology: Making the Right Choice, Coventry: NCET.

Newson, J. and Newson, E. (1977) Perspectives on School at Seven Years Old, London: Allen & Unwin.

Nicolson, R.I. (1996) 'Development Dyslexia: Past, Present and Future', Dyslexia: An International Journal of Research and Practice 2(3), pp. 190–207.

—— (2001) 'Developmental Dyslexia: Into the Future', in A. Fawcett (ed.), Dyslexia: Theory and Good Practice, London, Whurr.

—— (2002) 'Developmental Dyslexia: Into the Future', in J. Soler, J. Wearmouth and G. Reid (eds), Contextualising Difficulties in Literacy Development: Exploring Politics, Culture, Ethnicity and Ethics, London: Routledge.

Nicolson, R.I. and Fawcett, A.J. (1994) 'Comparison of Deficits in Cognitive and Motor Skills among Children with Dyslexia', Annals of Dyslexia 44, pp. 147–64.

—— (2000) 'Long-term Learning in Dyslexic Children', European Journal of Cognitive Psychology 12, pp. 357–93.

Nicolson, R.I. and Siegel, L. (1996) 'Special Issue on Dyslexia and Intelligence: Editor's Foreword', Dyslexia 2(3), p.153.

Norwich, B. (1990) Special Needs in Ordinary Schools, London: Cassell.

—— (1994) 'Differentiation from the Perspective of Resolving Tensions between Basic Social Values and Assumptions about Individual Differences', *Curriculum Studies* 2(3), pp.289–308.

—— (1996) *Special Needs Education, Inclusive Education or Just Education for All?*, London: Institute of Education, London University.

Oakhill, J. and Yuill, J. (1995) 'Learning to Understand Written Language', in E. Funnell and M. Stuart (eds), *Learning to Read: Psychology in the Classroom*, Oxford: Blackwell.

Office for Standards in Education (OFSTED) (1999) *The SEN Code of Practice Three Years On* (HMI 235), London: OFSTED.

OFSTED (1996) *Implementation of the Code of Practice for Pupils with Special Educational Needs*, London: HMSO.

—— (1997) *The SEN Code of Practice: Two Years On*, London: OFSTED.

Open University (2000a) 'How Should we Respond to Government Policy', in E829 Course Materials.

—— (2000b) 'Study Guide', in *E831 Professional Development for Special Educational Needs Co-ordinators*, Milton Keynes: Open University.

—— (2001a) 'Students with Special Educational Needs and Difficulties in Literacy in Irish Schools 1950–2001', *E831 Professional Development for Special Educational Needs Co-ordinators*.

—— (2001b) 'E831 Study Guide', *E831 Professional Development for Special Educational Needs Co-ordinators*.

Open University (2002) *E801 Difficulties in Literacy Development*, Milton Keynes: Open University.

Openshaw, R., Soler, J., Wearmouth, J. and Paige-Smith, A. (2002) 'Reading Recovery and Pause, Prompt, Praise: Professional Visions and Current Practices', in J. Soler and J. Wearmouth and G. Reid (eds.), *Contextualising Difficulties in Literacy Development: Exploring Politics, Culture, Ethnicity and Ethics*, London: RoutledgeFalmer.

Orton, S.T. (1937) *Reading, Writing and Speech Problems in Children*, New York: Norton.

Ott, P. (1997) *How to Detect and Manage Dyslexia – A Reference and Resource Manual*, Oxford, Heinemann.

Padmore, S. (1994) 'Guiding Lights', in M. Hamilton *et al.* (eds), *Worlds of Literacy*, Clevedon: Multilingual Matters.

Palincsar, A.S. (1986) 'The Role of Dialogue in Providing Scaffolded Instruction', *Educational Psychologist* (21), pp. 73–98.

Palincsar, A.S. and Brown, A.L. (1984) 'Reciprocal Teaching of Comprehension – Fostering and Comprehension-monitoring Activities', *Cognition and Instruction* 1(2), pp. 117–75.

Palincsar, A.S., Winn, J., David, Y., Snyder, B. and Stevens, D. (1993) 'Approaches to Strategic Reading Instruction Reflecting Different Assumptions Regarding Teaching and Learning', in L.J. Meltzer (ed.), *Strategy Assessment and Instruction for Students with Learning Disabilities*, Austin, TX: Pro-Ed.

Peacey, N. (2002) 'Examinations, Assessments and Special Arrangements', in J. Wearmouth, J. Soler and G. Reid (eds), *Addressing Difficulties in Literacy Development: Responses at Family, School, Pupil and Teacher Levels*, London: RoutledgeFalmer.

Peer, L. (2001) 'Dyslexia and its Manifestations in the Secondary School', in L. Peer and G. Reid (eds), *Dyslexia: Successful Inclusion in the Secondary School*, London: David Fulton.

Peer, L. and Reid, G. (eds) (2001) *Dyslexia: Successful Inclusion in the Secondary School*, London: David Fulton Publishers.

—— (2002) 'Dyslexia and Literacy: Challenges in the Secondary School', in G. Reid and J. Wearmouth (eds), *Dyslexia and Literacy: Research and Practice*, Chichester: Wiley.

Perera, K. (1979) *The Language Demands of School Learning*, Course material for Course PE232 Language Development, Milton Keynes: Open University Press.

Peters, M. (1967) *Spelling Caught or Taught?*, London: Routledge Kegan Paul.

Phillips, S. (1999) *Management Skills for SEN Co-ordinators in the Primary School*, London: Falmer.

Piotrowski, J. and Reason, R. (2000) 'The National Literacy Strategy and Dyslexia: A Comparison of Teaching Methods and Materials', *Support for Learning* 15(2), pp. 51–7.

Pringle-Morgan, W.P. (1896) 'A Case of Congenital Word-blindness', *British Medical Journal* 2, p. 1,378.

Pumfrey, P.D. (1996) *Specific Developmental Dyslexia: Basics to Back. The Fifteenth Vernon–Wall Lecture*, Leicester: British Psychological Society.

—— (2002) 'Specific Developmental Dyslexia (SDD): "Basics to Back" in 2000 and Beyond?', in J. Wearmouth, J. Soler and G. Reid (eds), *Addressing Difficulties in Literacy Development: Responses at Family, School, Pupil and Teacher Levels*, London: RoutledgeFalmer.

Qualifications and Curriculum Authority (QCA) (1998) *The Long-term Effects of Two Interventions for Children with Reading Difficulties*, London: QCA.

—— (2000) 'General Statement on Inclusion', *Curriculum 2000*, London: QCA.

Qualifications and Curriculum Authority (QCA) and Department for Education and Employment (DfEE) (1999) *Early Learning Goals*, London: QCA.

Rafferty, F. (1996) 'Labour Gets Back to Basics', in 'News and Opinion', *Times Educational Supplement*, 31 May.

Rassool, N. (1999) 'Literacy: In Search of a Paradigm', in N. Rassool (ed.), *Literacy for Sustainable Development in the Age of Information*, Clevedon/ Philadelphia, PA: Multilingual Matters.

—— (2002) 'Literacy: In Search of a Paradigm', in J. Soler, J. Wearmouth and G. Reid (eds), *Contextualising Difficulties in Literacy Development: Exploring Politics, Culture, Ethnicity and Ethics* London: RoutledgeFalmer.

Reason, R. (2002) 'From Assessment to Intervention: The Educational Psychology Perspective', in G. Reid and J. Wearmouth (eds), *Dyslexia and Literacy: Research and Practice*, Chichester: Wiley.

Reason, R. and Boote, R. (1994) *Helping Children with Reading and Spelling*, London: Routledge.

Reed, T. (2002) 'The Literacy Acquisition of Black and Asian "English-as-Additional Language" (EAL) Learners: Anti-racist Assessment and Intervention Challenges', in J. Soler, J. Wearmouth and G. Reid (eds), *Contextualising Difficulties in Literacy Development*, London: RoutledgeFalmer.

Reid, G. (1994) 'Specific Learning Difficulties (Dyslexia)', A *Handbook for Study and Practice*, Edinburgh: Moray House Publications.

—— (1998) *Dyslexia: A Practitioner's Handbook*, Chichester: John Wiley & Sons.

—— (2001) 'Specialist Teacher Training in the UK: Issues, Considerations and Future Directions', in M. Hunter-Carsch (ed.), *Dyslexia: A Psychosocial Perspective*, London. Whurr.

Reid, G. and Given, B.K. (1999) 'The Interactive Observation Style Identification', in B.K. Given and G. Reid *Learning Styles: A Guide for Teachers and Parents*, Lancashire: Red Rose Publications.

Reid, G. and Kirk, J. (2000) *Adult Dyslexia for Employment and Training (ADEPT)*, report commissioned by the employment service on best practice in dyslexia assessment, support and training, Edinburgh: Faculty of Education, University of Edinburgh.

—— (2001) *Dyslexia in Adults: Education and Employment*, Chichester: Wiley.

Reynolds, D. (1998) 'Schooling for Literacy: A Review of Research on Teacher Effectiveness and School Effectiveness and Its Implications for Contemporary Educational Policies', *Educational Review* 50(2), pp. 147–62.

Reynolds, D. and Farrell, S. (1996) *Worlds Apart? A Review of International Studies of Educational Achievement Involving England*, London: HMSO for OFSTED.

Richardson, A. (2002) 'Dyslexia, Dyspraxia and ADHD – Can Nutrition Help? All Kinds of Minds' (keynote lecture handouts), Helen Arkell 8th Cambridge Conference, 25–7 March.

Riddick, B. (1996) *Living with Dyslexia*, London/New York: Routledge.

—— (2000) 'An Examination of the Relationship Between Labelling and Stigmatisation with Reference to Dyslexia', *Disability & Society* 15(4), pp. 653–67.

Riding, R. and Rayner, S. (1998) *Cognitive Styles and Learning Strategies, Understanding Style Differences in Learning and Behaviour*, London: David Fulton Publishers.

Riedler, C.R. (1962) 'A Content Analysis of Rudolf Flesch's Book: Why Johnny Can't Read', unpublished graduate research seminar paper, School of Education, City College, City University of New York.

Riley, J. (2001) 'The National Literacy Strategy Success with Literacy for All?', *Curriculum Journal* 12(1), pp. 29–58.

Robertson, J. and Bakker, D.J. (2002) 'The Balance Model of Reading and Dyslexia', in G. Reid and J. Wearmouth (eds), *Dyslexia and Literacy: Research and Practice*, Chichester: Wiley.

Rosenthal, R. and Jacobson, L. (1968) *Pygmalion in the Classroom*, New York: Holt, Rinehart & Winston.

Rouse, M. and Florian, L. (2000) 'Effective Inclusive Schools: A Study in Two Countries', *Cambridge Journal of Education* 26(1), pp. 71–85.

Russell, P. (1997) 'Parents as Partners: Some Early Impressions of the Impact of the Code of Practice', in S. Wolfendale (ed.), *Working with Parents After the Code of Practice*, London: Fulton.

Rutter, M. and Madge, N. (1976) *Cycles of Disadvantage: A Review of Research*, London: Heinemann Educational.

Rutter, M., Tizard, J. and Whitmore, K. (1970) *Education, Health and Behaviour*, London: Longman.

Scardamalia, M. and Bereiter, C. (1986) 'The Development of Evaluative, Diagnostic and Remedial Capabilities in Children's Composing', in M. Martlew (ed.), *The Psychology of Written Language: Developmental and Educational Perspectives*, London: Wiley.

Schunk, D.H. (1989) 'Self-efficacy and Cognitive Achievement: Implications for Students with Learning Problems', *Journal of Learning Disabilities* 22, pp. 14–22.

Schunk, D.H. and Cox, P.D. (1986) 'Strategy Training and Attributional Feedback with Learning Disabled Students', *Journal of Educational Psychology* 78, pp. 201–9.

Schunk, D.H., Hanson, A.R. and Cox, P.D. (1987) 'Peer-model Attributes and Children's Achievement Behaviors', *Journal of Educational Psychology* 79, pp. 54–61.

Scoble, J. (1988) 'Cued Spelling in Adult Literacy – A Case Study', *Paired Reading Bulletin* 4, pp. 93 6.

Scribner, S. and Cole, M. (1981) *The Psychology of Literacy*, Cambridge, MA: Harvard University Press.

Sebba, J. with Sachdev, D. (1997) *What Works in Inclusive Education?*, Barkingside: Barnados.

SED (1987) *Curriculum and Assessment in Scotland: A Policy for the '90s*, Edinburgh: SED.

SEED (2001) *Assessing Our Children's Educational Needs: The way forward?*, Edinburgh: SEED.

Shelton, T.L., Anastopoulos, A.D. and Linden, J.D. (1985) 'An Attribution Training Program with Learning Disabled Children', *Journal of Learning Disabilities* 18, pp. 261–5.

Sigafoos, J., Kigner, J., Holt, K., Doss, S. and Mustonen, T. (1991) 'Improving the Quality of Written Development Policies for Adults with Intellectual Disabilities', *British Journal of Mental Subnormality* 37, pp. 35–46.

Silver, L.B. (2001) *Perspectives* 27(3), Summer, pp. 1, 4 (Baltimore, MD: International Dyslexia Association).

Simmons, K. (1996) 'In Defence of Entitlement', *Support for Learning* 11(3), pp. 105–8.

Sinclair, J. and Coulthard, M. (1992) 'Towards an Analysis of Discourse', in M. Coulthard (ed.), *Advances in Spoken Discourse Analysis*, London: Routledge.

Singleton, C.H. (1994) 'Computer Applications in the Identification and Remediation of Dyslexia', in D. Wray (ed.), *Literacy and Computers: Insights from Research*, Widnes: United Kingdom Reading Association.

—— (1997) 'Computerised Assessment of Reading', in J.R. Beech and C.H. Singleton (eds), *The Psychological Assessment of Reading*, London: Routledge.

—— (1999) *Dyslexia in Higher Education: Policy, Provision and Practice*, Report of the National Working Party on Dyslexia in Higher Education, Hull: University of Hull.

—— (2002) 'Dyslexia: Cognitive Factors and Implications for Literacy', in G. Reid and J. Wearmouth (eds), *Dyslexia and Literacy: Research and Practice*, Chichester: Wiley.

Singleton, C.H., Thomas, K.V. and Leedale, R.C. (1996) *CoPS 1 Cognitive Profiling System (Developmental Version)*, Beverley, East Yorkshire: Lucid Research Limited.

Smith, C.B. (1994) *Whole-language: The Debate*, Bloomington, IN: ERIC Clearinghouse on Reading English and Communication/EDINFO Press.

Smith, D. (1999) 'Books to Suit Everyone: Is There a Place for Reading Schemes within the National Literacy Strategy Framework?', in M. Hinson (ed.), *Surviving the Literacy Hour*, Tamworth: NASEN.

Smith, F. (1971) *Understanding Reading : A Psycholinguistic Analysis of Reading and Learning to Read*, New York: Holt Rinehart & Winston.

—— (1973) *Psycholinguistics and Reading*, New York, Holt, Rinehart & Winston.

Smyth, G. (2000) *I Feel this Challenge and I Don't Have the Background: Teaching Bilingual Pupils in Scottish Primary Schools*, paper presented at the European Conference on Educational Research, Edinburgh, 20–3 September.

Snowling, M.J. (1998) 'Reading Development and its Difficulties', *Educational and Child Psychology* 15(2), pp. 44–58.

—— (2000) *Dyslexia*, 2nd edn, Oxford: Blackwell.

Snowling, M.J. and Hulme, C. (1994) 'The Development of Phonological Skills', *Philosophical Transactions of the Royal Society* B346, pp. 21–8.

Snowling, M.J. and Nation, K.A. (1997) 'Language, Phonology and Learning to Read', in C. Hulme and M.J. Snowling (eds), *Dyslexia, Biology, Cognition and Intervention*, London: Whurr.

Snowling, M., Goulandris, N. and Stackhouse, J. (1994) 'Phonological Constraints on Learning to Read: Evidence from Single-case Studies of Reading Difficulty', in C. Hulme and M. Snowling (eds), *Reading Development and Dyslexia*, London: Whurr.

Snowling, M.J., Goulandris, N., Bowlby, M. and Howell, P. (1986) 'Segmentation and Speech Perception in Relation to Reading Skill: A Developmental Analysis', *Journal of Experimental Child Psychology* 41, pp. 489–507.

Snowling, M.J., Nation, K., Moxham, P., Gallagher, A. and Frith, U. (1997) 'Phonological Processing Deficits in Dyslexic Students: A Preliminary Account', *Journal of Research in Reading* 20, pp. 31–4.

SOED (1993) *Structure and Balance of the Curriculum 5–14*, Edinburgh: SOED.

SOEID (1991) *English Language 5–14: National Guidelines*, Edinburgh: HMSO.

—— (1996) *Children and Young Persons with Special Educational Needs: Assessment and Recording*, Edinburgh, Scottish Office.

—— (1997) *A Curriculum Framework for Children in their Pre-School Year*, Edinburgh: HMSO.

Soler, J. and Smith, J. (eds) (2000) *Literacy in New Zealand: Practices, Politics and Policy Since 1900*, Auckland: Addison Wesley Longman.

Solity, J. (1996) 'Discrepancy Definitions of Dyslexia: An Assessment through Teaching Perspective', *Educational Psychology in Practice* 12(3), pp. 141–51.

Stanovich, K.E. (1986) 'Matthew Effects in Reading: Some Consequences of Individual Differences in the Acquisition of Reading', *Reading Research Quarterly* 21, pp. 360–406.

—— (1988) 'Explaining the Difference between the Dyslexic and the Garden-variety Poor Readers: The Phonological Core Model', *Journal of Learning Disabilities* 21(10), pp. 590–604.

—— (1996) 'Towards a More Inclusive Definition of Dyslexia', *Dyslexia* 2(3), pp. 154–66.

—— (2000) *Progress in Understanding Reading: Scientific Foundations and New Frontiers*, London: Guilford Press.

Stanovich, K.E. and Stanovich, P.J. (1995) 'How Research Might Inform the Debate about Early Reading Acquisition', *Journal of Research in Reading* 18(2), pp. 87–105.

Stanovich, K.E., Siegel, L.S. and Gottardo, A. (1997) 'Progress in the Search for Dyslexia Subtypes', in C. Hulme and M. Snowling (eds), *Dyslexia: Biology, Cognition and Intervention*, London: Whurr.

Stein, J.F. (1995) 'A Visual Defect in Dyslexics?', In R.I. Nicolson and A.J. Fawcett (eds), *Dyslexia in Children: Multidisciplinary Perspectives*, London: Harvester Wheatsheaf.

—— (2002) 'The Sensory Basis of Reading. All Kinds of Minds' (keynote lecture handouts), Helen Arkell 8th Cambridge Conference, 25–7 March.

Stierer, B. (2002) 'Simply Doing Their Job? The Politics of Reading Standards and "Real Books"', in J. Soler, J. Wearmouth and G. Reid (eds), *Contextualising Difficulties in Literacy Development*, London: RoutledgeFalmer.

Stobart, G. (2000) *Examinations, Formal Qualifications and the Construction of Professional Identities: A British Case Study 1880–1940*, Budapest: IREX–Hungarian Academy of Sciences Conference.

Stone, C.A. (1989) 'Improving the Effectiveness of Strategy Training for Learning-disabled Students: The Role of Communicational Dynamics', *Remedial and Special Education* (10), pp. 35–42.

Street, B. (1995) *Social Literacies: Critical Approaches to Literacy in Development, Ethnography and Education*, London: Longman.

Strickland, D. and Cullinan, B. (1994) 'Afterword', in M.J. Adams *Beginning to Read: Thinking and Learning about Print*, London: MIT Press.

Swan, D. (2002) 'The Law in Eire', in K. Simmons, J. Wearmouth, D. Swan and T. Booth *Difficulties in Literacy Development: The Legal Framework*, Milton Keynes: Open University.

Tharp, R.G. and Gallimore, R. (1988) *Rousing Minds to Life: Teaching, Learning and Schooling in Social Context*, Cambridge: Cambridge University Press.

Thomas, G. (1992) *Effective Classroom Teamwork – Support or Intrusion?*, London: Falmer.

Tizard, J., Schofield, W.N. and Hewison, J. (1982) 'Collaboration Between Teachers and Parents in Assisting Children's Reading', *British Journal of Educational Psychology* 52, pp. 1–15.

Tod, J. (2002) 'Individual Education Plans and Dyslexia: Some Principles', in G. Reid and J. Wearmouth (eds), *Dyslexia and Literacy: Research and Practice*, Chichester: Wiley.

Tod, J. and Fairman, A. (2001) 'Individualised Learning in a Group Setting', in L. Peer and G. Reid (eds), *Dyslexia – Successful Inclusion in the Secondary School*, London: Fulton.

Tod, J., Castle, F. and Blamires, M. (1998) *Implementing Effective Practice*, London: Fulton.

Tomlinson, S. (1988) 'Why Johnny Can't Read: Critical Theory and Special Education', *European Journal of Special Needs Education* 3(1), pp. 45–58.

Topping, K.J. (1992) 'Short- and Long-term Follow-up of Parental Involvement in Reading Projects', *British Educational Research Journal* 18(4), pp. 369–79.

—— (1995) *Paired Reading, Spelling and Writing – The Handbook for Teachers*, London: Cassell.

—— (1996) 'Tutoring Systems for Family Literacy', in S. Wolfendale and K. Topping (eds), *Family Involvement in Literacy*, London: Cassell.

—— (2002) 'Paired Thinking: Developing Thinking Skills Through Structured Interaction with Peers, Parents and Volunteers', in G. Reid and J. Wearmouth (eds), *Dyslexia and Literacy Theory and Practice*, Chichester: Wiley.

Topping, K.J. and Lindsay, G. (1992) 'Paired Reading: A Review of the Literature', *Research Papers in Education* 7(3), pp. 1–50.

Topping, K.J. and Wolfendale, S. (eds) (1985) *Parental Involvement in Children's Reading*, Beckenham: Croom Helm.

Tunmer, W.E. and Chapman, J. (1996) 'A Developmental Model of Dyslexia. Can the Construct Be Saved?', *Dyslexia* 2(3), pp. 179–89.

Turner, M. (1990) *Sponsored Reading Failure: An Object Lesson*, Warlingham, Surrey: IPSET Education Unit.

Ulmer, C. and Timothy, M. (2001) *How Does Alternative Assessment Affect Teachers' Practice? Two Years Later*, Paper presented at the 12th European Conference on Reading, Dublin, Ireland, 1–4 July 2001.

UNESCO (1994) *Salamanca Declaration and Framework for Action*, Paris: UNESCO.

Visser, J. (1993) *Differentiation: Making it Work*, Tamworth: NASEN.

Vygotsky, L.S. (1978) *Mind in Society: The Development of Higher Psychological Processes*, London: Harvard University Press.

—— (1987) *The Collected Works of L.S. Vygotsky, Vol 1: Problems of General Psychology*, edited by R.W. Rieber and A.S. Carton, translated by N. Minisk, NY: Plenum Press.

Wade, B. and Moore, M. (1993) *Experiencing Special Education: What Young People with Special Needs Can Tell Us*, Buckingham: Open University Press.

Walkerdine, V. (1990) *School Girl Fictions*, London and New York: Verso.

Wearmouth, J. (2000) *Special Educational Provision: Meeting the Challenges in Schools*, London: Hodder.

Wearmouth, J. and Reid, G. (2002) 'Issues for Assessment and Planning of Teaching and Learning', in G. Reid and J. Wearmouth (eds), *Dyslexia and Literacy: Research and Practice*, Chichester: Wiley.

Wearmouth, J. and Soler, J. (2001) 'How Inclusive is the Literacy Hour', *British Journal of Special Education* 28(3), pp. 113–19.

—— (2002a) 'How Inclusive is the Literacy Hour', in J. Soler, J. Wearmouth and G. Reid (eds), *Contextualising Difficulties in Literacy Development: Exploring Politics, Culture, Ethnicity and Ethics*, London: RoutledgeFalmer.

—— (2002b) 'Reading Recovery and Pause, Prompt, Praise: Professional Visions and Current Practices', in J. Soler, J. Wearmouth and G. Reid (eds.), *Contextualising Difficulties in Literacy Development: Exploring Politics, Culture, Ethnicity and Ethics*, London: RoutledgeFalmer.

Wechsler, D. (1996) *The Wechsler Dimensions* (WISC III), London: Psychological Corporation.

Weedon, C. and Reid, G. (2001) *Listening and Literacy Index: Group Tests for Profiling Literacy Development and Identifying Specific Learning Difficulties*, London: Hodder & Stoughton.

Weiner, B. (1979) 'A Theory of Motivation for Some Classroom Experiences', *Journal of Educational Psychology* 71, pp. 3–25.

Welch, A.R. and Freebody, P. (2002) 'Explanations of the Current International "Literacy Crises"', in J. Soler, J. Wearmouth and G. Reid (eds), *Contextualising Difficulties in Literacy Development*, London: RoutledgeFalmer.

Wells, G. (1985) *Language Development in the Pre-School Years*, Cambridge: Cambridge University Press.

West, T.G. (1991) *In the Mind's Eye: Visual Thinkers, Gifted People with Learning Difficulties, Computer Images, and the Ironies of Creativity*, Buffalo NY: Prometheus Books.

—— (1997) *In the Mind's Eye. Visual Thinkers, Gifted People with Learning Difficulties, Computer Images and the Ironies of Creativity*, 2nd edn, Buffalo, N.Y. Prometheus Books.

Westwood, P. (1997) *Commonsense Methods for Children with Special Needs*, London: Routledge.

Wilkins, A.J., Evans, B.J.W., Brown, J.A., Busby, A.E., Wingfield, A.E., Jeanes, R.J. and Bald, J. (1994) Double-masked Placebo-controlled Trial of Precision

Spectral Filters in Children Who Use Coloured Overlays', *Ophthalmic and Physiological Optics* 14, pp. 365–70.

Wilkinson, I.A.G. (1998) 'Dealing with Diversity: Achievement Gaps in Reading Literacy among New Zealand Students', *Reading Research Quarterly* 33(2), pp. 144–67.

Williams, R. (1965) *The Long Revolution*, Harmondsworth: Penguin Books.

—— (1989) 'Hegemony and the Selective Tradition', in S. deCastell, A. Luke and C. Luke (eds.), *Language, Authority and Criticism: Readings on the School Textbook*, London/New York: Falmer Press.

Willinsky, J. (1990) *The New Literacy: Redefining Reading and Writing in the Schools*, London: Routledge.

Wilson, J. (1993) *Phonological Awareness Training*, London: Educational Supply Publishers.

Witkin H. and Goodenough, D. (1981) 'Cognitive Styles: Essence and Origins', *Psychological Issues Monograph 51*, New York: International Universities Press.

Wolf, M. and Bowers, P.G. (1999) 'The Double Deficit Hypothesis for the Development of Dyslexias', *Journal of Educational Psychology* 91, pp. 415–38.

Wood, D., Bruner, J.S. and Ross, G. (1976) 'The Role of Tutoring in Problem Solving', *Journal of Child Psychology and Psychiatry*.

Wragg, E.C. (1997) *The Cubic Curriculum*, London: Routledge.

Wragg, E.C., Wragg, C.M., Haynes, G.S. and Chamberlain, R.P. (1998) *Improvising Literacy in the Primary School*, London: Routledge.

Wray, D. (1994) *Literacy and Awareness*, London: Hodder & Stoughton.

—— (2002) 'Metacognition and Literacy', in G. Reid and J. Wearmouth (eds), *Dyslexia and Literacy: Research and Practice*, Chichester: Wiley.

Young, M. and McGeeney, P. (1968) *Learning Begins at Home*, London: Routledge & Kegan Paul.

Young, P. and Tyre, C. (1983) *Dyslexia or Illiteracy: Realizing the Right to Read*, Milton Keynes: Open University Press.

Ysseldyke, J.E. and Christenson, S.L. (1987a) *The Instructional Environment System*, Austin, TX: Pro-Ed.

—— (1987b) 'Evaluating Students' Instructional Environments', *Remedial and Special Education* 8(3), pp. 17–24.

Index